GREEKS BEARING GIFTS

bernard evslin

GREEKS BEARING GIFTS

the epics of achilles and ulysses

illustrations by lucy martin bitzer

four winds press
new york

LIBRARY OF CONGRESS CATALOGING IN PUBLICATION DATA

EVSLIN, BERNARD.
GREEKS BEARING GIFTS.

I. MYTHOLOGY, GREEK. I. HOMERUS. ILIAS.
II. HOMERUS. ODYSSEA. III. TITLE.
BL782.E89 1976   883'.01   76–16039
ISBN 0–590–17431–2

77-306

PUBLISHED BY FOUR WINDS PRESS
A DIVISION OF SCHOLASTIC MAGAZINES, INC., NEW YORK, N.Y.
PRINTED IN THE UNITED STATES OF AMERICA
LIBRARY OF CONGRESS CATALOG CARD NUMBER: 76–16039
1   2   3   4   5   80   79   78   77   76

For Hirsh W. Stalberg,
voyager on other seas

CONTENTS

GREEKS BEARING GIFTS

I

THE TROJAN WAR

тнε ρεddlεR

The man stooped under a huge bale. He passed through the castle gates and climbed the broad stone stairs that led to the women's quarters. The brass-helmeted sentries stood silently watching him go. Ordinarily they did a little playful torturing of peddlers before allowing them in—beat them a bit about the shoulders with their spearhafts, plucked their beards, and scattered their wares. They weren't really cruel, these sentries, but they were fighting men; it had been a long time between wars, and they were bored. But they had not bothered this red-headed fellow for some reason. Perhaps it was because his shoulders were so broad and his arms so knotted with muscle—and he had lifted the great bale of goods so easily off his white donkey. His grin was servile enough, and he had tipped them a greasy little bow like all peddlers. Nevertheless, they let him pass through the gates and across the courtyard without tormenting him.

It was strange too that the great guard dogs, the brindle mastiffs with their spiked brass collars, did not charge the stranger, nor even growl.

The peddler flung down his bale and knelt on the stone-flagged floor, pulling out garment after shining garment as the tall daughters of King Scyros crowded about him, chattering and laughing and shrieking with greed. They loved clothes, these daughters of the king, and Scyros was such a

3   THE TROJAN WAR

remote island, they felt themselves falling far behind the fashions. Besides, they had a visitor to impress: the tall yellow-headed silent girl—a country cousin who had been with them for three months now without ever telling them anything about herself. She listened to all they had to say, smiling her curious thin-lipped smile, but never told any secrets in return.

"Spread out your wares, man," cried Calyx, the eldest princess. "Don't pull them out one by one. Spread them so we can see them all."

"Yes, princess," said the peddler.

With a sweep of his arm he spread his goods upon the stone floor. Silks and furs and garments of wonderfully woven flax dyed with the colors of mountain sunset. Jewels flashed—rings, bracelets, anklets, necklaces. On a long cloak of black wool were couched a lance and a sword. Unjewelled these weapons, made for battle use, not ceremony; their blades were heavy and sharp, newly honed. The hilt of the sword was bull-horn, the haft of the throwing lance of polished ash, its head of copper. With gull cries of greed the girls fell upon the garments—all except their visitor. She leaped across the chamber and snatched up the weapons, flexed her long legs in a fighting stance, and whipped the sword through the air, decapitating a horde of imaginary foes.

The princesses fell silent and stared at their cousin, eyes huge. The peddler smiled. He arose. His stoop was gone and the little servile selling grin. He stood there massively, smiling and watching as the princesses' yellow-headed cousin shadow duelled—whirling, dancing, ducking, stabbing.

"It is well," said the peddler. And his voice was different, too. "By your choices shall you be known. I have come a long way for you, Achilles. Now you must come back with me."

"Achilles!" shrieked the maidens.

"Achilles," said the peddler.

He approached the tall girl, seized the shoulder of her tunic, and ripped it away, baring her to the waist, disclosing not another maiden, but a young man muscled like the statue of a god.

"A man," murmured the princesses. "She's a man."

The young man said nothing but seized the peddler by the beard and raised his sword.

"Softly, Achilles," said the peddler. "I too am unlike what I seem. We are kinsmen far back, you and I. I am Ulysses, king of Ithaca."

"Ulysses? You?"

Achilles let his hand fall.

"Ulysses," echoed the princesses.

Indeed, even before the Trojan War was fought, this name was known the length and breadth of Hellas as that of the boldest pirate-king of the Inner Sea, a master of strategy on land and water.

"But why do you seek me, cousin?" said Achilles. "My mother bade me dress in maiden's garb and hide myself in this court in obedience to some oracle or other. She said she would call me back when the Fates had been satisfied. Said it would be only a matter of weeks, but now you come first to fetch me away. By what right?"

"Oh, you may abide here among the maidens and wait for your mother," said Ulysses. "But I think I should tell you that there's a war on."

"A war?" shouted Achilles, snatching up his sword. "A real war?"

"Very real. With Troy. Against some of the most fearsome warriors of this age or any other."

"Why do we stand here conversing?" cried Achilles. "Let's go!"

Ulysses bowed to the princesses. "You may keep these garments, fair maidens. They are my gift to you. Accept too my apologies for the slight deceit I was forced to practice."

"Farewell, cousins," said Achilles. "Gentle maids, farewell. After this war is over, I shall return, in my own guise, and attempt to thank you for your hospitality."

The two men passed from the chamber and left the courtyard. The princesses watched from the embrasures, saw them disappear through the gates, and then appear again around the corner of the cliff where the road dipped to the sea. And that night nine of them dreamed of Achilles and three of Ulysses, but in the middle darkness their dreams crossed, and by dawn there was no counting.

Ulysses led the young man aboard his ship. They lifted anchor and set sail for Aulis where the war fleet was gathering. They sat on deck in the golden weather, and Ulysses told how enmity was born between Greece and Troy.

sEEds of WAR

"Actually, you and this war were meant for each other," he said to Achilles. "Your seeds were planted on the same night—when your mother and father were wed—at a wedding feast given by the gods themselves on Mount Olympus. Know you, Achilles, that your father, Peleus, was the most renowned warrior of his day, and your mother, Thetis, the most beautiful naiad who ever rose naked and dripping from the tides of the moon to trouble man's sleep.

Thetis, the immortal Thetis, queen of naiads, nereids, and sea nymphs, fleeing always the clutches of the amorous Poseidon, was coveted by Zeus himself who would have taken her to wife despite the ragings of Hera—except that an oracle foretold that the son of Thetis would grow greater than his father. Zeus had no stomach for this and abandoned his suit, as did all the other envious gods. And so she was given to the greatest of mortals, your father, Peleus."

"I'm aware of my own pedigree, man," said Achilles. "Get to the war."

"Patience, young friend. The marriage of Peleus and Thetis was celebrated by the mightiest revels in the memory of man or god. Now it is well known that the Olympians are infallible, but they are sometimes forgetful. And whoever it was of the High Ones who made out the invitation list neglected to include the Lady of Discord herself, Eris, queen of Harpies, sister to the war-god, who rides beside him in his chariot delighting in the cries of the wounded and the smell of blood. She was not invited to the feast. Oh, Achilles, and a terrible omission it was. When the rejoicing was at its height and the stars reeled on their crystal axes, shaken by the laughter of the gods, then it was that Eris made herself invisible, entered the great banquet hall, and rolled upon the table a gleaming heavy apple of solid gold. Upon the apple were written the words: "To the most beautiful." It glowed there like the heart of flame and was immediately claimed by Hera, Athena, and Aphrodite. The festivities were rent by their quarreling as they shrieked like fishwives over a beached mackerel. The feast was ruined. Gentle Hestia, goddess of the Hearth and protector of feasts, wept great tears. Eris stood among the shadows, chuckling. Hestia begged Zeus to settle things by awarding the apple to whomever he considered the most beautiful. But Father Zeus was much too wise to be caught in a trap like that. For Hera happened to be his sister and his wife, Athena his daughter, and Aphrodite a kind of half-sister—and, it is said, much else besides.

"Peace, good company!" boomed Zeus. "The question of choosing among three such enchanting beauties is too difficult to be undertaken by anyone who knows them well and has been exposed to their potent charms. We must therefore seek beyond our own small circle for a just decision. I shall search among the mortals of the earth for him of coolest judgment and most exquisite taste. Give me a few days to find him. In the meantime, I bid you cease your quarreling, my three fair claimants, and let the festivities resume. As for this little gem of contention, I shall just keep it myself until judgment is made." And his huge hand closed lovingly about the golden apple.

"The war, man, the war!" cried Achilles. "Enough of parents, weddings, and high vanities! When will your tale tell of war?"

"Hark now. These events I relate are the living seeds. They will bear bloody fruit, I promise, and you, my boy, will be there for the harvesting. Where was I?"

"Zeus was seeking one wise among mortals to give judgment upon the claims of the goddesses."

"It was Paris he chose. Paris, secret prince of Troy, Priam's youngest son, was thought to have been killed at birth because an oracle had warned that his deeds would destroy Troy."

"Reason enough for the king to drown him like a kitten. How is it he survived?"

"Oh, some plot of Hecuba's, no doubt. A mother's heart cherishes her sons, even those who endanger the state. It is said Queen Hecuba instructed her serving man to smuggle the babe out of the castle and give him to a certain shepherd to raise as his own. He grew up to be very beautiful. It's a handsome family anyway, and he is the fairest by far, they say, of Priam's fifty sons. The shepherd maids trailed him up and down the slopes like ewes in season. But he was yet unripe; he spurned the maidens. This, of course, recommended him to uneasy husbands and lovers, giving them a great opinion of his wisdom and moderation. So it was that he was called on to mediate their disputes, fix grazing rights, judge the point of cattle, and so forth. When Zeus bent his ear to earth to hear of a man of judgment, the strongest word came from Mount Ida, speaking the name, Paris."

The hot silver of a flying fish scudded suddenly out of the water followed by the black-silver hump of a broaching dolphin. For half a breath they hung in the air, long enough for Achilles to uncoil from the deck with a swift fluency that delighted the warrior heart of Ulysses, and to hurl a short lance through the air transfixing the winged fish so that it fell heavily before the dolphin—which drew out the lance, swam to the boat, and tossed the weapon aboard with a flick of its head, grinning up at the men like a dog, then turned and swam back for its meal.

Dolphins were even more intelligent then than they are now, and were friendly toward the Hellenes—mainly to annoy Poseidon with whom they had an old feud. They disliked his treatment of Amphitrite whom he tormented with his infidelities. She had been a nereid of the dolphin school before her marriage.

"Well thrown," said Ulysses.

"It thirsts for blood," said Achilles, wiping his lancehead. "I must appease it with hunting until it can drink of the enemy upon the beaches of Troy. Unless, of course, I am lucky enough to fall in with a private quarrel."

"Strictly forbidden," said Ulysses. "There's a war on. Private quarrels must wait. We have all taken an oath, and you must, too."

"Tell the tale, king of Ithaca. It shortens the journey."

The judgment of paris

They were fighting a headwind out of Scyros, and Ulysses saw that it would take some days to reach Aulis. He told the rest of the story in the old bardic way with many a trill and flourish, and taking every byroad. But we will shorten it.

In those days it was customary to bribe judges, which shows how far we have come since. And so Paris was offered bribes.

Hera offered him power.

"Great fleets shall sail at your nod," she told him. "Armies shall march when you raise your hand. Dominion shall be yours over land and sea. All men shall be as slaves to you. Your smile will quicken them, your frown kill. And power is wealth. Your slaves will delve the earth for gold and jewels. Your galleys will plunder far places and sail back with cargoes beyond dreams of piracy to stuff your vaults. All this shall be yours if you award me the apple.

"Reverence, you will agree, is the highest wisdom. How can you judge more wisely than by conforming to the judgment of Father Zeus, master of choices, who of all living creatures chose me, me, me as his wife? A more serious choice, you understand, than among you mortals, for neither of us can die and he must keep me to wife through all eternity.

"Be reverent then, Paris. Be rich and powerful. Choose me, Hera. Let the apple be mine."

Athena spoke, "Father Zeus, remember, has appointed you judge, meaning that he throws his own divine power behind your judgment; otherwise he would have judged for himself. As for Hera's argument, it signifies nothing. Anyone acquainted with affairs on Olympus knows that it is godly to keep titles within the immediate family. That is the only reason Zeus married his sister. And it has been amply proved —by which I mean almost every night for two thousand years—that he finds others more attractive than his wife.

"As for her offer, I can overbid that, too. I offer you wisdom. Born from Zeus's head I am Patroness of Intellectual Activities, you know, and wisdom is uniquely mine to offer. And without wisdom, power loses its potence and wealth grows poor. I can teach you to know, to understand, to penetrate to the innermost secrets of man's soul. I can disclose to you certain divine secrets which men call nature. With such knowledge you will have mastery over other men and, more important, mastery over yourself. As for Hera's glittering promises, remember this: I am also Mistress of Strategy. Before battle, captains pray to me for tactics. Give me that apple and I will make you the greatest soldier of the age. Everyone knows that power and wealth depend finally on victory in war.

"Be wise, Paris, choose the Goddess of Wisdom."

All Aphrodite said was, "Come closer. . . ."

When he approached, she touched him and the world changed. The sun dived into the sea and made it boil, and his blood boiled, too. He felt himself going red-hot like a poker in the fire. Then she touched him with her other hand, and a delicious icy coolness washed over him. He forgot everything but the touch of her hands, her fragrance, the music of her voice.

"I am Aphrodite, Goddess of Love. I give you the first of

two gifts now and ask no promise. This gift is your own body, wherein is contained the only true wealth, the only true power, the only wisdom. You shall receive the second gift after you have delivered judgment. There is a mortal woman on earth said to rival me in beauty. She is Helen, queen of Sparta, and I hereby promise her to you."

Without hesitation Paris awarded the apple to Aphrodite. Screaming like Harpies, Athena and Hera flew back to Olympus, flung themselves before Zeus, and tried to get Aphrodite disqualified for illegal use of hands. Zeus laughed at them. He agreed with Paris's choice and was thankful that it would be the young shepherd prince, and not himself, who would attract the savage reprisals of the goddesses.

Aflame with Aphrodite's touch, drunk with her promise, Paris dropped his role of shepherd and returned to Troy, storming into the great throne-room and sweeping the astounded Priam and Hecuba into his embrace. He demanded they recognize him as their son. All their hesitations and fears were burned away in the blaze of his beauty, and they received him with great joy. His forty-nine brothers were a bit more dubious, remembering what the oracle had warned, but Priam was king, and his wish was law. Besides, things had been dull and peaceful for some time, and the prospect of danger was not unwelcome.

Then Paris asked that a ship be fitted out so that he might make an embassy to the kingdom of Sparta.

"I can tell you no more, Venerable Majesty. I must speak no further, brothers. The purpose of my voyage is a secret between me and the gods. But I promise you this: When I return I shall bring with me a cargo such as no ship has ever carried—and with it undying fame for us all. Thus a goddess has assured me in secret, and that secret is my destiny."

A small fleet was fitted out, and Paris sailed away for Sparta. In a few weeks' time he returned with Helen aboard.

There, before all Troy, he declared her his wife, admitting that she was encumbered with a prior husband, but that this detail was beneath consideration. When Menelaus came to Troy, as come he must, then he, Paris, would engage the husband in single combat and with one thrust of his spear make Helen half a widow and wholly a wife.

Priam and Hecuba and Paris's forty-nine brothers and fifty sisters fully understood what was happening—Paris had not only stolen another man's wife, but even worse, committed a breach of hospitality, a much more serious sacrilege. They knew Troy would shortly be plunged into a bloody war with the most powerful chieftains of Achaea, Helles, Boetia, Sparta, Athens, and that entire warlike peninsula not yet called Greece. But when Helen smiled at them they forgot all their fears.

"It's true," they whispered to each other. "She's as beautiful as Aphrodite. Surely the gods will allow us to protect such a treasure."

The only dissenting voice was that of Cassandra, Priam's youngest daughter. Apollo had wooed her one summer past; his sunstroke caress left her with visions. The future painted itself in smoky pictures for her to read, but she had tired of the sun god's touch.

Apollo, maddened, had said, "Wicked girl, you shall choke with frustration even as I do now. I have given you the gift of prophecy, and now I make that gift a punishment. The more accurate your prediction, the less you shall be believed. The colder the disbelief, the more ardent your forecast."

Now, as Paris introduced Helen to the court, and the tall lovers stood in a blaze of acceptance and love, and Priam's fifty sons beat their spearhafts on their shields bawling defiance at the Greeks, then it was that Cassandra lifted her voice in prophecy:

"Hear me, Trojans, hear me. Return that harlot whence

she came, for she brings death with her. Your fair city will be rent stone from stone, your young men slaughtered, your ancients shamed, your women and children taken into slavery. Ship her back to Sparta before it is too late . . . too late . . . too late. . . ."

Helen, hearing only her name spoken, smiled at the girl. The crowd, seeing her smile, went wild with enthusiasm. Cassandra's words were heeded no more than if they had been the small wind rattling the leaves. The girl fell silent, moaning softly as the thwarted vision dug its fangs into her head.

"That is why we're off to Troy now," said Ulysses to Achilles. "The events I have related to you, young falcon, are the roots of this war."

"All this to retrieve a runaway bride," said Achilles. "One reason to fight is as good as another, so long as you do, but I would have expected a great war to have a greater cause."

"You haven't seen the lady," said Ulysses.

"Oh, I understand what you tell me, that she is enough to send the Trojans mad. But then they're half-mad to begin with."

"I repeat, you haven't seen the lady or you wouldn't talk this way. She's enough to send more than Trojans mad. She's maddened some very hardheaded Greeks that I know of, all of us, to be sure. We were all her suitors—every prince and chieftain of the Peloponnesus and its islands—so many of us and such a fierce brawling crew that her foster father, Tyndareus, didn't dare give her to any one of us for fear he might offend the others. So he kept fobbing us off with one excuse after another until we were ready to fly at each other's throats, but, finally, I came up with a little plan. It was this: that each suitor take an oath that we would abide by Helen's own choice of husband and forebear from attacking the lucky man or Tyndareus. Further, we would swear to a binding alliance, so that if anyone else attacked her husband and attempted to rob him of Helen, we would band together and punish the interloper. We swore a most sacred oath on the quartered carcass of a horse. And that is why we must all go now to the aid of Menelaus and pursue Paris even into Troy itself."

"Are they good fighters, the Trojans?" asked Achilles.

"The best—next to us. And, in their own minds, they have no such reservation. There will be keen fighting, never doubt it. I have told you of how we wooed Helen, the compromise that came out of it, and the alliance. But mark you now, within a general purpose a man does things for his own ends. I'm saying we might not have all been so eager to help Menelaus but that each of us sees something in it for himself. Fame, of course. A chance to use our swords before they grow rusty. Also slaves. And mountains of loot. Troy is a very rich city, far richer than any of ours. The city stands upon a headland commanding the straits which lead into the Black Sea and to the rich land of Scythia where there are boundless opportunities for trade, slave raids, robbery, piracy, and other commercial traffic. While Troy stands our fleets can never enter those straits, nor can we penetrate the lands of the Black Sea, nor the further mysterious reaches of Asia whose east winds fairly reek of wealth. These are considerations, too, lad."

"All I want to do is fight," said Achilles. "I'll leave the reasons to you."

"Well, you should get your stomachful. Our forces are to be led by Agamemnon, king of Mycenae and brother to Menelaus. He is a bold, practical leader, very aggressive, very ruthless. He is married to Helen's older sister, Clytemnestra, and so has a double motive for adopting his brother's blood-feud with the Royal family of Troy. . . ."

What Ulysses did not tell Achilles was that he himself had

used all his remarkable cunning to avoid the Trojan campaign. An oracle had said that if Ulysses went off to fight at Troy it would be twenty years before he could come home, and when he did so, it would be as a penniless vagabond recognized by no one. So when Agamemnon and Palamedes, king of Euboea, came to Ithaca to demand his aid against Troy, he tried to evade his vow by feigning madness. He put on a tall pointed fool's hat and harnessed a bull and a goat to his plow, sowing his furrow with salt instead of seed. After watching him for a bit, Palamedes, who was almost as crafty as Ulysses, decided to give him a sanity test. He plucked Ulysses' infant son from his nurse's arms and set him on the ground in the path of the oncoming plow. Ulysses reined his animals short and snatched the babe out of danger.

"You're fit for fighting," said Palamedes. "Drop the bluff and come along."

"A parent's instinct is stronger than reason—I mean unreason," said Ulysses, "but I assure you my wits are deranged."

"Nonsense," growled Agamemnon. "How sane do you have to be to make war? In this affair a touch of madness may help. You have the right sort of wits for us, Ulysses. Now keep your oath, and come away."

So Ulysses was forced to yield. As his first task, he volunteered to recruit Achilles who had disappeared. The same oracle had stated that the Greeks must lose the war unless Achilles fought, but that he would not survive the siege. Ulysses had a shrewd idea that Achilles' mother, Thetis, had hidden the boy away, preferring his survival to Greek victory.

tHE EVENTS AT AuLis

They found a thousand ships at Aulis and the greatest
gathering of heroes since the beginning of time. Their commander was Agamemnon, an angry bull of a man, burly as
the stump of an oak, with a dark red face and eyes cold and
hard as chunks of lava—until he became enraged, when they
glowed like hot coals. His voice of command was like the bellowing of a bull.

When Achilles smelled a fight, his blood did not heat nor
did excitement take him. A delicious chill prickled over all
his body, sweet cold airs wrapped themselves about his limbs,
cool fingers stroked his hair, and in his mouth was a taste like
honey. This is what made him so fearsome in battle; he
fought like other men make love. He fought with gleaming
chest and flashing arm and marvelously thewed leg, and he
smiled his lipless smile as he fought. He did not shout except
when summoning his men, but uttered a low crooning sound
like a love song. Men, fighting him, felt his blade at their
throats like an act of deliverance.

Now when he saw the bull-man, Agamemnon, he felt that
delicious chill touch his neck and he knew that this man was
his archenemy in all the world even though they were fighting on the same side, and that his main problem in the war
to come would be how to refrain from attacking his commander.

Agamemnon gazed at Achilles with no great favor when
Ulysses led the young man over to present him.

"Hail, great Agamemnon," said Ulysses. "I wish you to meet Achilles and to value him as I do. According to prophecy, it is his courage and skill that will bring us victory in the war to come."

"Oracles take delight in riddling," said Agamemnon. "Seems to me they never say things straight anymore. I welcome you, young man, and look forward to seeing you display that courage and skill of which the oracle speaks."

"Thank you," said Achilles.

"The oracle holds also that you will not survive this war," said Agamemnon. "I suppose that is why your mother hid you away among the maidens of Scyros."

"I suppose so," said Achilles, "but you know how parents are. How devouring their love can be."

Ulysses snorted with laughter. The blood flamed in Agamemnon's face. This was a shrewd rejoinder of Achilles; it related to a scandal in Agamemnon's family. It was his father, Atreus, who had committed one of the most unsavory crimes in history. He had butchered his nephews and served them up in a stew to their father, his brother, Thyestes, all so that he could seize the throne of Mycenae and rule unchallenged, the same throne that Agamemnon had inherited.

Ulysses eyed Agamemnon closely. He knew that the man was seething with rage, and was only a hairbreadth from striking out at Achilles.

He saw Achilles himself lightly balancing on the balls of his feet, ready to move in any direction, and smiling his lipless smile.

But Agamemnon mastered himself and said, "Truly, Achilles, if your sword is as sharp as your tongue you should do great damage to the Trojans. In the meantime, welcome. We shall converse again when your Myrmidons arrive. Then you may report for instructions about their quartering, forage for the horses, sailing order, and so forth."

"Very good, sir," said Achilles. "Thank you for your courtesy."

Thus, bloodshed was averted upon that first meeting, but the note of hatred was struck between them that was to devil the efforts of the Greeks, and almost lead to defeat.

Now Ulysses took the young man about the encampment, introducing him to the other great chieftains. He met Palamedes, king of Euboea, most skilled artificer since Daedalus; and Diomedes, king of Argos—a man, it was said, who had never known fear. He was presented to the two warriors named Ajax. One was Ajax of Salamis, strongest mortal since Hercules, head and shoulders taller than Achilles. Again, the young man, measuring the giant with his eyes, felt a breath of that sweet combative chill, but he could work up no fighting wrath.

The huge man grinned down at him, and said, "Stop puffing your chest like a rooster. You and I are going to be friends and fight only Trojans."

He clapped his great meaty paw on Achilles' shoulder—a blow hard enough to cripple an ordinary man, but Achilles accepted it as a friendly tap and nodded gravely back at Ajax. He never smiled his lipless smile except when angry.

He was pleased also to meet the Lesser Ajax, leader of the Locrians, a man famous for his speed afoot and his deadly spearmanship, two talents which Achilles himself fancied that he possessed beyond all men.

Standing with the two Ajaxes was Teucer, brother to Great Ajax and the best archer since Hercules. The three made a fighting team. In battle, Great Ajax would shelter the Lesser Ajax and Teucer behind his enormous bullhide shield. From there Teucer would shoot his venomous arrows and Lesser Ajax hurl his lances, and no one could approach them for Ajax whirled his huge sword making an impassable thicket of steel. Together, like this, they moved slowly upon the enemy lines, cleaving their way through a loam of dead bodies like a plowman turning soil.

He met Idmoneus, king of Crete, a swarthy pirate, savage as a wild boar, who shared command of the land forces with Agamemnon.

All these tested warriors received the young man with marks of esteem even though he had not yet proven himself in battle. They had heard startling reports of him from his old tutor, Phoenix, a man much feared by foemen, who was there at Aulis as a member of the War Council. Phoenix had told how he had managed the education of the young Achilles. He had taken him and his elder cousin, Patroclus, onto the wild slopes of Mount Pelion, Achilles being seven years old then, and Patroclus twelve. He had fed the younger boy on the bloody meat of courage itself, restricting his diet to the entrails of bear and wolf and lion, which Achilles had eaten greedily, but Patroclus had refused. He had recruited the centaur, Chiron, to help raise the boys, and Chiron had taught Achilles to run more swiftly than a staghound, to hunt down the wild boar without the use of hounds, and to split a willow wand with his spear at a hundred yards.

Patroclus he had tutored in the softer arts—the use of herbs and music for healing and how to play the pipe and psaltery. At the age of thirteen, Achilles had singlehandedly slaughtered a robber band that, for years, had terrified the villagers on Mount Pelion. He had been wounded in thigh and shoulder in this fight, and Patroclus had tended him, poulticed him, and nursed him back to health. With such tales had Phoenix stuffed the other leaders at Aulis, so it was little wonder they were ready to extend so hearty a welcome to Achilles.

The young warrior was overjoyed to meet his old tutor in this place and even more happy to learn that his dear cousin and playmate, Patroclus, was sailing toward Aulis at the head of the Myrmidons.

THE SIEGE BEGINS

Ulysses had warned that the war would be a long one, but Agamemnon, who always preferred to believe what was most convenient, was confident of a quick victory. When the Greeks landed on the Trojan beaches they met stiff resistance. A Trojan hero, Cycnus, son of Poseidon, a man who could not be wounded by sword or spear, captained the beach party and fought like a demon, almost driving the Greeks into the sea. Achilles it was who finally killed him without a weapon by twisting Cycnus's helmet so that he was strangled by his own chin strap. Then the Greeks rallied and fought their way to the Trojan walls, but met so savage a defence that they had to withdraw.

At the War Council, Ulysses said, "I was right, unfortunately. It will be a long war. Their walls are huge, their men brave, and they have at least three magnificent warriors, Prince Hector, his young brother Troilus, and his cousin Aeneas. Sheltered by such walls, led by such heroes, they are

too powerful for direct assault. We shall have to lay siege.
In the meantime, by using our sea power, we can raid the
nearby islands one by one. This will strip Troy of her allies
and provide us with food and slaves."

It was agreed, and Achilles was named commander of the
raiding parties. During the next eight years he attacked the
home islands of Troy's allies one by one, sacked their cities,
took much loot and many slaves. All this time the main body
of the Greeks encamped on the beach behind a stockade of
pointed stakes and laid siege to the mighty city.

But a siege is a tedious business, and quarrels flared among
the men who had grown tired of the war and longed for
home. The bitterest squabbles were provoked by the division
of slaves. One of these almost sent the Greeks home in defeat.

tHe quARRel

On one raid Achilles captured Cressida, one of the loveliest
young maidens of Troy. She was a smokey-eyed, honey-
skinned girl with a low hoarse voice. When Agamemnon
heard her speak at the Dividing of the Spoils, he felt her
voice running over nerve ends of his face—like a cat's tongue
licking him. And he immediately claimed her as his share of
the booty. Ordinarily, Achilles would have disputed this
claim and an ugly squabble would have flared, but upon this
raid, Achilles had captured a girl he fancied more, a tall

green-eyed maiden named Briseis. So Agamemnon's claim was allowed, and he took Cressida into his tent. She was hard to handle at first, but Agamemnon was an old hand at breaking slave-girls, and very soon she was content, or pretended to be.

But her father was not content. His name was Chryses; he was a priest of Apollo and a soothsayer. He came under a truce to Agamemnon's tent and begged the release of his daughter, offering a generous ransom. But Agamemnon would have none of it. He was infatuated with the girl, and he drove her father away with harsh words. The old man, furious and humiliated, prayed to Apollo as he hobbled back toward Troy.

"Oh, Phoebus, I implore you, curb that haughty spirit. Punish Agamemnon, who keeps my daughter in carnal bond and vile servitude. Today, he insults your servant; tomorrow, Apollo, he will insult your holy self. He is a most arrogant Greek, overbearing and imperious, ready to affront a god should his will be questioned."

It suited Apollo to hear this prayer. He favored the Trojans in the war and felt that it was time to do the Greeks a mischief. He descended that night and stood between the great wall and the Greek encampment on the beach. He shot arrows of pestilence among the tents. They were tipped with fever. They ignited the camp refuse; foul vapors caught fire. Again and again Apollo shot his arrows. Where they struck, plague burned. Man and beast sickened. In the morning they awoke to die. Horses died, and cattle. In three days the Greeks had lost half as many troops as they had in nine years of fighting.

Ulysses urged Agamemnon to call a council. There, the oracle, Calchas, was consulted because it was known that plague is sent by the gods in punishment for some affront, real or fancied. And it is always necessary to find out which god so that the insult might be undone. But Calchas balked when he was called upon for interpretation.

"Pardon, great king," he said to Agamemnon, "but I would far rather you called upon another oracle."

"Why should we?" said Ulysses. "You're the best we have, and the best is what we need."

Agamemnon said, "Read the signs, oh Calchas, and tell us true."

"I have read the signs, and the truth will anger you. And who will protect me from your sudden wrath?"

"I will," said Achilles, looking at Agamemnon. "I guarantee your safety."

"Hear then the reason for this pestilence. Our high king and war-leader, Agamemnon, has angered Apollo by insulting his priest, Chryses, who seeks the return of his daughter, Cressida. Agamemnon's angry refusal has kindled the radiant wrath of Phoebus who descended with a quiver full of plague darts which he flung into our tents so that we sicken and die."

"I don't believe it," roared Agamemnon.

"It makes sense," Achilles said. "Speak on, Calchas. Tell us how we can placate Apollo and avert this plague."

"The remedy is obvious," said Calchas. "Cressida must be returned to her father, without ransom. Then a clean wind will spring from the sea, blowing away the pestilence."

Agamemnon turned savagely upon Calchas, "You miserable, spiteful, croaking old raven. You have never yet in all the years I have known you spoke me a favorable auspice. Whether studying the flight of birds or examining their entrails or casting bones, by whatever secret contrivance you read the riddle of the future, it is always to my disadvantage. In your eyes I am always angering the gods, as if they had nothing to do but perch on Olympus and watch me night and day, seeking cause for anger in the actions of this one poor mortal, ignoring everyone else on earth.

"At Aulis you said I had angered Artemis by not invoking her aid in some hunt or other, and that it was she who had sent the northeast gale to keep us penned in the harbor and prevent our fleet from sailing for Troy. It was not until you prevailed upon me to sacrifice my own eldest, dearest daughter, Iphigenia, that you were satisfied. Now, you wish to rob me of even a greater prize, the smoky-eyed Cressida, so much more beautiful and skillful than my own wife, Clytemnestra. Now you seek to rob me of the one prize I value after nine years of bloody toil on these beaches, bidding me tear my very heart from my body to appease Apollo, and the Royal Council agrees with you. The chiefs agree with you. Very well, so be it. But, by the easily angered Gods, know this: I will not be left without a prize. If you take Cressida from me, I will take someone else's beautiful and clever slave-girl."

Achilles sprang to his feet. "From what common pen of slaves do you expect to draw your compensation?" he cried. "In your blind and matchless greed you have forgotten that each man takes his own prize as divided according to your own unjust decrees whereby you always get the lion's share, or should I say the swine's share? No, you must give up Cressida without immediate compensation. For no man here, I believe, will give up what is his own. Perhaps when we raid another rich colony, or when Troy herself finally falls, if ever she does, then you will be able to take booty that will glut even your greed."

"You are a mighty warrior, Achilles," said Agamemnon. "But your spear speaks more surely than your tongue. I am High King, chosen by all of you in a choice certified by the gods. To deprive me of any jot or iota of my rights is sacrilege—not only foolish, but impious. It is my duty to take someone else's woman to repay me for the loss of the lovely Cressida for a king deprived is half a king, and half a king means defeat in warfare. If I want your woman, Achilles, or

Ulysses', or that of Diomedes, or any creature I choose, all I have to do is reach my hand and take. But that will all be decided later. For the moment, I consent. Cressida shall be returned so that the plague may end."

"Why you great snorting hog!" cried Achilles. "You are more fit to king it over a pigpen somewhere than to try to lead a band of free men. So this is how you would arrange things—that the burden should fall always on me, while you grab the spoils for yourself. Well, I've had enough. I'm tired of fighting your battles and those of your brother, who wasn't man enough to keep his wife in his bed. I'm taking my Myrmidons and sailing back home. We will see how you make out against Hector and his brothers."

"Go where you will, you bragging brawler," said Agamemnon. "You're better at fighting your friends than your enemies anyway. Board your beaked ship and sail where you will —to Hades I hope. But I swear by my crown that when you go you shall leave Briseis behind. And I shall take her to replace Cressida."

Now the lion wrath of Achilles rose in his breast and choked him with its sulphurous bile. He could think of nothing but to cleave the crowd and kill Agamemnon where he stood. He drew his sword, but a strong hand caught his arm. It was Athena, heaven-descended, invisible to everyone but Achilles. She fixed him with eyes as hotly gray as the sun swimming through fog, so brilliant that they seemed to scorch his face. An unearthly musk came off her white arms. But Achilles was too angry to be intimidated.

"Great goddess," he said, "I love and venerate you. But if you have come to stop me from killing Agamemnon you are wasting your time. He has insulted me and must pay with his life."

"Where life and death are concerned," said Athena, "only the gods say 'must.' You are the greatest of mortals, Achilles, but I have come to teach you this. You are not to kill Agamemnon. Hera, queen of the gods, and I myself are mightily interested in the victory of Greek arms. We can allow no squabbling among your leaders, no division among your troops. As for your wrath, it is justified. I promise you this. Inside a space of days, great Agamemnon will humble himself to you and offer the return of your slave-girl, and gifts more valuable than you can reckon. I promise you this. Hera promises it. But you must obey us."

"I listen and obey," said Achilles. "I will hold my hand from him, and he shall live at least until the next time. But I shall never fight under his leadership again."

"Yes, tell him so," said Athena. "Attack him in words as fiercely as you will. The man has been blinded by greed to the detriment of his leadership, and he must be shaken up or victory will elude you Greeks whom the best gods love. Tell him what you will, say what you will, but do not kill him."

Athena disappeared. Achilles sheathed his sword again, saying, "You are a putrid cur, Agamemnon, unfit to lead men in battle. Only by the grace of heaven am I sparing your life now. I shall not follow your example and squabble over a slave-girl. Take her if you must, you besotted swine, and may you strangle in your own lust. But I tell you this: I will not fight against Troy. I will not contend against Hector and his brothers. Priam's brave sons and the Trojan troops shall go unchecked for all of me. From now on I pay no heed to battle, but fit out my ships for the voyage home. And when Hector is winnowing your ranks like the man with the scythe among the September wheat, when you see your troops falling by the dozens before that terrible sword, then, eat out your heart in remorse for having treated Achilles so."

Achilles stalked off, leaving the council aghast.

tHETis

Before the council broke up, the ancient general, Nestor, who had led three generations of warriors and was now Agamemnon's most trusted advisor, addressed the assembly. He tried to dissuade Agamemnon from the path he had chosen, but though the eloquence flowed sweet as nectar from his mouth, the high king could not be swayed. He sent two messengers to Achilles' tent to bear away the beautiful Briseis. Achilles watched them take the girl and did not offer them harm although they trembled at his shadow. He was too fair-minded to blame Agamemnon's messengers for the king's own evil, and he was forced to hold his hand from Agamemnon because of Athena's command. But he wept as he saw Briseis being borne off. He turned to face the sea.

"Oh, deep Mother," he prayed. "Thetis of the Silver Feet, you who rise from the tides of the moon to trouble man's sleep forever, you who led my father a chase through all the changes of beast and fish before you allowed yourself to be caught, you, Thetis, my mother, most beautiful and generous of naiads, help me now or I shall strangle here of a choler I cannot lance with my good blade."

Thetis was sporting then in the depths of the sea, fleeing the amorous clutch of Poseidon, allowing him almost to catch her, then escaping his attentions by dodging behind a giant squid, which she tickled, making the great jellied creature cast a curtain of black ink between her and her lustful pursuer. In the midst of her sport, her son's voice drifted down to her, and she arose from the sea like a mist.

"Oh, my brave Son," she cried. "Why these tears? Tell your mother so that she may share your grief."

"Welcome, gentle Mother," said Achilles. "Thank you for coming when I call. I suffer thus because Agamemnon, the high king, has offered me ignoble insult. Denied by the gods of his own bedmate, he has taken my beautiful slave-girl, Briseis, into his tent. And I am forbidden by Athena to draw my sword from its sheath and must stand helplessly by and watch myself despoiled."

"Ever meddlesome Athena!" cried Thetis. "Powerful you are, but I have powers, too."

"Yes, Mother, the owl-goddess has forbidden me vengeance. I must stand here choking back my wrath, and, oh Mother, it is too bitter to swallow."

"What would you have me do, my son? How can I help you?"

"You must intercede with Father Zeus, whose edict over-bears Athena's and all the gods'. Speak winningly to him, Mother, as you alone can do. Arouse his interest in my behalf. Let him nod toward Troy, infusing courage into the Trojan hearts and strength into the Trojan arms. Let haughty Agamemnon find himself penned on the beaches while swift Hector and his brothers slaughter the Achaean forces. Then, then will he rend his beard and weep for Achilles."

"I shall do so," said Thetis. "Swiftly will I travel to the Bronze Palace of the All-High and beseech his intervention in your behalf. Those two mighty hags, Hera and Athena, keep close watch upon him, seeing that he does not intercede for Troy. But he still has some measure of regard for me, no doubt, and I still own some powers of persuasion, I am told. Rest easy, Son. Wrap yourself in your cloak and taste sweet dreamless repose as your mother does your bidding. And

gladly will she do it, for, in truth, you are the loveliest, strongest son that any mother, mortal or goddess, was blessed with."

She disappeared into the sea. Achilles lay down and went to sleep and did not dream.

Upon that same night Cressida was returned to her father by Ulysses, who said, "Here, venerable Chryses, is your daughter returned. Now keep your part of the bargain and pray to Apollo to lift the plague which strikes among our tents killing man and beast."

Chryses embraced his daughter, and said, "Depart in peace, good Ulysses. This very night I will sacrifice nine bulls to Apollo. And with the ascending savor of their flesh will go my prayers. Since it was at my request that great Phoebus shot his plague arrows, no doubt at my request he will hold his hand. By dawn a wind will arise from the sea blowing the fever out of your tents."

His daughter Cressida stayed dutifully by his side, but said not a word. For, after some nights of trouble, she had fallen quite in love with heavy-handed Agamemnon. Although she pretended joy at her return, she was already planning how to get back to the Greek tents.

Now, like a great white sea bird, silver-footed Thetis flew to the Bronze Palace of Zeus high on mount Olympus. She found him seated on a throne of black rock in his garden, looking down upon the earth. He smiled when he saw her for she had long been a favorite of his. Then, remembering that Hera might be watching, he quickly changed his smile to a frown. But Thetis had felt the first warmth of his smile which melted snow out of season in the mountains of far-off Thessaly, starting an avalanche. She sank down beside him among the flowers that grew at his feet, hugged his legs, and spoke to him. As she spoke, she raised her long arm and stroked his beard and touched his face.

"Father Zeus," she said, "I, Thetis, daughter of the sea, present her warmest greetings to mighty Zeus, king of the gods, ruler of sky, air, and mountain. If I mention my name, oh heavenly one, it is because I fear you might have forgotten me. It has been so many long painful hours since we last met."

"I have not forgotten you," said Zeus in a thunderous whisper. It was this unfortunate inability of his to whisper softly that upset so many of his nocturnes by catching Hera's sharp ears—even when he was conducting his session in a secret place upon some remote marge of beach or shelf of cliff.

"Thanks be for that," said Thetis, "for I think of you constantly."

"Constantly, my dear? But I understand you have many distractions."

"Oh, yes. I am a goddess, and grief does not become me. But even among the most sportive of my diversions my dreams shuttle your image like a girl weaving who, no matter what gray or blue thread embroiders the detail of her design, still casts the strong scarlet flax which becomes the theme-line of her tapestry. Thus does memory of you, my king, run its scarlet thread through the shuttling and weaving of my dreams."

"Sweet words, Thetis, which your voice makes even sweeter. What favor do you seek?"

"All-knowing Zeus, you have read my heart. Pleasure and longing alone would bring me to you, but now, as it happens, I do have a petition. Not for myself, but for my son, Achilles, the son of Peleus, my mortal husband, whom you will re-member, no doubt. And you will remember, too, that Achilles' days are briefly numbered. It has been decreed by the Fates that he could choose between brilliant fighting and death at Troy or a long life of peace and obscurity far from battle cry and clash of spear. He chose Troy and death, of course. Since his days are to be so brief, I do not wish them clouded by suffering. And Agamemnon makes him suffer brutal injustice."

"I do not understand," said Zeus. "Why does he not kill Agamemnon? Your son is no man to allow himself to be insulted."

"Aye, his sword had leaped halfway from its scabbard when your daughter Athena intervened, bidding him swallow his wrath and allow Agamemnon to work his horrid will. He has obeyed her because she is your daughter and her strength derives from yours, as does that of all the gods. But he wishes to pay out Agamemnon all the same."

"What can I do at this juncture?" said Zeus.

"Inspire the Trojans to attack. Fire their hearts and strengthen their arms so that they are triumphant, so that Agamemnon must beg my son's pardon or face defeat. As you know, Achilles is the very buckler of the Greek forces; without him, they must surely lose."

The frown on Zeus's face was darkening. Sable night itself seemed to flow from his beard and hair. Darkness thickened upon earth. Men groaned in their sleep, and the birds stopped singing.

"If I grant your favor, oh Thetis, it means endless trouble for me. Night and day will Queen Hera rail and nag, haunt my pleasures and devil my repose. For she heavily favors the Greeks. And, knowing that I disagree, she has made me promise neutrality at least. But she is always accusing me of secret partiality for the Trojans, which is true, which is true. . . . Now, if I do this thing for you, her opinion stands confirmed, and she will reveal her aptitude as archcrone of the Universe."

"Please," said Thetis.

"I cannot refuse you," said Zeus, "but return to the sea,

now, quickly lest she spot us conversing here and her suspicions be prematurely aroused. One kiss, my salty minx, and then off you go."

"Here's a kiss with all my heart. You do promise?"

"I do," said Zeus. "We shall have another conversation, perhaps, after the Greeks lose their battle."

"Gladly. Do not keep me waiting too long, dear Zeus."

Thetis left Olympus and sank to the depths of the sea. Zeus went into the banqueting hall of his Bronze Palace where the gods were gathered, but Hera was not disposed to let him eat the evening meal in peace.

"King of Deceivers!" she cried. "You have been with that briny bitch, Thetis. And she has been asking you for favors. To help the Trojans, no doubt, because her bumptious brawling son has cooked up a grievance against the great Agamemnon."

"Good sister and wife," said Zeus. "Hera of the Golden Throne, please shut your nagging mouth, and keep it shut before I plant my fist in it."

"Abuse me! Beat me! You have the power and can do so, but you have not the power to make me stop telling you what you should hear. I know that deep-sea trollop has been flattering you, getting you to promise this and that. She's capable of anything, that one. Do you know how she spends her time? She hides behind reefs to capsize ships so that she can swim off with her arms full of sailors, whom she keeps in a deep grotto and wears them out in her service. Then, when they're all used up and as feeble as old men, she feeds them to the sharks and makes necklaces out of their finger bones. She probably tells you that she spends her time doing kind deeds and pining away for one more glimpse of your august visage. And you, with all your tremendous wisdom and your insight into men's souls, you swallow this flattery like a schoolboy and promise her to do mischief to my Greeks."

GREEKS BEARING GIFTS

36

Zeus said no word but frowned so heavily that the stone floor began to crack. His fingers tightened around his scepter which was a radiant volt-blue zigzag shaft of lightning. For he was also known as the Thunderer, Lord of Lightning—and, when angered, flung that deadly bolt the way a warrior hurls his lance.

Hephaestus, the smith-god, lame son of Zeus and Hera, who in his volcanic smithy had forged these lightning bolts and knew their awful power, ran to his mother in fear, whispering, "Mother, Mother, say something pleasant. Smile! Stop nagging! You'll get us all killed."

"Never," hissed Hera. "Let him flail about with his lightning bolt; let the brute do what he wishes. I shall never stop railing and howling until he disowns that trollop and her plots."

"Nay, Mother, you forget. He has reason to favor Thetis of the Silver Feet, whatever her amorous habits. Do not forget her ancient loyalty to him. When you and Athena and Poseidon plotted against him and tried to depose him from his throne—took him by surprise and bound him with a hundred knots—was it not she who called the hundred-handed Briareus, his titanic gardener, who sprang into the Bronze Palace and rescued his master, each of his hundred hands untying a knot? Do you not remember? It was upon that terrible night, too, that he showed what his wrath could be, punishing us all, particularly you, chaining you upside down in the vault of heaven until your screams cracked the crystal goblets of the stars?"

"I remember," muttered Hera hoarsely. "I remember."

"Then appease him, Mother. Say something gentle, quickly. His wrath is brewing. I see it plain, and terrible will be the consequences."

Hera arose then, and said, "Mighty Zeus, Lord of us all, I beg your pardon for causing you disquiet. It is only my concern for your peace of mind that sometimes leads me to hasty words. For I know how strong your honor is, how you value your word, and how you would hate to do anything to breach the promise of neutrality that you have given to me and Athena. Forgive my undue zeal in fearing that the trollopy tricks of moist Thetis would seduce you from your vow. Forgive me now, dear Lord, and I will not say another word no matter what your intentions in the war below."

"Seat yourselves all," boomed Zeus. "Drink your mead. We shall quarrel no more upon this night for it is the shortest of all the year and filled with the perfumes of earth."

THE WAR COUNCIL

Zeus sent a misleading dream to Agamemnon. The dream masqueraded as Nestor who came to the king's tent at dawn and said, "Awake! Awake! This is no time to be sleeping. Hera has persuaded Zeus to permit the fall of Troy. You must move immediately to the attack. Awake. Rouse yourself from slumber and advance upon Troy. For gods grow wroth when men waste their favor."

Agamemnon arose immediately and called together his council. He related his dream. Nestor climbed to his feet blushing with pride for it pleased him to appear in a dream sent by Zeus.

"It is a true auspice, oh King, and must be obeyed. You

know me well enough to realize I would never allow myself to appear in any dream that was not of the utmost authenticity."

Agamemnon said, "Nine years we have fought. We have killed Trojans, but Troy still stands. We have looted her colonies and sacked the cities of her allies, but Troy herself still abides fair and impregnable as the virgin goddess Artemis, who, indeed, favors the Trojan cause.

"After nine years our men are disheartened. Many of our finest have fallen to deadly Hector and his brothers, many others to Apollo's plague arrows. Now, I fear, too many of those left are on the point of mutiny or desertion. I have led men a long time; I know the signs.

"It is at this juncture that Zeus sees fit to promise me Troy. This means—and I interpret these matters not like an oracle but like a soldier—that he gives it to me if I can take it."

"Exactly," said Ulysses. "Therefore, let us take it."

"Yes, brave Ulysses. But consider this: If our men desert us in the midst of a general assault when we have committed our reserves to a headlong attack, then, indeed, we shall meet disaster."

"We must see that they do not desert," said Diomedes.

"Precisely what I propose," said Agamemnon. "What I mean to do is weed out the cowards and traitors beforehand. I shall call the men together and address them in discouraging terms, indicating that I am ready to abandon the war and sail back to Greece."

"Dangerous, very dangerous," said Ulysses. "They will welcome your words and stampede to the boats."

"And that will weed out the cowards and traitors."

"You may be weeding out the entire army, saving those present, of course. Your test is ill-timed, Agamemnon. The men are war-weary and legitimately so. The plague proves that. Despite the venom of Apollo's arrows, a man in good

39   THE TROJAN WAR

spirits is bucklered against disease. A sick body means a sick soul. They are battle-worn; they long for home. Your speech will send them scurrying off to the ships."

"Then what would you have me do," cried Agamemnon. "If things are that bad, we may as well fold our tents and raise our sails and skulk off for home."

"No," said Ulysses. "The important thing is to ignore the men's weariness. Show them a glad and confident face. Address the troops. Speak no discouraging word, but tell them your dream and order them to attack. Twenty years of warfare have taught me that the cure for fear is fighting."

"Too many words," growled huge Ajax. "Let's stop talking and start cracking some heads. If we crack enough outside of Troy, we'll soon be doing it inside."

But Agamemnon would not be dissuaded. Like all men of few ideas he clung bitterly to one when it occurred. And by now he had convinced himself that his notion was a brilliant one.

"I shall make the speech I planned," he said, "and depend upon you kings and chieftains of my War Council to keep the men from breaking."

Agamemnon issued orders. Nine heralds went through the camp blowing their silver trumpets, calling the men together. They came in a mighty swarm. Even after its losses, this army remained the greatest fighting force ever assembled in ancient times.

Agamemnon stood on a rock and raised his golden scepter. He had planned his speech for hours, but was able to utter only one sentence.

"Friends, my heart has been overwhelmed by our losses, and I have decided it is time to quit this war and sail for Greece."

No sooner had he said these words, then, as Ulysses had foretold, the vast crowd stampeded. With a wild moaning cry the men leaped to their feet and stormed toward the beach. Had the restless gods not been vigilant, the Greek cause would have died that day.

But Hera and Athena were watching from Olympus. "What's the matter with Agamemnon," cried Hera. "Has he gone quite mad? Oh, this is some treachery of Zeus, I'm quite certain."

"No, this is Agamemnon's own stupidity," said Athena. "Some idea of testing the men before battle. He shouldn't be having ideas; he's not equipped."

"They're stampeding like cattle," said Hera. "Look at the miserable cowards. When I think of the effort we've spent on them. Go, dear Stepdaughter. Descend to Troy, and stop them."

"Divine Stepmother, I go," said Athena, and flew down to Troy.

She did not reveal herself to the multitude, only to her favorite, Ulysses, saying, "Don't just stand there, man. Stop them."

She snapped her fingers. Agamemnon's heavy scepter flew from his hand and sailed over the heads of the mob. She caught it in mid-air and handed it to Ulysses.

"Here is the rod of power, the very staff and scepter of kingly authority, given only by the gods and taken back at will. Grasp the scepter, Ulysses. Use it. Stop the rabble's flight."

With great strides Ulysses leaped down to the beach, bearing his scepter. Divinely inspired, his shout of outrage rolled like thunder across the plain.

"Stop!" he roared. "Stop! I command it! I speak the will of the gods."

He rushed up and down the strand, guarding the beached ships so that no one could board them. His flailing scepter rose like a golden barrier before the men's astonished eyes.

THE TROJAN WAR

In truth, with his red hair blazing and his eyes flashing and the golden rod flailing, he looked like a god descended.

"Stop!" he shouted. "Back to the assembly-place. Agamemnon means battle, not retreat. You misunderstood his words; they were only a rhetorical device. You fools, you dim-witted dolts! Zeus himself has appeared to the king in his sleep ordering an attack upon Troy. Do you think this is the moment he would order us to sail home? You have misunderstood. You have listened with your fears instead of your intelligence. No wonder you heard things wrong. Back! Back! Back to the arena. Let the king declare your battle array."

Listening to Ulysses, seeing him blaze with that special creative rage which comes rarely in a lifetime and then only to extraordinary men, because it is a particle of the gods' own radiance, hearing Ulysses' clangorous voice, and seeing him guard the ships, the men felt courage slipping back into their hearts and began to drift away from the beach.

But a gifted troublemaker arose. Thersites was his name, a little hunched shuffling bald-headed man, very clever with a voice that brayed like a donkey's so that you could hear no one else when he wished to drown them out.

Now he said, "You stupid sheep, do you allow yourself to be herded this way by a man with a staff? For the first time in his life that lout, Agamemnon, speaks the truth. By accident, I know, but the truth all the same. This war is a disaster, and the sooner we get home the better. It's a bloody miracle there are any of us left to get home after nine years of so-called leadership by greedy, inept, cowardly, lecherous imitations of kings. So heed not this red-headed madman, my fellow soldiers, my fellow sufferers. But board the ships. And if any of these brave chieftains come after you, trying to drag you back, why then cut their throats and dump them overboard as a sacrifice to Poseidon, who will ensure us cloudless skies and a following wind."

It was part of Ulysses' wisdom always to listen to criticism, hoping to learn something thereby. He held his hand until Thersites finished his speech. Then, by way of comment, he swung his scepter. The knobbed end hit Thersites in the face, shattering his jaw. The man tried to keep talking, but the only sound that came out was the crackling of broken bone. He kept trying to speak, gagged on his own blood, and fell unconscious on the beach.

By this time the other members of the War Council—Ajax the Greater, Ajax the Lesser, Idmoneus, Nestor, Diomedes—had joined Ulysses and stood between the men and the ships, thrusting them back, exhorting them. The mutiny crumbled. The men turned and moved sullenly back to the field. Ulysses and the other chieftains followed, herding them. When they were again assembled he mounted Agamemnon's rock, still holding the golden scepter. Agamemnon himself, seized by bewilderment and rage, had vanished into his tent.

Ulysses said, "Our great king and war-leader, Agamemnon, has been so disgusted by your cowardly performance that he does not wish to address you again today and has asked me to say a few words. Let me say, men, that despite appearances, I do not view your recent abrupt withdrawal toward the beach as cowardice. I view it as a gigantic form of the fighting man's gesture, who, before he can strike his blow, must draw back his arm. You were not running away; you were coiling for the spring, the spring that will take you in one tigerish leap over the walls and into Troy. I promise you this, men, and I do not speak idly. We will have victory. For know that on the night that has just passed, Father Zeus himself condescended to visit Agamemnon in a dream, promising us victory if we attack, attack, attack."

On the third repetition of the word "attack," he flung up his arm, the sceptor flashed, and the men raised a great ferocious, joyful shout. Two brown vultures coasting the steeps of air off Mount Ida heard this yelling and planed down a way. They had heard this sound before and knew that it meant a battle, and a battle meant fine feasting afterward.

THE BATTLE BEGINS

The Greek forces advanced toward Troy raising an enormous cloud of dust. And the dust was the color of gold mixed with the color of blood for, at Ulysses' suggestion, they were advancing on the eastern wall of Troy that morning so that the Trojans would have to fight with the rising sun in their eyes. This was one of the oldest tricks in warfare but still effective, and Ulysses never overlooked the slightest advantage.

The great bronze gates of the eastern wall swung open, and the men of Troy came out to meet the attackers. The high gods settled down comfortably on the peaks of Olympus to watch the sport.

Through the dust-cloud Teucer, who had the sharpest eyes among the Greeks, spotted something strange. He reported to Agamemnon, who held up his hand in the sign of halt. The dust subsided, and the attackers saw an amazing spectacle. The Trojan line had stopped moving, was standing fast, weapons glittering in the slant rays of the sun. And a single man was coming forward to meet them, a tall, supple figure clad in a panther skin and carrying two spears.

It was Paris, who raised his voice in challenge, "Hear me, oh Greeks. I propose single combat between the lines to any one of you bold enough to come forward and meet me."

"Rumor travels fast," grumbled Ulysses to himself. "It's clear they've already heard about Achilles' defection. Otherwise that coxcomb would never be offering single combat."

Menelaus then split the air with his war-cry and shuffled forward. His shout was echoed by all the Greeks for it was very fitting that he, the offended husband, should respond to the challenge of the abductor.

"I'll fight you!" he cried. "And a short fight it will be. I'll tear out your guts with my bare hands."

Now Menelaus was no comfortable sight for an opponent. If his brother, Agamemnon, was a bull, he was a bear. Not very tall, but very wide and bulging with muscle, clothed in a pelt of black hair from neck to ankle. Black-bearded, wearing black armor—helmet, breastplate and greaves not of bronze like most of the others but of iron—too heavy for most men to wear—iron pieces smoky and black as if they had just issued from Hephaestus's forge. He carried an axe in one hand and a huge iron-bossed bullhide shield in the other. Truly he was a fearsome sight slouching out of the Greek lines like an iron bear.

Paris took one look and darted back into the Trojan lines, crying, "It's not fair! He has full armor. I am clad only in a panther skin. I'll fight any man alive, but a metal monster is something else!"

His brother Hector, commander of the Trojan forces, turned on him. "You miserable cringing coward, you yellow-bellied dog. The oracle was right. You will bring disgrace and ruin on us all. Here we are fighting a war started by your own lechery and when a chance is given for you to strike a blow for yourself—something you should have been praying to the gods for—you skulk away. My father was right in his

THE TROJAN WAR

original impulse. He should have garroted you with your own umbilical cord. Dreadful was my mother's misjudgment, saving you. Well, you are not free to disgrace yourself. You are a son of Priam, and when you bring shame on yourself, you shame us all. I will not permit this. Sooner will I break your pretty skull here and now, explain that you have met with an unfortunate accident, and take up your challenge to Menelaus myself."

Paris, who thought quickly, said, "Peace, brother. It was I who issued the challenge, unprompted by you, and it is I who will fight. Please do not scourge me with that tongue of yours. You are my elder brother, my leader, but you have no right to say such things to me because I chose to lighten the heavy moment with a jest or two. Truly, the thing I regret most about this war I started is that every day it makes the Trojans more like the Greeks. We are forgetting what laughter is, and that is a terrible casualty."

"I can't follow you," said Hector. "Speak plainly. Are you going to fight or not?"

"Certainly I'm going to fight. I didn't come to battle to exchange platitudes with you. But that man is clad in ugly armor from wooly pate to tufted toe, and I, too, must armor myself."

"Brothers, lend him some pieces of armor," said Hector. "I'll start. Take my shield."

"Nay, Brother," said Paris. "It is too heavy for me. Troilus here will give me what I need. We are the same size."

From Troilus, the brother next youngest to himself, also a very beautiful lad, he borrowed helmet, chestplate, and greaves. From Lyncaeus, an elder brother, he took a bronze-bossed oxhide shield.

While Paris was armoring himself Hector stepped out between the two armies and held up his arms for silence.

"Worthy foes," he said, "you have known me for nine long

years and know that I do not shrink from a fight. So you will not take my proposal in the wrong spirit. But I think there is a kind of inspired justice about the idea of Paris and Menelaus meeting each other in single combat. I suggest this: If Paris wins, we keep Helen and you depart, taking with you only the price of Helen's bride-gift. If, on the other hand, Menelaus leaves Paris in the dust, then he must take back his wife plus an indemnity to be reckoned by joint council between us. Then, your cause having been won, you depart on your black ships in honor and in peace."

There was a great clamor of joyful shouting on both sides. It was clear that Hector's proposal met with general favor from Trojan and Greek alike. Ulysses saw Agamemnon frown and knew that the hasty general was about to refuse Hector's offer and order a charge.

He went swiftly to Agamemnon and whispered, "Agree, agree. We'll have general mutiny if you refuse. And the end will be the same. The oracle has decreed that Troy must fall, and fall she must for the voice of the oracle is the promise of the gods. But for now, agree to the truce. There is nothing else to do."

Therefore Agamemnon answered, saying, "Well spoken, Hector. Let our brothers fight, and give my sister-in-law a chance to change beds again tonight."

Hector stepped out between the armies holding his helmet in his hand. In the helmet were two pebbles, a rough one for Menelaus and a smooth one for Paris. He shook his helmet; one pebble jumped out, the smooth one. A groan went up from the Greek lines because this meant that Paris would cast the first spear. The Trojans cheered wildly.

Paris danced out into the space between armies. Menelaus shuffled forward to meet him, covering himself with his bull-hide shield. Paris came, all glittering bronze, poising two bronze-headed spears. He stopped about twenty paces from his enemy and hurled his spear. Its point hit the iron boss of Menelaus's shield and fell to earth. Now the Trojans groaned, and the Greeks cheered. Menelaus immediately hurled his spear with tremendous force. It hummed venomously through the air and sheared through the Trojan's shield. Paris ducked aside, and the spearhead just nicked his shoulder. Before he could recover, Menelaus was upon him, hacking at him with his axe. Paris tried to back away, but Menelaus allowed him no time to recover. Raising his axe high, he smote the Trojan's horse-plume helmet. Paris staggered but the axehead shattered into three pieces.

"Cruel Zeus!" cried Menelaus. "First you raise my hopes by allowing me to close with the false-hearted home-breaker; then when he is in my grasp you save him from my spear; you break my axe; you leave me weaponless. But I have weapons still, these two good hands you gave me before you gave me sword or spear—they are enough to do the beautiful murder I have dreamed of for nine long years."

He grasped Paris by the crest of the helmet, swung him off his feet, and began to drag him back toward the Greek lines. Paris struggled helplessly; his legs were dragging, the chin strap of his helmet dug into his throat, strangling him.

Aphrodite could not bear to see her favorite being manhandled. Making herself invisible, she flew down from Olympus, broke the chin strap of his helmet and snatched him away, leaving the raging Menelaus with an empty helmet in his hands.

Paris felt himself translated into paradise. Instead of strangling beneath his enemy's hands, he was lying snug as a babe in Aphrodite's arms, cuddled against the fragrant billow of her breasts. The goddess kept herself invisible as the wind, but he recognized her by her intoxicating scent which was honey and baking bread. Aphrodite flew over the Trojan wall, past the painted wooden houses and the marble temple, to Priam's castle. She flew through a casement and deposited Paris in his own bed. Then, still invisible, she kissed him into a healing sleep.

Down on the battlefield the disappearance of Paris had ignited angry confusion. Trojan and Greek began shifting and muttering, but no one was quite sure what had happened.

Agamemnon then stepped between the lines, raising his arms for silence. "Honorable Hector, Trojans all, I declare my brother Menelaus, king of Sparta, the victor in the single combat we agreed was to decide the war. To this you must submit since your champion Paris has vanished, and Menelaus holds the field. Therefore Helen must be returned to us, and the entire cost of our expedition must be paid by you, plus a huge and fitting indemnity.

The Greeks shouted with joy; the Trojan lines were wrapped in bitter silence. Helen had been watching on the wall with Priam and the other elders of Troy, which was the habit of the court during battle. When she heard Agamemnon's declaration she hurried back to the palace to change her dress, perfume herself, and prepare to be retaken. She was amazed to find Paris in bed.

"What are you doing here?"

"Sleeping, waiting."

"For what?"

"For you, dear. What else?"

"I was watching from the wall. The last I saw you, you were fighting Menelaus more or less. Did you run away, darling?"

"More or less. Not exactly."

"You didn't exactly stay, either."

"Rough character, that ex-husband of yours. No one stays around him very long."

"What now, sweet coward?"

"Come here."

"But I'm about to be reclaimed. Agamemnon has declared the Greeks victorious."

"Agamemnon is hasty, my dear. The gods are just beginning to enjoy this war; they're not going to let it end so quickly."

"Are you sure?"

"Believe me, the real war is just beginning. So come to bed. We battle-weary warriors need frequent interludes of tender repose; then we return refreshed, and carry all before us. So come. . . ."

"Yes, dear."

Hera and Athena were now perched on the same peak whispering to each other. They did not like the way things were going down below.

Zeus called out teasingly, "Well, my dears, your gentle impulses should be gratified for it looks very much like peace will be concluded between Greece and Troy, and many brave men spared who would otherwise have died."

"You are hasty, sire," said Hera sweetly. "No peace treaty has been signed, only an armistice. And with two armies full of such spirited warriors, anything may happen to break a truce. Of course, we hope nothing does, but—after all—it has been foretold that Troy will fall."

Zeus frowned and did not answer. He knew better than to try to match jibes with Hera.

In the meantime the ox-eyed queen of the gods was whispering to Athena, "We must do something immediately or peace will break out. Get down there and see what you can do about ending this stupid truce."

Athena flew down and sought out a Trojan leader named Pandarus, a very vain and greedy man. Keeping herself invisible, she whispered to him, "Here is your chance to win undying fame. The man who sends an arrow through one of those famed Greek warriors will live in the annals of warfare for the next three thousand years, longer perhaps. Just imagine putting a shaft through Ulysses, or Agamemnon, or Achilles. No, he's not fighting today, is he? But look! There stands Menelaus, still searching for Paris. He's within very easy bowshot. What are you waiting for, man? If I were an archer like you, I wouldn't hesitate for a second."

Pandarus swallowed this flattery in one gulp as Athena knew he would. Now, Pandarus was a fine archer, although not as good as he thought he was, and he owned a marvelous bow made of two polished antelope horns seized together by copper bands and strung with ox sinew. Inflamed by Athena's words, he snatched an arrow from his quiver, fitted it to his bowstring, bent his horn bow, and let fly. The arrow sang through the air and would have finished off Menelaus right then and there had not Athena, still invisible, flashed across the space and deflected the arrow so that it struck through the Spartan king's buckle, was further deflected, and passed through the bottom part of his breastplate, just scratching his side. The wound looked more serious than it was because the arrow stuck out the other side of his breastplate as if it had passed through his body. He staggered and fell to his knees; blood flowed down his thighs. The Greek army gasped with horror, and the Trojans groaned, too, for they knew this must break the truce.

Agamemnon uttered a mighty, grief-stricken shout, "Traitors! You have killed my brother! You have broken the truce! Greeks, to arms! Kill the traitors! Charge!"

The dust was churned again as the whole Greek army, moving like one man, snatched up its weapons and rushed toward the Trojan lines.

diomedes

Athena could not be content with starting the battle; she wanted the Greeks to win it. And this was a problem, for they were fighting without Achilles. Now every battle needs a hero, an archkiller, someone filled with such successful rage that he seems transformed into a god. His headlong charge rebukes and inspires the laggards. Every thrust punishes the enemy.

Heroes in those days were of two kinds—god-born or god-made—either the son of a god or goddess, as were Hercules, Achilles, Theseus, and Jason, or man born of mortal parents who underwent the grim and passionate rite of hero-making. But hero-making was a very rare occurrence, having been enacted only three times since the beginning of the world. Now, Athena did it for the fourth time, and she chose Diomedes.

She plucked Diomedes from his chariot and flew with him to a secret grove. Holding him in one hand she stripped him of his armor, like shelling a nut, and ate him raw. Then the virgin goddess squatted and gave birth. She bore Diomedes, naked as a babe but full-grown, with a pearly moist skin and wet hair. She took him to her breast and suckled him. Holding that great teat he sucked in a curdle of honey and milk called hero-pap, meant for infant godlings, but which, when mortal drinks, fills him with either poetry or rage.

Diomedes was a warrior, and he was filled with divine rage.

Athena kissed him upon the mouth, kissed him upon each eye, and kissed him upon the forehead. Then she clad him in his armor again, flew back to the field, and set him in his chariot. Diomedes, who had been in a swoon the entire time of his rebirth, never knew that he had left the high seat of his war cart, but suddenly felt himself full of a giant's strength. Whooping with joyous rage, he whipped his horses and streaked toward the Trojan lines like a falling star. His eyes, which had been brown, were gray as Athena's now, misted with a milky light like moonstones, and his skin was moist and pearly. His rage was starry, beautiful. Every time he thrust his spear he killed a Trojan.

Pandarus, the archer who had broken the truce by wounding Menelaus, notched another arrow to his antelope-horn bow and shot Diomedes through the shoulder. Without drawing rein, Diomedes tended his wound. Shifting the traces to his left hand, he broke off the arrowhead with his right, then drew the shaft out of his shoulder. Blood spurted, but in his starry rage the blood was like wine. He twisted his head, licked his shoulder like a wounded lion, and grew even stronger.

He killed a Trojan warrior named Astynius with a single thrust of his spear. But the lance head stuck on a bone, and he could not pull it free. He drew his sword then and guided his chariot into a knot of Trojans. Sweeping his sword like a scythe, he delivered three strokes that carved the name of Diomedes into battle annals forever. It was the custom then for brothers to fight in teams, side by side. And with those three sword-strokes Diomedes killed six men, three sets of brothers, each single stroke passing through two necks and shearing off two heads—like a boy tramping through a field, sweeping the heads of dandelions with a stick. With the first stroke he killed Abas and Polydus, sons of a soothsayer who after that day, dreamed no more. With his second stroke he beheaded the twin sons of a rich Trojan who had no other heir. Then Diomedes sprang from his chariot into the chariot of two princes of Troy and scythed their heads off with a single stroke.

Now Aeneas, son of Anchises, seeing this slaughter, was filled with shame and rage, and determined to kill Diomedes. The mother of Aeneas was Aphrodite who had seduced Anchises when he was barely old enough to be of use to her. She caught him in a meadow, tending cows, stretched the beautiful youth on the grass, and taught him what to do. From this encounter Aeneas was born, whom Aphrodite returned to his father, bidding him raise the boy as a mortal prince. He grew up to be the most powerful warrior, next to Hector, in the whole Trojan confederation.

But Aeneas was a man of wisdom as well as strength, and knew that Diomedes now was filled with more than mortal prowess and could not be matched in single combat.

He went in search of Pandarus, and said, "Oh, strong archer, today you have sent your arrows through two kings, and it is not your fault that they still live. I urge you to return to your uncompleted task, and send another shaft through Diomedes. I will be at your side with my spear. Together, perhaps, we can finish him off. It will take both of us for I am sure he is being sponsored by a god in this battle."

"He dashes here and there in his chariot," said Pandarus. "We shall never catch him afoot. I have no chariot of my own; we must use yours."

"By all means," said Aeneas. "Let us use mine. In mounting that chariot perhaps we can partake of some small portion of the divine power which has been aiding the Greeks, for my horses are of the Olympian stud."

What Aeneas meant was this: Two generations before

Zeus had abducted a beautiful lad named Ganymede, son of King Tros, first of the Trojan kings, after whom the city was named. Zeus took Ganymede to be his cup-bearer, and in compensation gave two stallions to King Tros. They were of the string that draws Apollo's sun-chariot from its eastern palace to the western rim of the sky, its journey dividing day from night. Afterward, Aeneas's father, Anchises, helped himself to these stallions for a few hours—stole them right out of the Imperial Stables one night, led them to his own meadow, and had them cover a herd of his own mares. The happy mares dropped six fiery foals of which Anchises kept four, giving the other two to his warrior son to train as chariot horses.

Aeneas spoke of his marvelous steeds because he saw that Pandarus was afraid, and he wished to lull these fears. He held Pandarus by the arm and guided him to the chariot which was drawn by a team of huge white stallions—fire-maned, with glowing black eyes and coral nostrils, beautiful as their sires, the sun stallions which draw Apollo's golden chariot through the blue meadow of the sky. They mounted the chariot and flashed across the bloody field in search of Diomedes.

The Greek warrior in the heat of his battle-rage saw the beautiful team approach, and his love of horses pierced the blood-mist for a second. He resolved to have those horses for his own if he had to fight every Trojan on the field. It was his hour of splendor, an hour which comes but once in a lifetime, and upon such an hour a man kills his enemies and takes everthing of beauty he can find. These horses were the most beautiful he had ever seen. He did not know that on the walls of Troy something even more beautiful was watching him. Cressida. Newly returned from Agamemnon's tent, still secretly lusting after her memories of Greek ways, watching now on the wall with Helen and Priam and the elders and ladies of the court as the battle unreeled beneath them. She could not take her eyes off Diomedes. She had known him as a companion of Agamemnon and as frequent visitor to the high king's tent, but now in his starry rage he seemed like a different man, a man reborn. And she felt her very bones melting as she watched him kill.

Aeneas galloped his chariot toward Diomedes until he was some twenty paces away. Then he reined up abruptly in a superb piece of horsemanship, pulling his stallions back onto their hind legs and wheeling them in place so that his chariot swung around broadside, giving Pandarus a clear shot at Diomedes. The arrow struck Diomedes' breastplate, but he was twisting as it struck, and it glanced off. The Greek drew back his arm and cast his spear. It hurtled through the air, striking Pandarus full in the face. The spearhead went in under his nose, shattered his teeth, cut his tongue off, and came out the other side of his jawbone. He fell from the chariot, spouting blood.

Aeneas leaped out holding spear and shield and stood over Pandarus's corpse to prevent Diomedes from taking the armor. Diomedes sprang from his chariot also, but did not draw his sword. He scooped up a huge boulder, held it above his head like a Titan in their ancient war with the gods, and hurled it at Aeneas. It hit him low, crushing his hip bone and pinning him to the ground. Now Diomedes drew his dagger and advanced upon Aeneas to cut his head off.

Aphrodite, viewing the battle from on high, saw her son fall and for the second time that day flashed earthward. She snatched up Aeneas, cradled him in her white arms, and began to fly away. Diomedes, still berserk, saw himself being robbed of his foe's body which seemed to him to be rising on a spout of white mist. Boldly he sprang into that mist, slashing with his dagger, and stabbed Aphrodite in the hand. The goddess shrieked in pain; she had wounded countless others with her favors, but never before had she been wounded herself, and she did not know how to handle pain.

The body of Aeneas slipped from her grasp and was caught up by the god Apollo, who favored the Trojans. Apollo spread his mantle over Aeneas to protect him from sword-thrust or blow of spear. Diomedes hacked away at his enemy's body but each time felt his sword being turned. Then, realizing he was fighting some phantom power, he laid hold of Aeneas by arm and leg, trying to bear him off to the Greek lines. But he could not move the body; it was as if it had grown roots. Now appeared before him the tall radiant form of Apollo, with hair and beard of burning gold and storm-blue eyes. Apollo spoke; his voice was full of angry music.

"Son of Tydeus, today you have made the mistake of wounding one god; beware you do not offend another. Look at me, oh mortal. Regard me and worship. Then quit this field. Aeneas lives and shall live to fight again, for we cover him with the mantle of our power."

These words succeeded in piercing Diomedes' battle-fury without dispelling it. He retreated, but not far, and looked about for another foe to attack. Then he chortled with joy. He saw Aeneas's chariot drawn by those beautiful white and gold steeds descended from the sun stallions. The chariot was riderless, but the well-trained horses held their place, calmly munching the grass. He sprang into the chariot uttering a loud war-cry, and whirled toward the Trojan lines.

As this was happening, Aphrodite went to her brother Ares, god of war, and cried, "Look, Brother. I am wounded by a mortal. My arm drips ichor for he has wounded me with his dagger. He is filled with more than mortal strength, more than mortal daring. He is ready to storm Olympus itself, but before that means to destroy the Trojans single-handed. Help them, brother, help our suppliants, the Tro-

jans. Rid the earth of that ruffian, Diomedes. Awaken my gratitude. And you know I know how to be grateful."

Ares laughed his rough laugh that was like the grating of boulder against boulder.

"Keep away from battle, sister," he said. "You are framed for more tender encounters. Leave the fighting to me. See you tonight."

Ares leaped into his war-chariot and galloped earthward. Aphrodite proceeded toward Olympus, nursing her wounded arm and sobbing like a dove, but even as she sorrowed for herself, she kept plotting vengeance.

"Stab me, will he? Mark the perfect flesh of Aphrodite— how did he dare? He will suffer that wound. Its pain will be as nothing to the pain I shall inflict on him, pain compounded by puzzle. Torment wrapped in enigma. And I know my agent now—that little slut, Cressida. I spotted her watching him from the wall. Well, I'll stoke up those flames. And I'll work on him, the desperado, with dreams and secret promptings and fortuitous encounters. Yes, I will embroil those two beyond repair, and teach those piratical Greeks a lesson they'll never forget."

Ares put on the form of a Thracian chief named Acamas, a very swift runner and clever fighter, one of Troy's most effective allies.

So disguised, he berated the sons of Priam, crying, "When princes turn coward, what can you expect of common troops? No wonder the Greeks are pressing us back like a rabble toward the gates of Troy. Look, there lies the brave Aeneas wounded unto death, and no one of us is man enough to attempt his rescue."

Another ally grew ashamed at these words. He was Prince Sarpedon of Lycia, who called himself a son of Zeus, and had always been jealous of Hector. Now he turned upon Hector.

"Son of Priam, today's story shall be written in letters of shame for all the world to read. You Trojans are cowering back like curs and letting your allies do all the fighting. I have nothing at stake in Troy. My castle is on the river Xanthus. There my wife beds safely. She will not be raped by the Greeks. Nor will my little son have his brains dashed out by the invader. Nor will my treasury be sacked. Yet you, to whom all this will happen and more, stand aside and let the Greeks advance as they will. Set an example for your ally, Trojan! Or you will find us deserting you and sailing away to our home islands."

Sarpedon's words bit into Hector like envenomed snake fangs. Battle-rage danced hotly in his veins. Wielding two spears, he dashed up and down the ranks of the Trojans, urging them on with his fearsome war-cry. They needed no urging. They had heard the words of Ares and Sarpedon and threw off the stuporous fear which had been hobbling them since Diomedes had begun his inspired charge. And they were given fresh courage at the miraculous sight of Aeneas rising from beneath Apollo's mantle, hip bone mended and stronger than ever. For Apollo is the god of medicine, and he had laid hands upon Aeneas, healing him.

Aeneas was in a terrible fury because of the theft of his chariot and his marvelous team of horses. He joined with Hector, and together they led the Trojans in an irresistible charge that scattered the Greeks like dust.

All this time, while the battle was raging back and forth, Achilles kept to his tent and did not come out. He lay on his pallet trying to shut his ears to the sound of battle, but he could not. He heard it all—war-cry and answer, challenge and reply, spear-shock and the crash of shields, the rattle of sword against helmet, and the ping of dart against breastplate. Arrows sang through the air. Men shrieked and groaned; horses neighed and bugled. This sound had always been music to him—the best sound in all the world—but now it was a simple torment. For there to be a battle going on and Achilles not in it was a thing absolutely against nature. Great sobs wrenched Achilles, but Patroclus was in the tent with him, and he did not wish his friend to hear his grief.

Achilles bit down on his wrist till it bled, stifling his sobs that way. At last he could bear it no longer. He arose from his bed and washed his face in cold water that stood in a golden ewer which he had taken in some half forgotten raid. Oh, happy days they seemed now before his quarrel with Agamemnon, when he could allow himself to roam the seas raiding the home-islands of Trojan allies, raging into their very fastnesses, spearing men like fish and sacking the proud castles of their treasure—abducting women, taking slaves.

He stood now at the portal of his tent watching the battle. He saw Diomedes sweeping up and down, and it was like some memory of himself. He groaned aloud. Patroclus came to him and put his arm around his neck.

"Old friend," said Patroclus. "Beloved comrade, I can not see you kill yourself with grief. Forget your feud with Agamemnon. Go fight. Arm yourself and join the battle, else regret will tear your breast more surely than enemy spear."

"I cannot bury my feud with Agamemnon," cried Achilles. "False friend! How can you tell me to do that? He insulted me, took my woman. Do you think I will allow any man, though he be king a dozen times, to do such things to me. No! I would rather fight with the Trojans against the Greeks."

"A traitor to your own kind? You would never be that," said Patroclus.

"I'm a traitor to my own nature if I do not fight. And that's worse."

"You could never bring yourself to fight your old companions. How could you level your spear against either of the Ajaxes, or Ulysses, or Idmoneus. I do not even mention myself."

Achilles took his friend's head between his hands and looked deep into his eyes.

"Oh, Patroclus," he said. "You would be surprised to know the names of those I could bring myself to fight when the battle-fury burns. I like them well, Ajax, Diomedes, Ulysses, Idmoneus, even that crude bear, Menelaus. I have adventured with them, and raided with them, and fought the Trojans with them. I should regret killing them, perhaps, but I could manage the deed in the heat of battle. Only you, my friend, have a true hold on my esteem. You I will never harm. You I will always avenge should anyone else offer you harm. I feel myself being torn in two. I feel a fire inside my head that is scorching my very capacity to think. I feel a pain in my gut that is worse than any weapon that has pierced my armor. I don't know what will happen to me in the days to come, but take this pledge. You are my friend, my true friend, sweet cousin, and companion of my boyhood. Hear me, then. I shall never harm you and shall take vengeance upon anyone who does."

He shoved Patroclus away. "Go now. I know you do not wish me to stand alone, but I pray you, go. I do not wish you to see my grief.

"I go," said Patroclus. "But I shall not join the battle either until you give me leave."

He walked off, but not far. He circled in back of the tent and stood there watching Achilles. His heart was sodden with love for the mighty youth, and he was as loyal as a dog.

Hera and Athena watched, frowning, from their peak on Olympus as the Trojans beat back the Greeks.

"What ails you, Stepdaughter," said Hera. "You seem to be losing your touch. The strength you gave Diomedes appears to have ebbed and with it, the tide of Greek fortunes. Look at them; they're running like rabbits."

"It is because my brothers have broken their vow of neutrality," said Athena angrily. "Apollo has completely restored Aeneas who was felled by Diomedes in a glorious action, and the son of Anchises wields his weapon more powerfully than ever before. And Hector has suddenly become inspired and is raging like a wolf on the field. But it is no accident. Behind him I see the form of Ares, goading the Trojans to superhuman effort."

"Yes, Ares is chiefly to blame," said Hera. "Although I am his mother I must confess he is an incorrigible mischief-maker. Apollo will mend wounds and issue edicts, but he is too proud to fight with mortals. Ares, however, exults in battle, no matter whom he is fighting. It is he who harries the Trojans forward. It is Ares who must be driven from the field. And it is you who must do it, Stepdaughter. For Zeus would never forgive me if I took up arms against my own son. He is quite hidebound in some respects."

"Very well," said Athena, "then I shall do it. For many a century now I have been waiting to settle scores with that lout."

So saying, she sped to earth and, keeping herself invisible, joined the Greeks where they had set up a defense line near their ships. The Trojans were driving ahead viciously, but the toughest Greek warriors—Ajax the Greater, Ajax the Lesser, Teucer, Ulysses, Idmoneus, Agamemnon, Menelaus —all these ferocious fighters formed knots of resistance to the Trojans, who had breached the Greek line in many places and were advancing upon the beached ships.

Athena spoke to Diomedes, appearing before him in her own guise, but keeping herself invisible to the others. "Son of Tydeus," she said, "you are a great sorrow and disappointment to me. Today, I have honored you in a way that only

three other mortals have been honored since the very beginning of time. For I took you through the ritual of rebirth.
I became your goddess-dam, endowing you with godlike
strength. And what do I see now? After a few hours of
fighting, you grow weary. You fail. You leave the field to
Hector and Aeneas. It's incredible. Standing there on Olympus I could scarcely believe what I was seeing. I did not
know how to answer to Mother Hera, who chided me justly
for choosing so weak a vessel to hold the beautiful rage of the
gods. I am grieved, Diomedes. I am shocked and surprised."

By this time Diomedes' face was wet with tears. He tore
out his beard in great handfuls.

"Another word of reproof, oh Athena," he shouted, "and
I shall plunge this blade into my breast. And you will have
to find another to crush with your scorn. Why do you blame
me for that which is not my fault? You saw me overcoming
every Trojan I met, even Pandarus the shrewd archer, even
the mighty Aeneas. Why, I even wounded his mother, Aphrodite—and how many men have dappled with ichor the radiant flesh of the goddess of love? But in the midst of these
deeds I was stopped by your brother, Apollo, the sun-god
himself, who warned me that I must never lift my hand
against an Olympian again, threatening me with eternal
torment if I disobeyed. So what am I to do? It is your other
brother, Ares, who ranges behind the Trojan lines, filling
Aeneas and Hector with battle-rage, and making them invincible. Unless I lift my spear against Ares and chase him
from the field, he will never allow me to measure my strength
with Hector and Aeneas."

"You speak truly," said Athena, "but Apollo cannot stop
me from fighting Ares. I have the permission of Mother
Hera. As for Zeus, he detests his brawling son. Many a time,
in eons gone, he was moved to punish Ares himself. And
although Father Zeus tends to favor the Trojans, I know he

will not chide me overmuch if I chastise Ares. Let us go then. You will lift your spear against him, but I will ride as your charioteer and guide your spear. I will be your buckler, too, when the god of war aims his gigantic lance at your breastplate. Come, brave Diomedes, we will teach the Trojans that the Greeks must prevail even though great Achilles disdains to take the field. Yes, I will be your charioteer and guide this marvelous team you have taken from Aeneas, and you shall be able to devote your full time to fighting."

Athena sprang into the chariot and took up the reins. Diomedes stood beside her couching his spear and shouting his war-cry. Athena drove directly toward Ares who was snorting like a wild boar over a pile of dead Greeks, despoiling them of their armor. He wished to take back to Olympus the gear of twenty men of large stature to give to Hephaestus who would then melt the metal down and forge a breastplate and pair of greaves large enough for Ares. But when he saw the chariot approach, the somber pits of his eyes glowed with a new greed; he wanted those horses for himself. Also, he wished very much to square accounts with Diomedes, who had been so terrible against the Trojans that day. He picked up his twenty-foot spear, the haft of which was an entire ash tree, and rushed toward the chariot. It was a charge such as could batter down a city gate, but Athena reached her mailed hand and deflected the spearhead so that it whizzed harmlessly past Diomedes, carrying Ares within easy sword-reach. Diomedes' quick counterstroke half-gutted Ares. He fell with a horrid screech, holding his stomach together to keep his entrails in place. Had he been mortal man, the wound would have been fatal. As it was, he had to quit the field and fly back to Olympus. He visited Hephaestus first to tuck his mighty guts into place and sew up the wound with bullhide sinew.

Then Ares stormed into Zeus's throne-room, crying, "Justice! Justice! That harpy daughter of yours, that owl-hag Athena rides as Diomedes' charioteer, invisible, guarding him from all harm, and strengthening his hands so that he kills, kills, kills."

"Fancy that," said Zeus. "I had no idea that killing was so distasteful to you. These scruples seem to have developed overnight."

"You do not understand, oh Zeus. It is not only mortals he attacks. Earlier today he wounded Aphrodite. Just now he bloodied me with a lucky thrust. Me! Your son! God of Battle!"

"Who are you to complain," shouted Zeus. "Athena should not be taking a direct hand in the fighting, it is true, for I have forbidden it, but you were doing the very same thing on the Trojan side. I saw you. You were disguised as Acamas and, with your own weapons, were killing Greeks and despoiling them of their armor. You are equally to blame, and if I punish one I shall punish both. Besides, I think the god of war should be ashamed to publicize his defeat at the hands of his sister."

"Sister? That's no sister," muttered Ares as he left the throne-room. "That's a harpy out of hell."

Nevertheless, Zeus sent Apollo after Ares to make sure that his wound had been properly tended. Then he sent light-footed Iris to recall Athena from the battlefield, and issued another edict against direct intervention by any god on one side or the other.

HECTOR

The battle had begun at dawn, and it was now the hot middle of the day. The sun hung in the sky like a brass helmet; blond dust hung in the air hot as metal filings. The exhausted men gasped like unwatered cattle. They could feel their flesh charring where the sun hit their armor. Many of them threw off their armor and fought naked. Haft of spear, and shaft of lance, and hilt of sword were so slippery with sweat that they slid out of the men's hands. Without any orders being given the fighting subsided, and the armies drew off a little way from each other to await the cool of late afternoon.

During this lull Hector returned to Troy. He had two errands: First, to dig his brother Paris out of the boudoir, and get him onto the battlefield; secondly, to visit his wife, Andromache.

Andromache was not at home. The servants told him she was waiting on the Scaeian Wall. He went there to find her. They embraced.

She said, "I pray you, Hector, post some of your best fighters near this wall. It is the weakest one of all. See how low it is there, and crumbling? If we are breached, it will be here. Reinforce its guard."

Hector smiled. "You should be the general, my dear, not I. I see that you are absolutely correct. I shall strengthen these positions without delay."

"You're so hot and tired," she said. "Must you rush back to the battlefield? Can't you stay with me awhile? Stay only a little while, and let me make you comfortable again."

"No, I must get back there, dearly as I should love to stay with you and pass some cool and delicious hours in your matchless company. I am the commander, and I must lead my men."

"You look so solemn, so sad. Have you come to tell me something special?"

"I have had a vision of Troy's defeat. Among all the scenes of carnage and disaster it drags in its wake, all I can see is one picture: You in time to come, have been borne away by some mailed conqueror to far-off Greece. There in Argos, or Attica, or Sparta, I see you dressed in dull clothing, spinning at the loom or drawing water under the eye of your mistress who will not be partial to you for you will be too beautiful, more beautiful than she whoever she be. And her husband, your master, will be spending his nights with you rather than with her. I see you a servant, a slave; that is what losing means, to be enslaved. And that sight of you there fills me with such sorrowful rage that I feel a giant's strength, feel that I, personally, could interpose my body between Troy and all the Greek hordes, even if my comrades are cut down, and kill and kill until there is not one Greek left. And so the vision brings its own contradiction—and what do you make of that?"

"What do I make of that? That you are very brave and very dear. And that I am blessed beyond all women in my husband, for you, I believe, are the mightiest man ever to bear arms and the noblest heart ever to bear another's grief. And when you meet Achilles or Ajax, the gods will favor your cause for you are living proof that their handiwork is excelling itself."

"Thank you for those words," said Hector. "They are the sweetest I have ever heard in all my life. It is true, whether I can conquer Achilles or not, I must challenge him to single combat. These pitched battles waste our forces too much, and we do not have as many men to spare as do the enemy. Yes, I shall combat the strong Achilles, and when I do, the memory of your loving words will make a victor's music in my ears."

He took up his infant son, who was being held in a nurse's arms, lifted him high as if stretching him toward the heavens, and said, "Great Zeus, father of us all, hear a lesser father's prayer. I am a warrior; some call me a hero. As you know, a degree of self-esteem attaches to that condition. Instead of sacrificing a bull to you, let me sacrifice my self-esteem which, I assure you, is as huge and hot-blooded and rampaging as any bull. Let me ask you this: That when my son is grown and fights his battles, as all men must, and returns therefrom, that men will say of him only this. 'He is a better man than his father was.'"

The baby was frightened by his father's nodding horse-tail plume and burst into tears. Hector smiled and kissed him and gave him into his mother's arms. Then he kissed her, and said, "I must be off now, good wife. I must rout out lazy Paris and try to prevail upon him to do a bit of fighting in this war that he started. Farewell."

It took him a while to press through the mob in the streets to get to the mansion where Paris dwelt. It seemed all Troy was out. Since he was their special hero, the crowd jammed about him, shouting questions, trying to touch him. He kept a smile on his face, but forced his way steadily through the mob. However, his servant who had been on the wall, his son's nurse, had been so moved by his words that she had rushed off to tell everyone she could find what her master had said. By the time he reached Paris's house, all Troy was buzzing with his speech to Andromache, and no woman who heard it could refrain from bursting into tears and thinking critically of her own husband.

He found Paris with Helen, polishing his armor.

"It's clean enough, Brother, too clean. I should prefer to see it bloodied a bit."

"Ah, the old complaint," murmured Paris.

"Yes, the old complaint. You do not fight enough in your behalf, Paris. You set a bad example to the troops and create rancor among your brothers. The word has spread that you are a coward. I, too, have called you that in the heat of my displeasure, and yet I know that you are not. You are too proud for cowardice. What you are is irresponsible. You cannot bear the discipline of warfare, the compulsion, the iron urgency. You are like some magic child who can do anything but views his own caprice as the basic law of the universe. Well, you must drop that. The cruel necessity of war is upon us, a war prompted by your own desires. You must play not only an honorable role, but a hero's role. Zeus knows we need all the heroes we can muster."

"You keep saying these things, Hector," said Paris, "but I haven't uttered one syllable of objection. Why do you think I'm polishing my armor. I never wear it to bed. A rumor, incidentally, that is whispered about you, big brother. No, I mean to go to battle; I just want to look nice when I'm there."

"Dear brother Hector," said Helen, "honorable commander, I know you think little of me. I know you consider me a shameless bitch who seduced your brother and plunged Troy into a dreadful war. Nevertheless, let me say this: I, too, am always after him to do his share of fighting. I am of warrior race, too, you know. In fact, it is said that a very prominent belligerent, Zeus himself, is my father. I don't know how much truth there is in it, but they say he wooed my mother in the shape of a swan and that I was born from a swan's egg, which accounts for my complexion."

She smiled at Hector, and he could find no word of reproach to say to her. In the blaze of Helen's smile no man could think of anything but how it would be to lie with her. Even iron Hector was not immune.

"I heard what you said to Andromache," said Helen. A single pearly tear trembled on her eyelash without falling. "I think it was the most beautiful thing any man has ever said to any wife. This scoundrel here could never in a million years find such sentiments on his tongue, and he is famous for sweet speech. Truly the thought of being raped and enslaved is something that haunts every Trojan woman and devils every Trojan warrior."

"Truly," drawled Paris, "no man likes to think of his wife being enslaved by anyone but himself. Quite intolerable."

"See, he jokes even at that," cried Helen. "What is one to do with him?"

"Make a soldier of him," growled Hector. "Come on, pretty boy, enough talk. Let's fight."

Paris knelt before Helen, took both her hands, turned them over, and kissed each palm. Then he closed her hands.

"Keep these until I come again."

The sight of Hector and Paris emerging from the gate fresh and shining brought new heart to the Trojans, and they charged the Greek positions again. Led by Hector, Paris, and Aeneas, they wrought great havoc among the enemy who lost some of their best warrior's in that flurry.

Athena, despite Zeus's edict, flew down from Olympus to help the Greeks. This time she was intercepted by Apollo, who said, "No, sister, you must not. You are Zeus's favorite daughter, as everyone knows, and you should be the last to flout his commands. You see that I am keeping aloof from the battle, and so must you."

"I can't," cried Athena. "I won't! Too many Greeks are being killed."

"Come away. Listen to me. I have a plan to end this slaughter without any direct intercession on our part."

Athena joined Apollo under a huge oak tree.

"Owl-goddess," he said, "we can stop this killing by arranging that the battle be settled through single combat. This was attempted earlier in the day when Paris challenged Menelaus, but Paris fled, and the idea came to nought. Now, however, we shall have great Hector issue the challenge, and you may be sure that he will fight to the finish."

"I agree," said Athena. "Let us send Hector the idea."

Gods send ideas to men in different ways. But, whatever way they choose, it is necessary to create the illusion of personal authorship—that is, that each man believe the idea is his own. They sent this idea to Hector as a dart of sunlight glancing off the tall helm of Ajax, which towered above his companions. Seeing that high helmet gleam, Hector said to Paris, "Listen, brother, I have an idea."

Paris was willing enough to stop fighting and listen. Aeneas drew close, too. So did the other sons of Priam. And the fighting was eased again as the Trojans held a council on the field.

"We have fought valiantly this day," said Hector, "and have prevented the Greeks from storming our walls which was their intention this morning. So, in a sense, we have won the battle. In another sense we have not. Nor can we win any head-to-head battle with the Greeks. For if our losses be equal or anywhere near equal, they will contribute toward our final defeat. The Greeks outnumber us, and we dare not match their losses, or even match half their losses, or by and by we shall find ourselves with no fighting men at all while they will have a force capable of taking the city. What I propose then is this: That I challenge one of their champions to single combat, and that the honors of the day rest upon the result. If I win I shall do this each day until either I shall have run through all their champions and so dishearten them that they must depart, or I myself am killed, leaving the decisions to someone else. Let me add that the absence of Achilles should be no little help to this project."

His words met with general favor. He stepped in front of the Trojan lines, and addressed the Greeks.

"Honorable foemen," he said, "you have fought long and well upon this day, and have killed many of us. We have fought no less honorably and have killed many of you. But the sun sinks now and we have supplied the vultures with food enough for this day. Let me be a surrogate for the Trojan deaths, and choose you a champion who will meet me and be a surrogate for your deaths. Upon our combat let rest the honors of the day. If I lose, the victor may strip me of my armor, nor will any of my brothers oppose him. All I ask is that my body be returned to my father, Priam, for decent burning. But if the gods favor me in this combat, then I will act in the same way toward my fallen foe. Come, then, let me hear! Who of you will fight me? I await your reply."

His voice blared like a trumpet across the lines, leaving silence after it. The Greek champions looked at each other. No one, it seemed, was rushing to volunteer.

Finally, Menelaus dragged himself to his feet, and said, "Well, I won one duel today. Maybe this is my day for winning. If none of you offer to fight him, then I must."

But Agamemnon pulled him back, and said, "No, brother, not you. In plain words, if you fight Hector, you will die. The man belongs with the greatest warriors of all time.

Everyone acknowledges this. Even our own Achilles, for all his murderous pride, has never seen fit to engage Hector in single combat."

"Someone must fight him!" cried Menelaus. "If not I, then someone else."

"For shame!" cried old Nestor, rising and berating them in his dry voice like an angry cricket. "For shame. How the generations have shrunk. There were mighty men in my day. How they would laugh and scoff to see you sitting here like a circle of schoolboys awaiting the master's rod. Come. If there is no one to volunteer, then we must draw lots and let the gods choose."

He took chips of wood and inscribed the names of the Greek champions—nine of them—the two Ajaxes, Teucer, Idmoneus, Diomedes, Ulysses, Agamemnon, Menelaus, and Nestor's own son, Antilochus, a very skillful charioteer. He shook the chips in his helmet, then selected one and read the name inscribed in a piercing voice. "Ajax," he said. "Ajax of Salamis, known as the Great Ajax."

To Hector, Ajax looked as big as Ares prowling out of the Greek lines. The westering sun cast his gigantic shadow back over the massed Greeks, and beyond them over the beaked ships drawn up on the strand. His shield looked enormous as a chariot wheel. It was made of nine bullhides bound in brass. And he was using Ares' own spear, twenty feet long, its shaft made of a single ash tree, which he had picked up after the god of war had dropped it upon being wounded by Diomedes. Ajax was the only mortal large enough to wield this spear.

Hector did not wish to give Ajax a chance to hurl that huge spear, so he cast his own javelin first. It sped through the air and hit Ajax's shield, shattering its brass boss and penetrating all but the last bullhide. Ajax shivered like a tree under the blow of a woodman's axe, but he steadied himself, drew back his knotted arm, and hurled Ares' spear. Now Hector was using a smaller shield, also made of bullhide bound in brass, but he preferred a shield he could move about to cover himself rather than one to hide behind, because he depended more on speed and agility than size. When he saw the ash-tree lance hurtling through the air toward him, he lifted his shield which was immediately shattered by the spear. His left arm fell to his side numb. He swerved his body avoiding the spearhead, and suffered only a scratch on his shoulder, but that cut spurted blood, and the Trojans groaned.

Ajax did not pose on his follow-through, but let it take him into a wild-boar rush upon his foe, his signature in battle. Hector barely had time to scoop up a boulder; he did not have time to hurl it, but bowled it across the ground. He cast it so skillfully that it took Ajax's legs out from under him, and the big man sprawled on the ground. Hector whipped out his sword and rushed toward the fallen Ajax to cut his head off.

Ajax, seeing him come, picked up the boulder which had felled him and, still lying on his back, hurled it at Hector. It hit him on the breastplate and knocked him off his feet. Both men pulled themselves up and stepped toward each other, swords flashing. Blades clanged against breastplate and helmet. Ajax stood still, pivoting, aiming huge scything blows as Hector circled him, half-crouched, darting in and out, using edge and point. Both men were bruised, shaken, and bloody. Neither yet had the advantage.

It was at this point that Apollo intervened—without meaning to. He had not intended to meddle in the fighting. There had always been some coldness between him and Father Zeus, and he did not dare defy the high god's orders the way Athena did. So, after his consultation with the owl-goddess which had resulted in Hector's challenge and Ajax's reply, he had flown off to intercept his sun-chariot which, in his absence, was driven by Helios, his charioteer. The sun-god took Helios's place in the chariot, gathered the reins in one hand, and whipped up the fire-maned stallions. They set off in a swinging trot across the blue meadow of the sky, heading toward its western rim.

But when Apollo heard the shouting of Greek and Trojan far below, heard the clang of sword against shield, he dipped lower to watch the fighting. The duel was so exciting, he grew so fascinated that, for the first time in memory, he neglected his duties as the sun's coachman and allowed the stallions to stay in one spot grazing on the fluffy white cloud-blossoms. He kept the chariot reined in, burning a hole in the air, charring the earth below, until he smelled something burning. He saw great clouds of smoke pierced by dancing flames where the lingering coach had set forests ablaze. He put his horses to a gallop and fled, bright as a comet, toward the stables of night. But the land below had been charred over great distances, making a waste place which today men call the Sahara.

His gallop westward had drawn a curtain of night across the earth. Greek and Trojan, amazed, saw the afternoon sun drop like a red-hot coal, hissing, into the sea beyond the western wall of the city. Hector and Ajax groped for each other in the darkness.

Heralds bearing long willow wands rushed forth from the Trojan lines and the Greek lines, calling, "Night! Night! Sudden night! Leave off fighting and seek your tents for the light has flown."

This was the way they ended battles in those days. Hector and Ajax stopped fighting. They felt the night wind on their

77   THE TROJAN WAR

hot brows. All at once, these duelling warriors who had avoided killing each other only by the blunder of a god felt closer to each other than to anyone else on earth.

"Noble Hector," said Ajax, "I have never met a worthier foe."

"Nor have I, sir," said Hector. "Truly I am glad that the light was so magically brief. I welcome this pause."

"We shall resume tomorrow, no doubt," said Ajax. "In the meantime let us sleep. But, pray, take this as a gift and a remembrance."

He unbuckled a purple belt from about his waist. It was of thick soft wool embroidered in gold and black with the figures of dolphins that play off Salamis and do odd favors for men.

"Thank you, great Ajax; it is a beautiful cincture. I shall wear it proudly. Now take you this. It has never been yielded, sir, but now it is freely given."

Hector, then, whom a generous gesture always moved to an excess of generosity, handed Ajax his silver-hilted sword. The two warriors embraced, turned, and went back to their own lines as the first stars trembled steel-blue in the black sky.

тHuNdeR oN тHe RiqHт

Morning light revealed the battlefield so littered with corpses that Greek and Trojan agreed to a truce so that they might honor their dead—build pyres, offer to the gods, and consign the bodies to decent flame.

That morning, too, Zeus called a council of the gods on Olympus. All the members of the Pantheon were required to attend.

Zeus spoke, "Brothers and sisters, sons and daughters, wife, many a time have I warned you, gathered here in sacred convocation and individually to your faces, that I permit no direct intercession on the part of any god in the war below. We may keep our favorites, we may grant godlike dispensations and civilities from the privilege of our godheads, but we are not permitted to descend upon the field and actually handle arms like brawling mortals. Yet, as often as I have issued my edicts, that many times have they been disobeyed.

"Gods, I am not accustomed to being disobeyed. The very notion violates not only my principles but my identity. There can be no Zeus where there is defiance of Zeus. You have violated my decrees, some of you, and have intervened on both sides of the battle. Only yesterday my eyes were offended by the unseemly spectacle of brother and sister actually spearing each other on the reeking plain. Do you not know that this is the way that gods destroy themselves? Not by being conquered, not by invasion, through no act of foe, but by stooping beneath themselves, by behaving like mortals. To behave like a mortal is to forfeit immortality. To behave like that animal called Man is to forfeit divinity. What is mankind to think when it sees Athena fighting with Ares—in other words, Wisdom in conflict with Warfare? Man seeing this can no longer be either wise or warlike. And since this race of man was created for our edification and amusement, such a falling away from the great creative principles of survival will provide us with an earth full of dull automata whose antics we will find most boring through eternity.

"I repeat my edict then, and for the last time. If I catch any of you—and I mean anyone, no matter who he is or what high domain he rules—if I catch any god or goddess directly aiding either Greek or Trojan, then I shall take that offender and cast him or her down into the depths of hell. Yes, I will plunge that one into the blackness of Hades. There I will fork him with the roots of a mountain, as a boy catches a snake in a cleft stick, so that he cannot budge but must lie there with giant worms passing in and out of each eye socket, still alive, still possessing all his strength and all his desires but unable to move, unable to turn or shift, unable to be comforted. And this through eternity. Any questions?"

There was only silence. Finally, Poseidon, who always stood on his dignity with his brother Zeus, said, "Really, these mortals and their affairs are so petty, so unsavory. I don't see how any god can concern himself overmuch with this breed. Oh, we play favorites, to be sure. I suppose that I tend to prefer the Trojans simply because the Greeks have offended me more in times past. Yet really, to choose between them would be like discriminating among columns of ants as they converge upon a bread crumb one has shaken from one's beard."

Then, casting a sidelong look at Zeus, he continued, "Look at them now. Those Greeks are so arrogant and impious. Why they are building their funeral barrows and none of them has thought to sacrifice to Zeus, lord of life. Have the Trojans sacrificed to you, Brother? Oh, yes, I believe they are doing so now. Aren't those white bulls they are slaughtering? Yes. Well, as I said, little as there is to choose between them, yet the Trojans do seem a bit more courteous. But for a god to intercede? Folly."

Poseidon arose, shook the billows of his green garments, combed his beard with his fingers, and struck three times with his trident upon the marble floor, summoning a tidal wave which curled its awful cold green tongue over Olympus. He slipped into the cusp of that enormous wave and, upon his command, it subsided, rolling him down into the ocean depths where stood his castle of coral and pearl. But the sea-god left behind him, slyly kindled, a wrath in the heart of Zeus because he had been given the idea that the Greeks had neglected sacrificing to him.

Dismissing the council after his tirade against intervention, Zeus decided to do a little something himself to discomfit the Greeks. He translated himself to Mount Ida where he had a summer home. He sat on the peak of Ida looking down upon the battlefield. Poseidon's jibe had worked; he was full of rancor against the Hellenes. Now Mount Ida is to the north of Troy, and the Trojans faced westward as they tried to drive the Greeks into the sea, so that when Zeus thundered, he thundered from the Trojan right, an ancient sign of good fortune.

When Hector heard the thundering, he leaped to his feet and cried,

"Enough of truce, brothers! I hear thunder on the right!

Hear it? It is a sign from Zeus; he favors us in the battle to come. So let it begin! To the attack!"

The Trojans armed themselves and began a furious attack upon the Greek positions driving them backward upon their ships. Diomedes tried to lead a counterattack and indeed breached the Trojan lines. His chariot was drawn by the marvelous team of Aeneas, and this get of the sun-stallions were faster than any horses ever foaled. But as he sped toward Hector, spear poised, Zeus spotted him and hurled his lightning bolt. Thunder crashed. Lightning struck directly in front of Diomedes' chariot. There was an eerie flash, a suffocating smell of sulphur. The horses reared. Diomedes tried to whip them through the smoke, but Zeus threw another thunderbolt. Again the heavens crashed on the Trojans' right flank, again the searing flash of lightning in Diomedes' path, again the sulphur stench. The stallions reared again, whinnying in fright. Diomedes realized that Zeus had decided to favor the Trojans that day or that hour. He reined in his steeds and drove back to the Greek lines.

Hector led another savage charge toward the ships. They were protected by a deep ditch called a fosse. Behind the ditch were earthworks of sand. On top of the sand hummocks and entrenched behind them were Greeks. Hector and his brothers began to throw rocks into the fosse and to throw planks across it, so that they could cross over. Sword in hand they fought their way over their rude bridges and began to climb the earthworks.

Watching from Olympus, Hera cried, "My Greeks are being defeated! I can't bear the sight of it! Will no god help me? Then I shall go alone to save them."

Apollo said, "No, Stepmother, it would not be prudent. Do not tempt the wrath of Zeus. Every word he said to us this morning was freighted with the promise of eternal humiliation and torment for the god who would defy him. I know him well. You should know him better. If he sees you crossing the sky in your chariot, he will transfix you with a lightning bolt. Alas, I know those lightning bolts. I know how they can kill, for did he not slay two of my sons. Phaeton, who borrowed my sun-chariot and, careless youthful impetuous driver that he was, drove too high, too low, alternately scorching and freezing the earth. Yes, Zeus toppled him from my chariot with one cast of his fiery spear. There was some justice to it, I suppose. It is the duty of Zeus to protect his realms. But how cruelly and with what little cause did he send his shaft through my son Asclepius, the marvelous physician whose only transgression was that he saved so many of his patients from death that it displeased dark Hades, king of the underworld, who saw himself being deprived of clients and complained to his brother, Zeus. And Zeus complained by killing my wonderful son. So, Stepmother, I beg you, do not dare that awful wrath. Do not attempt to help the Greeks. It is not their day today. Return to your peak and abide the question."

Hera was convinced. She returned to her peak and sorrowfully watched the Greeks being routed below. Now the Greeks were driven back upon their ships. If they allowed the Trojans to advance any further, the ships would surely be burned and with them all hopes of sailing homeward ever again. Agamemnon tried to exhort his men, and his phrasing was as tactless as ever.

"Cowards!" he bellowed. "Empty braggarts. Are you those who claimed one Greek was worth a hundred Trojans? A hundred Trojans? Stand the numbers on their head and we may arrive at something more sensible. Have I not seen one Trojan, Hector, driving a hundred of you at spear point like a shepherd dog herding sheep?"

His voice broke into hoarse sobs. Tears streamed from his eyes. He turned his face to the sky, and said, "Oh, Father

Zeus, why are you punishing me so? Have I not always sacrificed bulls to you, the very finest I could cull from my herd. Great white bulls with black eyes and polished horns and coral nostrils. Swaying broad-backed white oxen, too? Or did I perchance by error neglect some sacrifice or libation to you? Is it for this your hand falls so heavily upon me and my men, delivering us to the enemy? Did not you yourself send me a dream bidding me attack the Trojans, promising me victory? Is this the price of my obedience? Oh, Father Zeus, have mercy. Let me at least drive the Trojans a little way from my ships if you can vouchsafe me no greater victory."

Although Zeus was still annoyed at the Greeks and still intent to keep his promise to Thetis that the Greeks would be denied victory until Agamemnon should plead for Achilles' help, still he was touched by the Mycenean king's plea and relented a bit. This took the form of fresh courage firing the Greek hearts. Crude as Agamemnon's words were, still they responded to his speech and launched a counterattack. They hurled down the plank bridges and drove the Trojans back from the lip of the fosse.

Teucer now became the most effective of the Hellenes. Hiding behind the enormous shield of his brother Ajax, he shot arrow after arrow, and it was as if Zeus himself personally guided each shaft. He loosed nine arrows, and each one of them killed a man. Nine Trojans fell, nine of the best.

With his genius for saying the wrong thing, Agamemnon now rushed up to Teucer, crying,

"Hail, great archer! Every arrow you let fly kills another Trojan. You must redouble your efforts. Snatch your arrows faster from the quiver. Notch them more speedily to your bowstring, and shoot one after the other without delay. You must kill as many Trojans as possible while Zeus smiles on you. His smiles are brief, as well we know."

"Why flog a horse that is breaking his wind galloping for you?" said Teucer. "I cannot shoot any faster."

"Certainly you can. You want an inducement. Listen, I promise you this. As high king and commander of the forces, I pledge that when finally we take and sack Troy you shall have the woman you choose for your very own, no matter how many princes contend for her, and you may take your choice from among all the daughters of Priam and the other beautiful maidens of the court."

"Thank you for nothing," said Teucer. "When we take Troy I'll do my own choosing. Now please, king, break off this discourse, and let me continue to send my bolts into the ranks of the enemy. As we stand here talking, they're regrouping. If we linger like this the only thing we'll be taking is a ferry across the Styx."

Sure enough, by the time he had notched another arrow to his bowstring, Hector had approached close enough to hurl a boulder that caught Teucer square, toppling him and crushing his collarbone. That would have been the end of the superb little archer except that Diomedes scooped him up into his chariot and galloped to safety behind the Greek lines.

This was a turning point again. Zeus felt that he had responded sufficiently to Agamemnon's prayer and withdrew his favor.

The Trojans crossed the fosse again and forced the Greeks step by step back toward their ships.

Hera, watching on high, was again seized by a savage dissatisfaction, with that imperious burning displeasure that was a hallmark of her character.

"Come, Athena!" she cried. "We must go help the Greeks!"

"No, Father Zeus has forbidden it," said Athena.

"My conduct is defined by my neglect of his decrees,"

said Hera. "Am I a wife for nothing? Forbid it or not, we must go down there, or the Greeks are doomed. And after all our efforts, it's intolerable!"

"Be patient but a little while, Stepmother," said Athena. "I know that Zeus in the larger measure of things means to abide by his oath of neutrality. He, too, as much as any of us, is bound by the anciently woven edicts of the Fates, who are older than the gods and less changeable. He knows that Troy must fall."

"It will never fall while Trojans are killing Greeks," said Hera.

"Patience, Mother. Zeus is but keeping the promise he made to Thetis, the silver-footed, that Greek fortunes would ebb until Agamemnon should be humbled and have to come to Achilles' tent to plead with him to drop his grudge and enter the lists again. When that happens, and the time is drawing near, then Zeus will resume his impartiality and let the Fates work."

"I can't wait that long," said Hera, "or there will be nothing left down there but Trojans. If you don't join me, I'm going alone."

But Hera had no sooner climbed into her chariot than Zeus made his power felt. Before she had a chance to whip up her horses, swift-winged Iris, the messenger-goddess, flashed across the sky from Mount Ida where she had been sitting at Zeus's feet, awaiting errands.

"Father Zeus is watching you," she said. "He is listening. He sees and hears across great distances. He knows your intentions. And he instructs me to say that if the wheels of your chariot leave this peak you will be transfixed by a thunderbolt which even now he holds poised, ready to hurl."

Hera threw down her reins and pulled herself from the coach, weeping. Athena tried to comfort her.

"Take heart, Mother," she said. "Night is falling, and the

fighting must stop. Perhaps in the watches of the night Father Zeus will relent and tomorrow turn his favor to the Greeks. Or, perhaps allow us to aid them if he will not. He is changeable, you know. His moods are brief as they are violent."

Hera, still sobbing, allowed herself to be led into her chamber.

Night

Sentries watching from the walls of Troy were comforted by the sight of a hundred fires burning on the beach. Trojan fires. They meant that the Trojans had penned the Greeks onto a narrow marge between fosse and ocean. Hector ranged among the fires, exhorting his men.

"Tomorrow!" he cried. "Tomorrow is our day! I feel it in my heart. Tomorrow we will finish what we have begun so well today. We will force them back, back, back, upon their ships, and slay them every one. And teach haughty invader never again to dare the beaches of Troy."

On the Greek side, the scene was much different. Dismay hung like a pall, and no watch fires gleamed. A solemn conclave was going on in Agamemnon's tent.

"Kings and princes," he said, "members of the council, I pray your forgiveness. As commander, I must take supreme responsibility for our defeat. And now I ask for your advice. Do you think we should try to save what we can—that is—

launch our ships under cover of night—this night I mean—
and sail for home? Tomorrow, remember, the enemy may
cross the ditch and burn our ships, cutting off our retreat.
That is the question we must resolve here and now. Do we
depart tonight or gird ourselves for tomorrow, knowing that
this morrow may be our last among the living?"

Diomedes spoke briefly. "The rest of you can leave, every
one, but I stay. I and my charioteer, Sthelenus. If all the rest
of you go, together we will mount the chariot and drive
Aeneas's marvelous horses against the Trojans, killing as
many as we can before we are killed in our turn. If you want
my real recommendation, Agamemnon, it would be for us to
burn the ships ourselves tonight, cutting off our own retreat
and giving every doubter among us the great gift of no al-
ternative. Better to be cut down here like men than to skulk
home defeated, dishonored, disgraced."

"Diomedes, you are a very young man," said Nestor, "but
you speak like a sage. Your words are golden, my boy.
Golden. I cannot quite hold with you on burning our ships,
but this much is sure, we must not sail home tonight. Of
course, we must stay and fight. And, by the gods, if we face
the enemy without dismay, we will win. The Fates have foretold it, and not even the gods may alter their decree. But I
have this to say. We must decide on a very important step
tonight. By this I mean we must coax Achilles back into the
fold. Agamemnon, the burden is yours. You must apologize to
him and make amends, and I know how this will torment
your proud spirit, but you have no choice, truly. You must
take upon yourself that humiliation; you must eat your arrogant words, return the slave-girl you took from him, and give
him rich compensation besides. Then, perhaps, we can convince him to fight tomorrow. My Lord Agamemnon, this is
absolutely necessary. Without him we are just an army; with
him we are an irresistible force."

Agamemnon said, "Honorable Nestor, dear sage, adept councilor, I speak no word in objection. I will humble my spirit and do everything necessary to persuade Achilles to join our ranks once again. I was wrong to quarrel with him, wrong to take the tall Briseis—wrong, wrong, wrong! I can ascribe my actions only to some hostile god addling my wits and doing us more harm thereby than if he had supplied the Trojans with a company of slingers, a company of archers, and a cavalry troop. Now I have come to my senses again. Harsh defeat has restored my balance. I see how misguided I was, and this is what I propose to do for Achilles if he consents to stand beside us tomorrow. Hark now to my gifts of appeasement: First, cooking ware, rich enough to prepare a feast for the gods—seven bronze kettles and twenty huge pots of burnished copper, each of them big enough to boil an ox in. Ten gold ingots, each of them weighing almost a hundred pounds. Six teams of matched stallions that in a chariot race would press the sun-bred stallions of Aeneas. Seven girl-slaves, the most beautiful of all those captured in nine years of island raiding, all of them contortionists, and very good at embroidery, too. Lastly, I shall return to him tall Briseis— and with her my oath that I have never tried her as bedmate. She will come back into his hands untouched by me. Generous? Yes, but this is only the start, good sirs. When we return to Greece I shall bestow upon him other gifts, beyond the dream of avarice. I shall consider him my son, an elder brother to Orestes, with all the privileges appertaining to a prince royal in Mycenae. He will choose a wife from among my three beautiful daughters; her dowry will be seven cities, the richest in the land. I pray you, inform Achilles of my offer, and bring me his answer."

"Very well," said Nestor. "On behalf of the War Council let me thank you for the remarkable generosity you now display. I have no doubt it will make Achilles forget the insults he suffered at your hands. I propose that the overtures be made to him by the men he respects most: Phoenix, his old tutor, Ulysses, and Ajax. And I myself will accompany these three for, in all modesty, he esteems me also."

When the delegation came to the tent of Achilles they found a very peaceful scene. There was a driftwood fire burning and the smell of roasting meat. Achilles was playing a silver-chased lyre and singing a boar-hunt song of Phthia. Patroclus lay back listening dreamily. Achilles sprang to his feet when he saw his guests.

He embraced them, calling to Patroclus, "See, my friend, how we are honored. Our companions, battle-weary, come to visit us instead of refreshing themselves with sleep."

"Oh, son of Peleus," said Patroclus, "I believe you misread their intent. They come not to exchange amenities and to pass the time, nor even to indulge themselves in your warm hospitality; they come on business, grim business. Am I right, friends?"

"Your wits have always been as sharp as your sword, good Patroclus," said Ulysses. "And, unlike your sword, have been given no chance to grow rusty. Yes, we come on business, grim business. Survival is always a grim affair. It is particularly grim when your enemies have you penned on a narrow stretch of beach threatening to slaughter you like cattle and burn your ships."

"Business or not, grim or not," boomed Achilles, "nevertheless we shall preserve the amenities. You have come on a visit to my tent, and it is my custom to feed visitors. Patroclus, will you do the honors of the table, sir?"

Patroclus served the savory roast meat and the rich purple wine. The guests fell to greedily for Agamemnon had neglected to feed them at the council.

When they had fed, Achilles said, "Now, sirs, say to me what you will. I am all attention."

Then Ulysses, always the spokesman in any delegation, told Achilles how greatly Agamemnon desired to make amends and the rich gifts he was offering.

Achilles answered, "If anything could convince me to drop my feud with Agamemnon and join battle against the Trojans, it would not be his bribes, but the feelings of comradeship, respect, and affection I have for you, great Ulysses, you Ajax, you Nestor, and you, Phoenix, beloved friend and mentor. Nevertheless my answer must be no. I loathe and despise Agamemnon. In open meeting before all the troops, he insulted me repeatedly. He spoke to me as if I were the seediest of camp followers rather than what I am. Laid rude hands upon Briseis and dragged her away. So, my friends, when you report back to him, tell him to keep his cook pots and his ingots and his talented slave-girls and his seven cities in Mycenae. As for his kind offer to wed me to one of his daughters, I can say only this: I have not met any of the three young ladies. I hope for their own sakes they resemble their mother, Clytemnestra, or their aunt, Helen. Nevertheless, heredity is a quirky thing. Lineaments and traits of personality have been known to skip generations. Ask my lord, Agamemnon, if he thinks I would risk having a son or daughter with his pig face and verminous disposition. No, gentlemen. The answer is no. Tomorrow, at dawn, my Myrmidons and I board our ships and sail away to Phthia. Patroclus comes with me. And you Phoenix, old teacher, do not stay and sacrifice yourself in this vain war. Come on board my ship, and sail home with me."

Phoenix could not speak; his voice was strangled with tears. He simply nodded to Achilles, and embraced Nestor, Ulysses, and Ajax in farewell. They said not a word in protest knowing it would be futile, but took courteous leave of Achilles and left his tent.

on the wall

It was as though the gods, heavy with business, had pressed the sky low that night between battles. The stars hung low, pulsing, each one big as a moon; the moon itself was a golden brooch pinning folds of darkness which were night's cloak. The gleaming watch fires on the field looked like star-images dancing in water. Standing on the west wall it was hard to tell where the sea ended and the beach began. Under the immense jewelry of the summer night lay the corpses of the day's fighting—bodies pierced and broken, smashed heads of beautiful young men, severed arms and legs. They bulked strangely now; they were heaped shadows. Pools of blood stank and glistened in the moonlight. Birds came down to drink.

The night is beautiful on the Dardanian plain when the sky presses low, flaunting its jewelry. Not a night for sleeping though you be battle-weary, or love-weary, or devilled by hope, or torn by fear. On both sides of the fosse the men seethed restlessly. Men and women still lingered on the walls of Troy where they had watched the battle all day. Usually, by night, the walls were bare of all save sentries, but this night pressed with too many hot lights. People trying to sleep were pressed between flaming sky and reeking earth, and were tormented by dreams that drove them from sleep.

Helen and Cressida lingered on the wall. They were

wrapped in long cloaks; their hands and faces glimmered in the weird light.

"I have been wanting to talk to you," said Cressida.

"Indeed?" said Helen, frowning slightly.

She was the daughter of kings and the wife of a king, paramour of a prince, and was being fought for by all the kings of Greece. She was proud. And Cressida was only a priest's daughter, but recently a slave in Agamemnon's tent. The difference was great between them.

"Forgive me for addressing you so familiarly, Queen Helen," said Cressida in her odd, furry voice. "I know the distance between us. But, you know, you are a heroine, a demi-goddess. When you go out on the streets of Troy, not only princes admire, but the populace cheers itself hoarse, too. I am not too humble to esteem you. And being here on the wall with you this way after a day of such sights, I cannot forbear from addressing you. There is something old in our hearts that tells us wisdom is allied to beauty, and I need the counsel of someone wise."

"Nay, put aside these ceremonial forms of address," said Helen, reaching her long arm and putting her hand on Cressida's shoulder. "We are two women together."

For admiration was soul's food to Helen, and the clever words of Cressida fired her vanity and made her ignore social distinctions.

"Two women together," murmured Cressida. "Yes, and we have watched the battle all day. With what mixed feelings women watch! Men are lucky; they're so simple. Their alternatives are so few. Kill or be killed. Good or bad. Noble or cowardly. Their simplicity is what gives them power over us. Oh, queen of Sparta, for we are poor weak divided creatures, torn by distinctions. We see our loved ones fighting, and we want them home safe. Yet, if they kill—and they must kill or be killed—it is other beautiful young men they are destroying. And we are dismayed by the waste. Lusty handsome young men who might serve women in their loneliness—who might make so many women bloom. And they fall like logs of wood. Look at that field covered with bodies—most of them young, most of them beautiful. It is a waste, a waste, and waste is what women cannot abide. We are a thrifty lot. We like to make and keep. We hate to see things thrown out while there is still use in them. And there was use in those young bodies, glorious hot-blooded use. Forgive my babbling, Queen, but I am more affected than others, I suppose, because, as you know, I lived among the Greeks. There were no strangers to me today on either side of the fighting."

"Ah, you forget," said Helen. "I, too, know Trojan and Greek."

"It is different with you now, beautiful queen. For your heart and soul reside in that radiant young prince, Paris. You must wholeheartedly follow his fortune. Although, when he dueled with Menelaus, your former husband, your thoughts then must have been interesting."

"Too interesting for gossip," said Helen, "much as I enjoy your conversation, but I will tell you one thought. When Menelaus wounded Paris I thought, 'Why it is my fault; he has gored my boy with the horns I myself gave him.' "

Cressida laughed. "In you, pain becomes wit, oh Queen. You are a very brave woman."

"Enough of flattery, or rather let me return the compliment. I think you are the most beautiful maiden in all Troy."

"Maiden no more," said Cressida. "You forget I was taken by Agamemnon."

"I know. It doesn't matter. One uses the word 'maiden' as a polite form rather than anything else. As a condition it is rare in any city and not too frequent in villages."

"Tell me why you think I'm beautiful."

"That is a question one asks a man," said Helen.

"Forgive me. There are no men here, and the question burns. Besides, whom could I better ask than the queen of beauty herself."

"I find your phraseology most persuasive," said Helen. "Very well. In your sojourn among the Greeks, Cressida, did you learn the word 'perprowktian'?"

"All I learned were very short words. 'Lie down,' 'Roll over,' 'Meat,' 'Wine,' 'Rub harder,' 'Shut up.' That was about the extent of it. I was there only a few weeks, you know."

"Well, you seem to have picked up a good practical vocabulary," said Helen. "However, 'preprowktian' is an interesting word. What it means is the undulant bulge-and-slide view a woman presents to a man as she walks away. Something grossly counterfeited by harlots and dancing girls and the like, but in a woman gently bred and well reared it is an extremely provocative display. I have always admired your walk, Cressida."

"Any bitch with an itching tail wags her hindquarters," said a voice. "What's so wonderful about that?"

It was Cassandra, almost invisible because she was cloaked in black, but her eyes, like a cat's, were burning holes in the darkness.

"You know my little sister-in-law, no doubt," said Helen. "And do not feel offended. What would be the most unpardonable rudeness in anyone else is genius in her. The sign of genius, apparently, is a systematic and ruthless discourtesy."

"Spartan whore," said Cassandra, "you have good reason to dislike me. The moment I saw you I knew you meant the destruction of Troy. Every breath you exhale poisons Ilium. Every lewd glitter of your leman's eye kindles a flame for that night of flame when Troy will be sacked. In your voice that coos of love is the death-rattle of brave men."

"You see how wise one is in accepting flattery when it

comes," said Helen to Cressida. "So soon afterward one hears something else."

"Good Cassandra," said Cressida. "For years I have seen you about the court. You were wrapped in so formidable a reputation of prophecy and god-given insight that I dared not make myself known to you. Yet on such a night, between battles, when the darkness itself seems pregnant with events struggling to be born, on such a night, there is an appetite, I think, for prophecy—more than for food or drink or love. Tell us what will happen. Who will be killed tomorrow and who survive? Will the Trojans drive the Greeks to the sea and burn their ships? Will the Greeks drive back the Trojans and storm these walls? Will Achilles return to the fray? Will Hector rage again like a lion in the field? What of Paris? And young Troilus—so like Paris in beauty of face and form, yet shy where his brother is bold—what of him? He escaped death by a hairsbreadth a dozen times today. Will he be as fortunate tomorrow—and return to bed some lucky girl?"

Helen was gazing at the moon, seemingly absent, but listening hard all the same. For she recognized in these last words of Cressida not an address to Cassandra but a message to herself. Cressida fancied young Troilus among all the Trojan men, and was obliquely asking Helen to drop a hint to the lad, the most naïve and inexperienced of all Priam's fifty sons.

"Do not plague me with your sordid little queries," said Cassandra to Cressida. "You say one thing but mean another. You seek to entrap my brother, Troilus. Very well. If he thinks the leavings of that wild boar, Agamemnon, make savory bed-fare, he is welcome to you."

"I do not understand what you mean, dear Cassandra," murmured Cressida, "but then it is said that you often prophesy in riddles. Are you doing that now, riddling us?

Please tell us what will happen in the battle tomorrow, but in plain words so that we can understand."

"In plain words, shut up, Whore Number Two," said Cassandra. "I will not speak of the battle tomorrow. I will not speak at all. But wait. I see something. A bloody thing is about to happen right now. Not tomorrow, *now*. My vision, god-poisoned, pierces distance. I see Ulysses and Diomedes preparing for a foray upon our lines."

"Diomedes," said Cressida. "A very likely man. He was another Achilles in the field today. He seemed like a god descended, bright as a star. I've never seen anything like it."

"Yes," said Helen. "He is too young to have been one of my suitors. Today I rather regretted it. He put on a remarkable performance. Remarkable."

"Ulysses dons a skullcap of boarhide and a half cloak of polished boarhide to serve as an arrow-proof vest. Diomedes, despite the warmth of the night, wraps himself in a wolf-skin cloak. They costume themselves like this to cast bulky shadows for the moon is very bright, and they wish to steal among our men and Ulysses is a master of artifice. They carry short hunting spears and knives at their belts, no swords to rattle against their legs. No bows and arrows for they will be working in close. They seek to raid our lines, capture a Trojan, and extract information from him. And into the jaws of this trap the gods are sending one of our officers named Dolon. He seeks to invoke the aid of darkness by putting on a mole-skin cloak and mole-skin cap for moles are blind and cannot see, and their hide, he believes, will protect him from being seen as he scouts out the Greek positions. Foolishness. The whole art of magic is the exchange of attributes through invocation, and he has no magic. Poor Dolon, he must die."

Helen and Cressida were so wrapped up in this tale told by the staring girl that they almost forgot to draw breath.

THE TROJAN WAR

Cassandra paused. Unwinkingly her cat's eyes burned holes in the darkness.

"Tell. Tell," whispered Helen. "What are they doing? Please tell."

Cassandra resumed her tale in a low monotonous voice. She cared nothing for her listeners; she never cared for listeners—she told things to herself, but she knew that others overheard.

"The Greeks pick their way among fallen bodies and pools of blood. At their approach birds flutter away. When they pass by, the birds return to drink. There is a rustling as rats scurry amid the corpses. O things of night do feed richly upon the battle's fruit."

She fell silent again, and the others, listening, thought they heard rats gnawing and birds sipping. And these tiny sounds were the most terrible they had ever heard.

"Listen well, my slothful sisters, and I will tell you a tale of this busy night, of this vast and starry, bloody night. Ulysses and Diomedes pick their way among corpses to spy upon the Trojan lines while Dolon skirts pools of blood to spy upon the Greeks. They will meet, they will meet, and sad will be the tale thereof, for Dolon knows a secret. Upon this night allies have come to join our forces—King Rhesus of Thrace with a thousand henchmen from that land behind the north wind where men grow large and fierce. Drawing the chariot of King Rhesus is a pair of horses unmatched by any in the world except those that Diomedes took from Aeneas earlier today. A pair of milk-white mares sired by Pegasus upon one of the white-maned gray mares that draw Poseidon's chariot when he raids the beaches. And so with gorgon blood in them, they can gallop as fast as those falcon-swift, brass-winged sisters who pursued Perseus, can gallop as tirelessly as the waves of the sea that break upon the shore. They are white as milk, tall as deer, with black manes and brass hooves. Mounted in his chariot, drawn by such mares, King Rhesus is a fearsome warrior. The wheels of his chariot wear no simple hubs, but a sheaf of scythes that turn with the turning of the wheel, mowing down his foes who fall like summer grass. Their coming should be a joy to us. Oh watchers upon the wall, sister harlots, the coming of Rhesus should be an occasion for rejoicing. For anciently it has been told that our city cannot fall once these mares drink of our river. Once these thirsty steeds dip their muzzles into the waters of the Scamander and drink therefrom, the walls of Troy must stand and its inhabitants be undisturbed. Will Rhesus arise in the rose and pearl dawn of the Dardanian plain? Will he start the bronze dust as he drives his chariot toward the Scamander and allow his mares to drink before the thirsty work of battle begins?

"Alas, alas, Dolon knows that the Thracians have come with Rhesus at their head. He knows they guard the right flank, that they have put out no sentries, and that they sleep soundly after their exhausting journey. He knows the tale of the prophecy. Dolon steps quietly, but Ulysses has ears like a fox; he hears someone coming. He pulls Diomedes into the shade of a tamarisk tree, and there they wait. They seize Dolon when he comes. Yes, now they have him. He has fallen into their jaws like a mole taken by a night-running hound. They tie him to the bole of the tamarisk tree. He pleads with them; they do not answer, but speak to each other in grunts. Now he is ready. Ulysses takes out his knife, saying, 'We are Greeks. We are after information. You will please answer what we ask, or we will carve you like a joint of meat. You are dead already, you see, because we will not leave you alive, but you can spare yourself some pain. Why not spend your last minutes without pain?'

"Dolon sobs. He is a brave man, but not brave enough for this. He is brave in the sunlight, but now they are under the

THE TROJAN WAR

cold lamp of the moon. He has been ambushed by shadows, by men big as shadows who speak to him in a strange language that he understands, saying nightmare things.

"Diomedes grows impatient while Dolon hesitates. He wields his knife and slices a finger off Dolon's hand. Dolon's screams are stifled by Ulysses' hand clapped over his mouth.

" 'That hurts, does it?' says Diomedes. 'Don't forget you have ten of those, not to mention your toes. Why don't you tell us what we want to know?'

"Dolon cannot bear this; few men could. He begins to babble away telling them more than they wish to know. Ulysses slaps him across the face, bidding him be still and just answer the questions.

" 'Have you posted sentries?'

" 'No.'

" 'Why not?'

" 'We thought you were too beaten, too disheartened to make any forays this night.'

" 'How are you encamped? What are the disposition of your forces?'

" 'We Trojans hold the center. To the left, toward the sea, lie the Lelegians, the Cauconians. On the left flank are those raiders from Crete, the sea-harassing Palasgians. To the right of us are stationed the Lycians, the Mysians, the Phrygians, and Maeonians. On the extreme right flank are those newcomers, the Thracians, under King Rhesus.'

" 'The Thracians? Are you sure?' said Ulysses. 'I know of no Thracians here.'

" 'They have joined us only tonight. I was a member of the welcoming party. I am sure. Pray let me go, good sirs. My father is the herald, Eumedes, and heralds grow rich in times of war. He will pay a large ransom for me. I will tell you what I know, but then let me go.'

"Diomedes prods him with the point of his dagger.

" 'Speak on,' he says. 'We have more questions. Who leads these Thracians?'

" 'I told you, King Rhesus.'

" 'Is he accounted a good fighter, this Rhesus?'

" 'The finest. Ranks with the best. And in a chariot is perhaps the very best for his steeds are matchless.'

" 'Indeed?' asks Diomedes. 'Better than those of Aeneas?'

" 'As good, as good. Some say better. They were sired by Pegasus upon one of Poseidon's own surf-mares. They are tall as stags, milk-white, with black manes and brass hooves. And they run like the wind. I have never seen them, but so I am told. And his chariot is made of silver and gold with brass wheels, and his axle sprout six long knives which scythe down the enemy. The Trojans rejoice to have him as an ally. Am I not a good informant, oh captors? Do I not report fully, fully? Pray, accept a ransom and let me go.'

" 'Anything else about him? How many men does he lead?'

" 'A thousand Thracians come with him, but best of all, I know something else! Don't kill me yet, don't kill me yet! I have something else to tell!'

" 'Tell away. The night grows old, and our patience short.'

" 'Don't kill me yet, not yet! Just listen to this!'

Cassandra broke off her tale, eyes huge and staring.

"Go on, go on," said Helen.

"Don't stop now. Tell. Please tell," whispered Cressida.

"Oh, no!" muttered Cassandra to herself, pressing her knuckles against her mouth. "He must not! No, Dolon, do not tell them! Do not inform them of the prophecy! It will be fatal! Oh, coward! He tells! He tells!"

"Tells what?" cried Helen.

"What I told you, you fat-hipped fool! Has it fled your memory so soon? The prophecy concerning the mares of Rhesus—that if they drink of Scamander's waters, Troy shall

THE TROJAN WAR

not fall. Dolon is blabbing this to those men of steel. He tells this to Diomedes and Ulysses; that is all they have to know. Ulysses thanks him and signals to Diomedes who with one swift movement cuts Dolon's throat as if he were a sheep. They leave him bound to the tamarisk tree and set off to their left, toward the extreme right flank of our lines where sleeps Rhesus and the Thracian host, and the fatal mares."

poseidon decides

The god of the sea was vexed. Unlike the other gods he had held himself aloof from this war. He had preened himself on being so far above the affairs of petty mortals that he might not stoop to take a hand in their quarrels. This was a unique position in the Pantheon: all the other gods had lined up one way or the other. For a while, this sense of uniqueness served his pride. But now of late he had felt a difference. The combatants, Trojan and Greek, were offering him fewer prayers, less sacrifices, adorned his statues more meagerly, built him fewer altars, and implored his intercession only in specific sea matters—voyages and piracies, and the like. But this had developed into a land war, so Poseidon was feeling neglected.

"It's all because of my impartiality," he raged to himself. "An attribute I have always held truly divine. But instead of being thankful that I do not meddle in their battles, killing this one, saving that one, turning all their plans awry—in-

stead of being thankful for my benign indifference—they have dared to neglect *me*. The Trojans, knowing that Athena is against them, sacrifice to her constantly. Just yesterday Hector sent all the women of Troy in great droves led by Hecuba to the Palladium to pray to Athena to turn a less furious face upon them. Similarly, the Hellenes court Apollo who favors the Trojans. Yes, they pray and sacrifice to him and to his cold bitch of a sister and to that blundering bully, Ares. They crawl to all the gods who favor Troy. The Trojans fill the air with supplications to Hera, whom they know loathes them. It's getting so a god has to punish a nation to get its respect. Well, I'm weary of being neglected. I shall take sides, too. Those I favor shall thank me; those I mistreat shall implore me. Yes, I shall have my mede of mortal attention—without which, it is curious to say, we gods, even the most powerful of us, are apt to shrivel and waste.

"Now who shall it be, Trojan or Greek? Very difficult. No instantaneous bias suggests itself, only a mild dislike for each."

The trouble here was that Poseidon for all his tempestuous bluster had a strong feminine side to his nature. He was incapable of loving or hating people in groups. Generalization irked him. He could form a powerful attachment to an individual as he had to Theseus, for instance, said to have been his son, and keep an eye on him through all circumstance and crown his deeds with glory. Far more often, he could hold an implacable grudge against someone and pursue him with storm, tidal wave, sea-monster, and every type of marine catastrophe. But, as he thought about things, he found himself incapable of preferring either Greek or Trojan en masse.

"Let's see," he said. "Let me consider this carefully. Certainly I can find cause to favor one side or the other, especially as it doesn't matter which. Now, if I have a grudge against any people as such it is the Athenians. Faced by a direct choice between me and Athena, they preferred her and her olive tree to me and my sea dower. Well, they've paid for that. They're paying still, and will pay in time to come. I founder their ships, scatter their fleets, drown their sailors. Still, the Athenians form only one small part of the Greek forces. Certain others, of the islands in particular, who study my moods closely, find favor in my eyes. The pirate kings of Rhodes, Cnossos, Sephiros, Ithaca, have all tickled my nostrils with the rich smoke of flayed oxen. The ancient misdeeds of the Athenians alone are not enough. Besides, was it not a Trojan, King Laomedon of olden times, who offered me an enormous offence? When Apollo and I were punished by Zeus for conspiring against his throne that time, we were exiled to Troy in the guise of mortals and were there bidden to serve King Laomedon. He worked us hard. We were the busiest slaves any king ever had. We built three walls of Troy before our year was up. Some mortal later built the west wall, which is by far the weakest. And Laomedon was a terrible taskmaster—never a civil word, no word of thanks, nothing but kicks and blows. Yet, he's long dead, Laomedon. Gone these many generations—just a dusty memory now, hard to hate. Besides, the real offence did not reside with him, who did not know us, but with Zeus who fastened so ignominious a penalty on other gods.

"I still cannot choose. Greek or Trojan, Trojan or Greek? Shall I have to draw straws? Seems a paltry device to decide such potent favor. Perhaps the clue to my intercession should lie not in mortal acts of grace or offence, but in my preferences among the gods, who have all involved themselves in this fray. Here again it is very difficult. I have reason to dislike all my brothers and sisters, nieces and nephews. My sister, Demeter, has always pleased me the most, I suppose. On the other hand, she takes the least interest in this war among all the Pantheon. She dislikes war too much. It means the de-

THE TROJAN WAR

struction of crops, whoever wins. And she is the Lady of Growing Things.

"I have this old feud with Athena, and her espousal of the Greeks might lead me to choose the Trojans. Against this, though, those mealy-mouthed high-stepping twins, Apollo and Artemis, help Troy, and I should not wish to be on the same side of any question as they are. Apollo's flaming nuisance of a chariot parches my waters whenever it can catch them in shallow pools. While that grasping bare-thighed male-hating icicle sister of his has the gall to meddle with my tides. Her keen whistle pierces to the underwater kennels where the sea-dogs sleep. She summons them, leashes them with a chain of silver light, and swings them high, low, despite my dominion of the sea. Her I will destroy one day. I don't quite know how, but I will find a way.

"Difficult—a most difficult question. Quite gives me a headache."

And he spit a tidal wave that covered an ancient island with a wall of water a hundred feet high. When the wave subsided the island had disappeared and has never been seen since.

All this time he had been hovering over the face of the waters. Now he whistled up his chariot, not the beach-raiding one drawn by his white-maned gray mares, but the sleek, green sea-going chariot drawn by dolphins. He sped to his palace of coral and pearl. Seated on his great throne which was of whalebone lined with mother-of-pearl, he felt more at ease and resumed his thought.

"I am unable to decide this way," he said to himself. "That is clear. Perhaps it is better so. Weighing this, calculating thus—that has never been my style. My rage is storm. My kindness a fall of light, sudden bliss of blue weather. I am sudden, capricious, king of tempest. The sea itself takes its famous changeableness from my moods. I shall watch the battle then as it shapes up this morning and, as I watch, take inspiration from what I see. Yes, that will relieve me of this head-splitting meditation and provide some diversion also. For I find uncertainty pleasing—and have always diced with dead men's bones. Very well, then, I shall watch the battle and decide. Woe be to the forces, Greek or Trojan, whom I decide against."

He took a great bowl made from a single chrysoprase, the largest in all the world. It is a light-green jewel pure as a child's eye holding much light. This bowl of chrysoprase he had filled with clear water. Watching the water and thinking about the Dardanian plain, he saw cloudy pictures form and dissolve, and they were the images of battle.

Poseidon, like all gods was intensely amused by the sight of men fighting. The fiercer the fighting, the more he enjoyed it. A good killing sent him into peals of laughter. This laughter of the gods at the sight of death and suffering is sometimes dimly heard by men—as a natural sound, usually— the wind howling on a peculiar note, the cry of an owl striking, a scream out of nowhere waking the sleeper who tries to identify it and fails, and certain sounds heard by children, the sourceless creaking of doors late at night, trees scratching at the window with long gray fingers—all these are that cruel laughter of the gods, disguised, heard always with great astonishment.

Thus, Poseidon on his whalebone and nacre throne rocked with laughter as he saw the battle rage on the Dardanian plain, saw the cloudy images form and dissolve in his chrysoprase bowl of pure water. So much blood was spilled in these scenes that the bowl was tinged with red, and this pleased Poseidon.

He saw Agamemnon, clad in gorgeous armor, goaded to fury by the whisper of Athena. Agamemnon clove the Trojan ranks, thrusting with his long spear, shearing through shield, breastplate, helmet, crushing bone, drinking blood.

"How gaudy he is, this commander," said Poseidon to himself, "this wild boar from Mycenae who cannot utter a word without creating dissension. How splendidly he is clad, and how splendidly he fights, to be sure. Marvelous his armor of lapis lazuli, of bronze, and of pure beaten tin. He glitters like a beetle on the dusty plain. And, like a beetle, can be crushed."

Just as Poseidon said these words the picture in the green bowl dissolved from that of Agamemnon spearing the elder son of Antenor to the younger son of Antenor spearing Agamemnon. The younger son, Choon, drove his spear through the king's shoulder. Agamemnon's counterthrust pierced the lad's eyesocket, and split his skull. But Agamemnon, bleeding sorely, was forced from the field.

Grinning, Poseidon signaled to a naiad who took up the bowl, poured out the blood-tinged water, refilled it with clean water, and returned it to the laughing god. Now Poseidon, conning the waters in the bowl, saw Hector rally the Trojans for a counterattack that carried them back over the field halfway to the fosse.

Here at the lip of the fosse the best of the Greeks took a stand against the Trojan's hurricane charge. Diomedes flung a rock at Hector that crushed the crest of his helmet and hurled him to earth, stunned. But Aeneas straddled the fallen Hector and covered him with his shield, and Diomedes could not follow up his advantage. Such was the fever of combat burning in Hector that his dizziness fled, and he sprang to his feet ready to fight again. As Diomedes hesitated, seeking a way to get at Hector, Paris slithered near. Sheltering behind a tree, he notched an arrow to his bowstring and let fly. It was a splendid shot. Had he ventured closer before shooting he would have killed Diomedes, but the tree was a long bowshot away, and the arrow struck downward, piercing

Diomedes' foot, pinning it to the ground. Seeing that Diomedes could not get at him, Paris laughed and came closer, fitting another arrow to his string.

"It was you, was it, prince of sneaks!" roared Diomedes. "Hiding behind a tree like a mountain bandit and shooting arrows at your betters. Miserable ambusher! Puling abductor! Dare to come within my reach. Dare to meet me with spear or sword. I'll send you back to the lap of your whore unfit for anything except cremation."

Diomedes stooped and pulled the arrow out of his foot despite the awful pain of the barb tearing backward through his flesh. Paris was so disconcerted at this stoic feat that he melted into the crowd again without shooting his second arrow. But Diomedes had lost much blood; he had to quit the battle.

Now Hector, flanked by Troilus and Aeneas, swept like a brush fire along the bank of the Scamander where the Thessalians were making a stand. Paris had hastened to join this group because he preferred to shelter himself behind an impenetrable hedge of such shields. But he was welcome. His archery was inspired. It was as if Apollo himself had tutored him in bowmanship between one day's fighting and the next. Every arrow he shot found its target in Greek flesh. He sent a shaft through the shoulder of Machaon, who fell where he stood. A shout of despair arose from the Thessalians. Machaon was their king, not only their king, but the most able healer in the Greek camp. Son of Aesclepius himself, he had been taught by the great surgeon and had mastered his father's art. This made him a grandson of Apollo, of course, but he had lost Apollo's favor by fighting on the wrong side.

It was old Nestor who leaped out of his chariot, lifted the fallen Machaon, and drove him safely back to the Greek lines. The Thessalians were disheartened by the loss of their

leader and would have crumbled before the Trojan charge
had not Great Ajax come rushing up and rallied their waver-
ing ranks with a loud war-cry.

All this time Poseidon was watching the battle in the
visionary waters of his chrysoprase bowl. Octopi wrestled
beyond the huge windows set in his palace of coral and pearl.
Sharks glided, smiling their hunger. Shoals of long-legged
naiads swam by, hair floating. Balloon fish, giant rays, the
artful twisted glyph, the only sea-creature that can outma-
neuver an eel—all the rich traffic of the sea swam past his
window—which he so loved in his ordinary hours, but which
he failed to notice now, absorbed as he was in the shifting
images of battle.

He saw Ajax standing among the broken Thessalians,
steady as a rock, with streams of Trojans dividing upon him
as waves break upon a rock. The Thessalians gave ground;
the Trojans swarmed. Ajax, for all his huge strength, was
about to be overwhelmed. Then Poseidon's heart bounded
with pleasure as he saw Ulysses storm up in a chariot drawn
by a pair of magnificent mares. Milk-white they were, with
red manes and brass hooves.

"How did Ulysses come by that team," said Poseidon to
himself. "They belong to Rhesus. They are the get of my
own surf-mares, sired upon them by Pegasus. He could not
be driving them and Rhesus alive. What could have happened?"

He shook the waters in the bowl until they darkened into
images of the night before. He saw Ulysses and Diomedes
acting upon the information they had tortured out of Dolon,
steal into the Thracian lines, cut the throats of Rhesus and
twelve companions, leap into his chariot and whip up the
beautiful steeds to a windlike rush back beyond the fosse.

"So that's how they did it," said Poseidon to himself.
"What devils they are, those two—crafty, bold, imaginative,

ruthless. How can the Trojans possibly stand against such men? How could they have withstood them for nine years? Zeus secretly helps the Trojans; that's the only explanation. Despite his oath of neutrality he is sending signs and portents to hearten the Dardanians beyond the limits of their own mortal strength. Yet he threatens with awful punishment any of the other gods who intercede."

Poseidon shook the waters in the bowl again, and returned to the day's fighting. Ajax and Ulysses, shields locked, were making a stand on the banks of the Scamander. But they had each suffered wounds and, step by step, were being forced back. Finally, Ulysses grasped Ajax, who was more seriously wounded, about his waist, thick as the trunk of a tree, and with an enormous effort hauled the giant into his chariot. Then he whipped up the white mares who galloped so fast they seemed they were flying. With one bound they leaped the Scamander, pulling the chariot through the air after them, and sped behind the Greek lines.

Now the Trojans were free to ford the river, storm the fosse, break the ramparts, and burn the ships. With the flight of Ulysses and Ajax, with Agamemnon, Diomedes and Machaon wounded, and Achilles still refusing to fight, the battle had definitely turned in favor of the Trojans.

But now Poseidon had decided. He could not retrace the process by which he had made the decision, but he recognized an enormous urgent partiality to the Greeks. He lost no time. He sent a message by a naiad, who swam underwater to a marge of the Inner Sea where a river cuts its way to the shore. There the naiad rose to the surface and sang a summoning song which was answered by a nereid, a river nymph. She arose, tall, naked, brown-haired and dripping, to meet her green-haired cousin. The naiad whispered the message to the nereid who swam upstream to the source of the river, a spring on the slope of the mountain. She arose from the water, sleek as an otter, naked and dripping, and sang a summoning song. A song answered—far and coming near. Running over the fields came a troop of dryads, or wood nymphs. The nereid spoke to their leader, a tall black-haired nymph with suave satiny muscles tightening her brown skin.

"I will bear the message, cousin," cried the dryad, laughing."

She ran up the slope again, followed by her troop, screaming and laughing. The nereid watched them until they disappeared into a grove of trees, then dived back into the river and floated downstream. The tall dryad ran to a certain grove on the slope of Olympus where she knew Hera was wont to hunt. There she found the goddess holding a hooded falcon on her wrist, instructing it which she did quite fluently. Being queen of the air, she spoke the language of falcons and of all birds. The dryad knelt before her.

"A message from Poseidon, oh Queen."

"What have you to do with Poseidon, hussy?" cried Hera, who like her falcon, would not be in good humor until their first kill. "Has he been hunting on these slopes again? Does he not have naiads aplenty, that he must seek my dryads of the Sacred Grove? Why, he's as insatiable as his elder brother, if that is possible."

"Pardon me, Queen," said the dryad, "but I was not given this message by him, personally. It was brought by a nereid who swam upstream from the Inner Sea, and she had it from a naiad sent by the Lord of the Deep with this message to be given to you, and you alone."

"What is it?"

"He wishes to meet with you on a matter of much urgency. He will meet you halfway on the isle of Patmos."

"Urgent for him or for me?"

"A most important affair, he said, which he could confide to your ear alone, but that you would rejoice to hear."

"Thank you then for the message," said Hera.

She uncinched the falcon from her wrist and gave it to the dryad.

"Take him back to the palace for me. Catch a rabbit and dismember it; feed it to him, fur and all, but take care of your fingers."

Hera whistled. A chariot appeared, drawn by eagles. She mounted the chariot, uttered a piercing eagle scream, and sped away off the mountain toward the blue puddle of the sea.

Poseidon's residence on Patmos was a great cave. He received Hera very courteously.

"Sister, forgive me for bringing you this distance. Had I come to visit you on Olympus, the wrong ear might have heard us speak, and a tattling tongue borne our business to Zeus."

"Ah, this is to be a secret from Zeus then," said Hera.

"A heavy secret. Heavy enough to crush us both if we are not prudent. I have observed, Sister, that your husband has broken his oath of neutrality in this war between Trojan and Greek. He has now tipped the balance in favor of the Trojans, though their numbers be fewer and their heroes less splendid. Therefore, I, who abhor dishonest dealing, have resolved to abandon my own posture of impartiality—by which you know I have truly abided, alone among the gods—and to cast my influence on the side of the Greeks, whom, I know, you favor also."

"That is well known," said Hera. "At the moment it's not helping them much, but I haven't played out my string yet."

"Precisely," said Poseidon, "and now I give you a new melody to play on that string. A most seductive one."

"Speak plainly, sir. I do not like this deep-sea riddling."

"Plain as plain, gentle Hera. I mean to intervene actively in the battle for there is no time to waste. The Trojans have crossed the fosse, are about to burst through the rampart and drive the Greeks into the sea, thus ending the war. I mean to visit that beach myself and tip the battle the other way. But Zeus must not see me do this, else he will hurl his thunderbolt and nail me to the indifferent earth with a shaft of light, and then send his Titans to drag me to Hades and chain me to the roots of a mountain in awful blackness, in choking dryness, there to abide for that endless sleepless night called eternity."

"And you dare to defy him like this knowing the penalties? Truly, this is a change of heart, Brother of the deep."

"It is that, high Sister. But the success of my venture depends, as I said, on his remaining ignorant of what I am doing."

"How will he remain ignorant? He sits on his peak on Olympus or a more private one on Mount Ida and studies the battle below with keen and vigilant eye. If you even approach the Dardanian plain he will see you."

"Then we must get him off that peak, Sister. We must close that keen and vigilant eye. And of all the creatures on earth, of air, or in the sea, mortal or immortal, you are the one to do this. For you are the most beautiful, the most sumptuous, the most regal, the most intoxicatingly seductive personage in all creation. You must woo him off his mountain, hold him tight, and beguile him with wanton delight—so strenuous that when you have finished with him all he will want to do is sleep. This will give me time to help the Greeks."

"I have never realized you thought me so attractive," said Hera. "We have known each other since one generation past the beginning of time, and never have you looked upon me with ardent eye or spoken such words."

"The modesty of a younger brother, oh lady of the luxurious hips and plum-dark eyes. I knew you were destined for our elder brother, who was to be king of the gods and deserved the best. So it seemed to be decreed. I have always thought you the most desirable of all the Pantheon, not to mention lesser breeds, but it was not my purpose to create family bitterness."

"Well, it's a dangerous, dangerous game," said Hera. "Old Zeus is a male, true, and like all males vulnerable to a low blow. Nevertheless, he is very wise, very cynical, very mistrustful, very difficult to deceive for any length of time. However, I find you oddly persuasive this hot afternoon, and I will try to do as you ask."

"Trying is not enough; you must succeed," said Poseidon. "Don't forget, you were the first to espouse the Greek cause, and have kept it alive these nine years, you and Athena, against all the stubborn resistance of your husband."

"That is true. I hate Paris, loathe the Trojans, dote on the Greeks. And, suddenly, dote on you, dear Poseidon. I shall return to Olympus and do what you want done."

"It is just before the noon-day meal," said Poseidon. "Would it not be better to approach him after he has dined? Like all males he has difficulty managing more than one appetite at a time. This gives us an hour or more."

"An hour or more for what?"

"For rehearsal, sweet sister."

"You are full of ideas today, my wet lord. One of them better than the next."

Hera and Zeus

Poseidon was marvelously sleepy after Hera left, and would have much preferred to nap the afternoon away in the flowery grove on Patmos. But he knew that the Trojans were pressing hard and that he must act immediately. He mounted his chariot and hastened to Troy.

Down on the field the Trojans had crossed the fosse and were storming the rampart which they were trying to knock down with battering rams. A squad of them lifted a log and rushed toward the wall at a dead run, smashing it against the wooden palisade. The timbers groaned and shuddered but still stood. The Greeks were thrusting down with their long lances from the top of the rampart. At each battering-ram charge the Trojans were losing men. Then Zeus sent a sign. He swerved an eagle in its path so that it crossed the sky to the right of Hector, dipping closer to the beach than eagles ever fly. And Hector knew that the god of air and mountain had sent the eagle as a sign.

Filled with joyous strength at this signal of divine favor, the Trojan leader then did something no man had ever done before. He ran to a wrecked chariot and with a mighty heave pulled off one of its wheels. As Greek and Trojan watched him in disbelief, he lofted the enormous copper-spoked brass wheel and whirled as if he were hurling a discus. The wheel flew on a flat trajectory like a discus well thrown and struck the rampart beyond the fosse, knocking a huge hole in it. Hector uttered a loud war-cry and charged toward the gap in the wall followed by his men. They crossed the fosse, climbed up the other side through a cloud of darts and arrows and rushed toward the breached wall, still following Hector who was several paces ahead, his brass helmet flashing light.

It was then that Poseidon came to the beach. All in gold he came, in a golden chariot, wearing goldern armor, carrying a golden lance.

"Too soon, too soon," he said to himself. "Hera will not have had time to woo brother Zeus from his vigil. If I appear like this he will see me and hurl his thunderbolt. Yet, if I delay, the Trojans will overrun the Greek camp. I must act now, but in disguise. Let us hope that Hera on her part does not delay, and that her husband is not immune to her wiles. For Zeus sees quickly through disguises."

Poseidon then put on the form of Calchas, the Greek soothsayer, and appeared on the other side of the rampart among the Hellenes. He stationed himself near great Ajax and faced Hector who, with the eagle-rage still upon him, face and body glowing like a demi-god, was charging the center of the Greek line, held by Great Ajax, Little Ajax, and Teucer.

Hera had not been wasting time. She knew how desperate the situation was, but for all her haste she made careful preparation. She knew that after a thousand years of marriage Zeus found her charms something less than irresistible. His changeableness in these matters had become a fact of nature and, indeed, had produced a large variety of demi-gods and heroes. But Hera was ferocious in her moods, too, had a volcanic temper, and time had never made her accept the ways of Zeus. So they had bickered down the ages with increasing rancor—and for the last few centuries had not slept together at all. Therefore, she fully understood how difficult was the assignment given her by Poseidon.

She visited Aphrodite, and said, "We have quarreled, Cousin, but I think it is time to forgive each other. I will forgive you for having so shamelessly suborned Paris's judgment and forced him to award you the golden apple as the most beautiful of us all. It is done now and cannot be undone. It will not change. But I will forgive you if you will forgive me for all I have done and said against you, and for my ardent espousal of the Greek cause which also will not change."

Now, Aphrodite had a passive easy-going nature, especially in the summer. She was quick-tempered and vengeful like all the gods, but did not have the patience for feuds. Besides, she feared Hera who was much stronger than she.

"Queen Hera," she said, "you could not have uttered words to give me more pleasure. Long have I wearied of this quarrel between us. I apologize for any harm I may have done you and, with a full heart, I forgive you for any injury you may have done me."

The two goddesses embraced, but not too closely.

"Since we're friends again," said Hera, "I am emboldened to ask you a favor."

"Ask away. I am sure the answer will be yes."

"Will you lend me your girdle, that magic garment which arouses desire in any man or god you fancy?"

"Girdle? I wear no girdle. Look at me."

She pirouetted before Hera. "Do I look like I'm wearing a girdle, oh Queen? And what would I do with such a thing after my charms worked on this man or god? It would just get in the way."

Hera frowned. "Come now," she said, "don't trifle with me. Everyone has heard about your magic girdle."

"That which everyone knows is most likely to be wrong," said Aphrodite. "I deny that any such girdle exists. What you

refer to is simply the essence of those attributes which make me Goddess of Love and Beauty and Carnal Desire. Do not forget that I can make myself irresistible, as you say, not only to any man I fancy, or any god, but that my favor extended to any other female creature makes *her* irresistible to any god or man *she* fancies."

"Are you going to help me? Yes or no?"

"Yes, yes, yes! Let me prepare you for love, and no man or god will resist you, no matter what his inclinations are. Once I have scented you with the distilled attar of these flowers in whose amorous cups bees linger longest, once I have kneaded into your flesh my secret ointment which makes any hag as sleek and supple, as shiny with pent juices, as a sixteen-year-old virgin with her first man—once I have tangled the poppies of sleep in your hair and tipped your fingernails with the sweet venom in which Eros dips his darts so that you have merely to scratch your paramour to plunge him straightway into the deepest abyss of desire—once I have so prepared you, Hera, then you can approach what god or man you will, knowing that the more powerful he is the more helpless he will be rendered by his hunger for you. And since Zeus is all-powerful. . . ."

"Sounds promising," said Hera. I place myself in your hands."

Poseidon had not dared to exert his full efforts in helping the Greeks until Hera had been given time enough to distract Zeus. What the sea-god did was to stand as close as possible to the center of the Greek line where Great Ajax held the field, aided by his brother, Teucer, and Little Ajax. There, disguised as Calchas the soothsayer, Poseidon flung his arms heavenward and pretended to raise his voice in prophecy, crying: "Great Ajax, Little Ajax, Teucer the archer, stand fast, stand fast. Resist the Trojans, and you will finally prevail. A great god is coming to aid you. A great god I cannot name seeks your victory. He cannot come yet, but he will come, will come, and cover you with his mantle, and you will be invincible. So stand fast, stand fast."

The three warriors, heartened beyond their own knowledge by the keen gull-cry of the pretended Calchas, fought more savagely than ever and held back the Greek advance.

Hera flew to Mount Ida, to its tallest peak, Gargarus, where Zeus sat watching the battle unfold.

"Greetings, dear lord and husband," she cried. "Forgive me for breaking upon your solitude, but I am departing on a long journey and did not wish to leave without saying good-bye."

"Where are you going?" said Zeus without turning around.

"Off to the bitter margin of the earth where our uncle, Oceanus, and his wife, Tethys, reside. Lately it has come to my notice that they live in terrible loneliness with each other, keeping a cold distance between them because of some ancient quarrel, never exchanging a kind word, never dining together, nor warming each other with a caress. I go to reconcile them so they can live together again as man and wife."

"Who do you think you are? Aphrodite?" said Zeus. "Lovers' quarrels, reconciliations, bedding people down—she takes care of all that."

Hera came very close to him.

"I am moved by pity for my aunt Tethys," she murmured, and in her voice was the song of birds. "I know what it means to be denied a husband's caress. To long for him with all my heart and soul and to be denied, denied."

Zeus turned then. When he did, his head was almost between her breasts. She gave off a powerful fragrance of sunshine and crushed grass.

"Besides," she whispered, "Aphrodite has lent me her bag of tricks, has tutored me in certain arts that are bound to reconcile that stupid feuding man and wife."

By this time Zeus was completely enraptured by the sight of his wife who looked as beautiful to him as she had when the world was very new and they had hid from their parents, old Cronus and Rhea, wrapping themselves in a cloud and making love with such hunger that the cloud had burst and the valley of Olympus was flooded—and Cronus and Rhea had been forced to give permission for the brother and sister to wed. He stood up and clasped her in his arms.

"Before you trundle off to the ends of the earth," he said, "there are a husband and wife here who have some arrears of intimacy to make up."

"Right here?" she whispered. "Here on the highest peak of Ida? All the Pantheon will see us. I am proud, proud to be loving you again, my lord, but such revels as I plan are better done in privacy."

"Privacy we shall have," said Zeus, "without moving from this spot."

Thereupon he caused the rock to grow anemones and roses and hyacinths and sweet grasses to a height of three feet, making a soft bed for the lovers. He pulled down a fleecy cloud to cover them like a quilt, quite concealing them from view, shielding them from the sun with a delicious moistness, bathing their nakedness with the lightest of dews.

And the folk who lived in the village at the foot of the mountain felt the solid rock shake, saw their slopes tremble, heard the giant sounds of Zeus's pleasure. They fled their village thinking their mountain had turned volcanic and was about to erupt.

As Hera lay down with Zeus she released a dove which she had been carrying on her wrist like a falcon, a swift-darting blue-and-gray bird specially trained to bear messages and keep secrets. It darted to earth, and found Poseidon where he stood on the Trojan beach disguised as Calchas. The bird cooed to him, relating Hera's message. He could help the Greeks as much as he liked because Zeus would be too busy for the rest of the afternoon to notice what was happening on earth.

ATTACK AND COUNTERATTACK

Bellowing and dancing in his exultance, the Lord of the Deep cast off the guise of old Calchas like a tall tree twisting in the wind, shedding leaves. He made himself invisible, all except his golden trident. When he wielded the great three-tined staff it was like the sun fighting clouds, sending spears of light through the cover. Invisibly he approached Ajax, Little Ajax, and Teucer and goaded them with his trident. A great salt wave of health broke upon their blood, filling them with the surging strength that the god of the sea can bestow. They led their men forward in a mighty rolling battering charge that smashed against the Trojan line like the ocean sending its white-plumed breakers to pound a foundering ship. And the Trojans, who had been so triumphantly victorious just a few moments before, now began to retreat.

Hector went purple in the face with rage, smacking his men with the flat of his sword, trying to harry them forward. Ajax, knowing his strength multiplied, stooped to pick up an enormous boulder lying half-buried in the sand, a massive rock seemingly rooted in the beach that twelve men had been unable to move. He raised it above his head with an easy motion and hurled it straight at Hector. It hit the Trojan hero's shield, driving the shield against his chest, knocking him flat. He seemed to be crushed like a beetle; he lay under the rock, legs kicking feebly. But then, with a last indomitable effort he thrust himself from under the boulder, and lay there, unable to raise, vomiting blood. Aeneas it was who lifted him onto his shoulders and rushed back toward Troy. Prince Troilus covered their flight, fighting like a young lion.

When Hector left the field, the Trojans were shattered. The retreat was becoming a rout. By this time Poseidon had ranged behind the Greek lines where the wounded leaders stood in a cluster watching the battle. Agamemnon was there, Diomedes, Ulysses, Machaon. Patroclus was there, too, tending their wounds. With Machaon out of service, the comrade of Achilles was the most skilled surgeon among the Hellenes. Poseidon, keeping himself invisible, spoke to them in sea-whispers. A huge salt wave of health broke upon their blood, healing them, knitting bone, mending flesh. With loud glad cries they leaped into their chariots and lent such strength to the Greek countercharge that the Trojans were driven back through the breach of the rampart, scrambling back over the fosse. Troilus tried to make a stand, so did Antenor and a few other of the most redoubtable Trojan warriors, but they could not stem the Greeks alone, and finally had to flee after the Trojan force which had fled before.

Bedded on flowers and sweet grass, wrapped in a fleecy cloud, Zeus slept in Hera's arms. This immense coupling of the sovereign gods had put all the beasts of Mount Ida in rut. Bears wrestled amorously in their caves on the slope; eagles sought each other in high nuptial; everywhere, except on the Dardanian plain where the battle wore on, lovers touched each other in sleepy rapture. Everywhere in field and meadow, cows mooed invitation, bulls swelled with joyous ire; mares strutted, stallions bugled. Everywhere over field and meadow hung a haze of pollen thickening to a golden drift under the slant rays of the afternoon sun—so that lovers moving toward each other through the grass felt themselves cleaving a heavier substance than air, felt their very blood fusing into a golden generative heat.

But on the Dardanian plain men killed each other. Heavy metal blades cracked bone, sheared through flesh. Beautiful young men, naked in their armor, drowned in their own blood. And still Greeks pursued and Trojans fled.

High upon Mount Ida, on a peak called Gargarus, Zeus slept in Hera's arms. But Hera did not sleep. Drowsy though she was after her volcanic session with Zeus, still her interest in earthly affairs kept her from joining her husband in slumber, which turned out to be a mistake.

Moving very carefully, very slowly, she slipped out of his embrace, slithered out from between flower bed and cloud cover, and walked to the edge of the precipice. All naked, pink, and dewy she was, like a larger version of her cousin, Aurora, rosy-fingered goddess of dawn. Hera looked down upon the Dardanian plain; what she saw made her forget her caution and laugh aloud in triumph. The Trojans were in full flight, pursued by furiously yelling Greeks whose swords and spearheads dripped with blood.

With Hector gone, Paris fled, Troilus and Aeneas wounded, the Trojans were a disorganized rabble instead of an army. It appeared as though the Greeks might be able to storm the walls of Troy there and then. Again Hera laughed.

Too loudly! She heard Zeus grumble. She had thought him deep asleep. She whirled about. To her horror she saw him sit up, stretch, yawn, and scratch his monumental chest. She ran back to him and knelt upon the flower bed, stroking his shoulders.

"Do not awake, dear lord!" she murmured. "Sleep, sleep. Plunge back into the sweetest sleep of all wherein you restore yourself after mountain-shaking acts of love, and can return afresh to the delightful fray."

Zeus stood up. He was unmoved by her plea. The habit of vigilance was strong upon him. Besides, into the depths of his sleep had wound a skein of mocking laughter. He put her aside gently and walked to the edge of the precipice.

"Don't look down there!" she cried. "Why trouble yourself with mundane affairs? Rest, rest, great lord of creation! The rusty old earth will turn a few turns without you."

Zeus was looking down upon the plain. His huge brow was furrowed like striated rock. He whirled and took Hera's throat in those enormous hands that crack stars like peanuts.

"Things have changed," he said softly, "since we two lay down together. I left the Trojans ascendant. They had breached the rampart and were driving toward the Greek ships. But now, after a session of your embraces, what do I find? Poseidon down there, my treacherous brother, who has turned the tide of battle so that the Greeks are everywhere triumphant. Tell me, was it coincidence, sweet sister, steadfast wife? Was our sudden encounter after all these centuries one of those happy accidents? Or perhaps part of a deeper design?"

"I can scarcely follow what you are saying," said Hera. "Poseidon at Troy? The Trojans winning? But this is a very abrupt change, as surprising to me as it is to you. What can Poseidon be thinking of to defy your edicts this way? It's dreadful."

"Be still! Don't try to play with me. I am very angry."

"Angry at me? Do you so soon forget the delicious hour we spent?"

"No, I do not forget. I may even look forward to other such hours—unless, of course, I decide to punish you so painfully that you will seek to avoid my company. However, we can postpone that decision. Let me attend to Poseidon first."

The god of the sea stood tall in his golden armor just beyond the beach, balancing himself on the surf like a child on a skate board. From time to time he uttered a great north-wind yell to hearten the Greeks. But matters were going so well now, he had little to do but watch the battle. Suddenly the sky growled. He looked up. No storm clouds at all, but a wide fair expanse of blueness.

Out of the blue sky shot a thunderbolt, a hooked shaft of white-hot light burning the air as it passed. It plunged into the water just missing Poseidon, immediately turning the sea to steam.

"What are you doing?" cried Hera, pleading with Zeus above. "Are you trying to destroy your own brother Poseidon, Lord of the Deep? Think of the consequences."

"He should have thought of the consequences," growled Zeus. "I *am* consequence."

"Consider his record," pleaded Hera. "He may have transgressed a bit this afternoon, but after all, up until now he has been the most neutral of the gods in this war, has been the one who has obeyed your edicts most strictly."

"That is why my first bolt missed," said Zeus. "As you know I usually hit what I aim at. I hope it serves as a warning. For my second bolt will not miss; it will gaff him like a fish."

There was no need for another bolt. When Poseidon saw the white-hot zigzag shaft of lightning hit the water, he was bathed in steam, felt that he was being broiled like a lobster. He knew that Zeus had seen him and was angry. Pausing only to flick a quick idea at Ulysses, he uttered a whistle which evoked his dolphin chariot in the wink of an eye. Instantly he had mounted the chariot and was gone—down, down into the depths of the cool sea where all the creatures are too busy eating each other to bother about such things as war.

Poseidon's last idea flew like a dart and hit Ulysses pain-

THE TROJAN WAR

lessly in the neck, passing into his head, nestling just beneath his consciousness ready to sprout as a full-fledged idea when its time should come.

"I cannot tell whether you are guilty or innocent," said Zeus to Hera. "Perhaps I do not want to know. It is the essence of a beautiful woman that she bewilder—and in this a goddess is a woman—so let it be. But do nothing from now on to change my opinion of your innocence. In other words, dear wife, keep your meddling hands off that war below, or I'll cut them off."

"Yes, my husband," murmured Hera.

"Now fly back to Olympus and send Apollo to me. We must undo the harm you have done. Let him come immediately."

Hera was frightened. She did not take the time to fly but translated herself back to Olympus where she said to her stepson, Apollo, "Go, go. Go swiftly to Zeus. He awaits you on Mount Ida, on the peak called Gargarus. He wants you immediately."

Apollo appeared before Zeus, who said, "That briny uncle of yours has played us false. He has appeared among the Greeks, endowing them with such strength and courage that they are about to overwhelm the Trojans. I suspend my act of neutrality now—or at least amend it—so that we may be neutral on the Trojan side. Go to work, dear Phoebus. Rally the Trojans. Make them fight again and prevail."

Now, Apollo, of course, had watched that afternoon's fighting and had been much impressed by the feat of Hector with the chariot wheel. He took a spare wheel of his sun-chariot, one of those glittering golden disks that, trundling across the blue meadow of the sky, refract the eternal fire as they turn, flashing, and that fire falls to earth in a benign glow that men call sunshine. He took this heavy glittering wheel and, holding it as a shield, flew to earth.

He appeared among the Trojans, flashing his sun-shield at them, kindling their courage, burning away fears and hesitations. He went to where Hector lay on a litter, pale and crushed and unconscious, almost dead from the blow of Ajax's boulder. Apollo focused light upon the fallen hero who, in the clammy grip of his swoon, felt the cockles of his heart warming, felt every vessel of his manhood filling with sap, putting forth buds. The amazed Trojans saw Hector arise, flushed with heat, eyes glittering.

"What are we doing here?" he cried in a voice like a trumpet. "Why here in the shadow of our walls? For shame! For shame! The last I remember we were beyond the rampart, advancing upon the Greek ships, ready to put them to the torch. And now, and now. . . . How could we have retreated so far? So soon?"

Troilus spoke. He had refused to be carried beyond the walls for treatment despite grievous wounds. "I'm with you, brother!" he cried. "Both my arms are broken, but I can still lower my head and charge like a stag."

Aeneas, also wounded, said, "A breath ago we were gripped by despair, ready to yield the city. And now, such a change! It is obvious, good friends, that a god is among us, that we have again earned the support of heaven which we lost for a bitter interval this afternoon. But the favor of gods abides only among the brave. So, forward under Hector! Forward! Forward!"

"Each prince to his chariot!" shouted Hector. "We will mount a chariot charge such as our fathers mounted in days of old—and still lie about. . . ."

Now, the Greeks, who had been enjoying themselves chasing the Trojan rabble across the field, spearing them like rabbits, found everything changed. Instead of a fleeing mob scurrying toward Troy, they saw a rank of bright chariots rushing toward them with terrible speed. They heard the squeal of wheel against axle, heard the clank of weapons, heard the bugling neigh of the chariot-steeds, and their eyes were assailed by splintering light. They saw light gathered in their enemy; light in sheaves, in quivers, in darts and lances, light splintering off breastplate and helmet, and brass wheel and brass coach, and the brass corslets of the chariot-horses. Light splintering, quivering, dancing, refracted by Apollo's sun-shield which, keeping himself invisible, he wielded behind the Trojan lines, harrying them forward with bright cries. And the Greeks, seeing these phalanxes of light, hearing the bright trampling triumph of the chariot charge, knew indeed that the god who had been helping them had deserted the field, and that a god who loved their enemy had descended in his stead. They turned and fled. Fled from the shadow of the city wall over the corpse-littered field, in their fearful haste stepping on the bodies of men fallen, not caring whether they were friend or foe.

Back the Greeks swarmed, back over the field, scrambled across the fosse, streamed through the breach in the rampart and took a stand only when they had reached the first line of ships. The Trojans, doubtless, would have stormed through and begun to burn the ships had it not been for the superb courage of great Ajax, Ulysses, Diomedes, and Agamemnon, who kept their heads through all the dismay of the rout, and rallied their men to beat the Trojans back from the ships. Great Ajax sprang on board his own ship which had been drawn farthest up on the beach. The Trojans charged through the thin line of Greeks and lit torches of pitch pine which burned with a pale flame in the hot sun and with aromatic smoke. They began to swarm over the hull of Ajax's ship, brandishing their torches.

Ajax, then, snatched up his thirty-foot mast from where it nested in its cradle on deck and flourished the enormous shaft as if it were a light throwing-lance. He swept it over the gunwales of his ship, breaking Trojan skulls like eggs, helmets and all, and swept the deck clear. But as fast as he cleared the gunwales, so swiftly did other Trojans swarm aboard.

Then it was that the glinting dart of Poseidon's last idea which he had planted in Ulysses' head began to flower. Ulysses, close-hemmed between Diomedes and Little Ajax, locking shields with both, thrusting with his spear, suddenly whispered to them, "Dear comrades, I quit you only on a matter of strategy. Lock your shields."

He backed away, took the shields of Little Ajax and Diomedes in his hands, and lapped them with each other and no gap appeared in the line. He then simply walked away from the battle, walked toward the tent of Achilles which stood with the Myrmidon fleet at the other end of the beach.

"This is it!" he said to himself. "A master notion. Achilles still sulks in his tent ignoring our mortal peril, ignoring the death of his comrades, the humiliation of Greek arms, and the certain destruction of the fleet. But he is still nourished by that poison pride of his and by his justified rancor against Agamemnon, and he still refuses to fight. Nevertheless, suppose his dear friend Patroclus were to impersonate him—don his armor, wield his weapons, ride his chariot, and lead his Myrmidons into the field? Why, that would be a superb stroke. One of two things must happen. Either the Trojans will believe that Patroclus is Achilles and seeing him, flee in terror, as they always have; or, it may be, they will see through the disguise and kill him. Then, if he falls, Achilles will have to choose between two passions—his pride, which is an overweening species of self-love and his love for Patroclus. And, I am sure, with his dear friend fallen that great heart will burst with spleen, and he will take arms and sweep the field like plague. Either way, we can't lose. All I have to do is convince Patroclus to persuade Achilles to lend him arms and armor."

Achilles' tent was cool after the hot sun. And the young warrior, seeing Ulysses so battle-worn, refused to let him say a word of business until a slave-girl had been summoned to loosen his armor, bathe his feet, swab his face and neck with a cool scented cloth, and bring him a restorative drink of barley steeped in honey.

"Thank you, great Achilles," said Ulysses. "As all men know, your courtesy is equalled only by your courage—by the memory of your courage, that is. For, indeed, no man has seen you recently performing those feats of arms which made you famed among the famous before you were old enough to grow a beard."

"Your conversation is always stimulating, friend Ulysses. The gloss of your compliments always conceals a sharp-edged gibe. But you are, as usual, justified. I know that I have been a noncombatant recently, know it well. Do you not think that I chafe at this inactivity? I am like a tiger playing with a ball of wool, hearing a lion roar as he hunts my deer. My desire for battle is so fierce I feel that I could drink blood by the goblet like some ancient ogre who ate men raw. But I am bound by an oath never to fight on this field as long as Agamemnon leads the Greeks; so I must abide here in my tent listening to the sounds of battle, being beguiled by my beloved friend Patroclus, and, occasionally, having the honor of entertaining such fighters as you."

"A truce to compliments," said Ulysses. "I have not come here to urge you to fight. In the past few days you have been begged to do so in more eloquent phrases than I can lay tongue to. No, I come with another suggestion: that you, Patroclus, play Achilles. We need an Achilles, even a counterfeit one. And what more fitting than that you, friend of his heart, pivot of his idle hours, should put on his armor, take his weapons, mount his chariot, and lead his Myrmidons in a charge against the Trojans?"

"Ridiculous!" said Achilles.

Patroclus said nothing.

"Perhaps you don't appreciate the gravity of our situation," said Ulysses. "We are at our last gasp. Even now the Trojans would be firing our fleet did not Great Ajax, like a Titan of old, fight them off with a mast he is using as a spear, carving a place for himself in the history of arms that will never fade as long as men love courage. But, when Ajax falls, as fall he must, then they will burn the fleet, not excepting your own ships unless you set sail immediately. Yes, they will put our proud beaked ships to the shame of the torch, and then, in all leisure, penning us between fire and sea, will slaughter us like cattle. You refuse to fight, Achilles. Very well. You are bound by an oath, fettered in your pride. You will not fight. But, in the name of all the gods, lend us your shadow. Allow Patroclus to impersonate you. It is our only chance."

"What do you say, Patroclus?" said Achilles. "Do you wish to do this thing?"

"I do," said Patroclus.

"Then you shall. I will be your squire and dress you myself in my own armor that I never thought any other man should wear."

"Thank you, great Achilles," said Ulysses. "Thank you, gallant Patroclus. I must hasten back to the fighting now. Even the whisper of what is to come, I'm sure, will hearten our comrades so that they can withstand the Trojans yet a little while—until Patroclus shall appear on the field."

pATROClus

Patroclus stripped himself then in Achilles' tent, and put on his friend's armor. Achilles acted as squire, helping him don corselet, breastplate, greaves, and plumed helmet.

"Beloved friend," said Achilles, "I wish I could clothe you in my invulnerability instead of these pieces of metal. Oh, they are beautiful pieces of metal—cast of molten gold and brass, with inlay of copper and tin—made by Hephaestus himself as a wedding present for my father, Peleus. The enemy, seeing this armor, know that it is Achilles they must face, and are disarmed by fear before they can begin to fight. But, friend, let me tell you a secret that no man knows and no woman either, except my mother Thetis. I can fight without that armor; and no spear, no sword, nor arrow can pierce me. For my mother, queen of the nereids, ranks as a goddess, and she wished to give me, her son, sired by a mortal, her own immortality. When I was just nine days old she dipped me into the River Styx, that black stream that separates the land of the living from the land of the dead whose waters have magic power. Every part of me the water touched was rendered beyond hurt, tough as nine layers of polished bullhide stiffened with brass, without losing the delicacy of human skin. Thus, no blade can cut me, no wound kill—all except one place."

Achilles lifted his foot and tapped the great tendon over his heel.

"She held me right here as she dipped me into the river. Where her fingers clasped, the waters could not touch. In this one spot I am vulnerable."

Patroclus laughed. "Not an easy spot for an enemy to reach," he said. "To expose it you would have to be running away. And that is a sight no man has ever seen, or ever will."

Achilles laughed, and embraced his friend.

"Truly," he said, "you are a gallant fellow. Here you are about to meet the Trojans in the full exultant tide of their victory, when their courage burns hot and they fight better than they know how, and you behave as though you were at a banquet, smiling and jesting."

"Dear friend," said Patroclus. "Clad in your armor I feel as safe as though I were at a banquet, reclining on a couch, being served wine by the slave-girls, chatting with the other guests. As Ulysses said, clad in your armor I go forth as your shadow, and even the shadow of you, mighty warrior that you are, is enough to chase the Trojans the best day they ever saw."

"One word of advice," said Achilles. "You will be followed by my Myrmidons, who, having been kept out of battle, are rested and fresh. They will give a good account of themselves. The Trojans should break before you. But please, I implore you, when they break do not pursue them. Let them retreat in their own way. If you follow them, keep with your troops. Do not charge ahead. Do not seek to despoil a fallen foe of his armor, no matter how rich it is. Above all, do not seek single combat. The Trojan heroes will not be seeking to encounter with you, either, clad as you are, so such duels should be easy to avoid. Avoid them! Most important of all, do not seek to engage Hector in hand-to-hand conflict. Now go, dear Patroclus. And may the fickle gods go with you."

He embraced him again, led him to his chariot, and helped him mount. Then he walked quickly away to the edge of the tide and stood there looking out over the sea. His heart was heavy with foreboding.

Patroclus, shining like the morning star in Achilles' armor, vaulted gaily into Achilles' chariot. It was of burnished bronze drawn by a pair of stallions named Xanthus and Balius. They were of divine breed. Their dam was not a mare at all, but a harpy named Podarge who had become amorous of the West Wind and would mount his warm currents, coasting like a gull on her brass wings. The West Wind is the wind that dries the wet fields in the spring so that the seeds can grow. Finally, he started seeds in Podarge. She foaled, dropping two colts. Matched blacks they were, with golden eyes, silver hooves, mane and tail of silver fleece. They ran as swiftly as their sire, the West Wind; in their temperaments was the loving ferocity of their dam, Podarge. They were loving to their master, but savage in battle. Achilles had trained them to rear back and strike like a boxer with their silver hooves; one blow of a hoof could crack a warrior's helmet like a nutshell. They used their great yellow teeth also, snapping like crocodiles. No man dared handle them except Achilles and Patroclus. Achilles boasted of their intelligence, saying they could speak if they wished, but preferred to remain silent. Drawn by these stallions, driven by Patroclus, the burnished bronze chariot of Achilles whirled into battle.

The Trojans were still trying to burn Ajax's ship. Hector had mounted the deck where the giant still wielded his thirty-foot mast. Ajax swept the deck with the huge staff trying to crush Hector. But each time the mast swept toward him Hector either ducked beneath it or leaped above it. Each time he did this he struck at it with his sword, each time hacking off a piece of it until Ajax was left holding only the fat stump of the mast. He hurled the butt of the mast at the

Trojans, who were again swarming over the gunwales and killed two of them. Then Great Ajax leaped off the deck and tried to rally his men for another stand.

Gleefully the Trojans set Ajax's ship to the torch and began to fire the other ships of the first line. Hector pressed forward swiftly after Ajax, wanting to finish him off. So swiftly that he became separated from his men. Suddenly he heard the shouts of triumph change to cries of bawling fear.

"Achilles! It's Achilles! Flee! Flee!"

He turned and saw his men break and flee before a chariot of burnished bronze drawn by those stallions he recognized as Xanthus and Balius. Riding the chariot was a tall figure in golden armor, his crest a plume of eagle feathers. Hector's men, chased by the bright chariot, were like a swarm of field mice and hares fleeing a grass fire. Brave Hector himself was sucked up in the wind of that going and fled before that chariot to the walls of Troy.

Patroclus, riding in his bronze car, felt the armor of Achilles clinging as lightly and intimately to him as his own skin. Yes, it was as if by some stroke of the gods he had been given a hide of supple bright armor, had been fanged with glittering blades, and had come among the Trojans terrible as a tiger among deer.

He swerved his chariot toward where the enemy was thickest. They fled before him always; they could not outrun his stallions. He scythed down the Trojans like summer grass. Everywhere he led, his Myrmidons followed, wheeling, charging, moving like one man, their brown-mailed ranks opening like jaws, closing upon the Trojans. When the jaws opened, crushed bodies fell.

These Myrmidons of Achilles were the best-drilled squadrons among the Greek forces. They were descended from those first Myrmidons captained by Achilles' grandfather, Aecus. This Aecus was the son of Zeus and a river-nymph named Aegina. In order to escape Hera's vigilance Zeus had put on the guise of an eagle, snatched up Aegina from the river, and carried her to an island in the sea which he named Aegina in honor of the nymph. She stayed on her beautiful little island—which was quite deserted—and after Zeus left gave birth to a boy whom she named Aecus. This boy grew to be a comely and strong young man. He was king of the island, but he had no subjects. He ached to wrestle and joust with other young men and to lead them in battle, but he and his mother dwelt alone upon this island, except for a huge golden eagle which occasionally visited the place. At such times his mother disappeared with the great bird for a night and a day, and the boy was lonelier than ever—until she came back, tremulous and soft and happy.

"Where do you go, mother?"

"I cannot tell you."

"Why not?"

"You're too young."

Finally, he was not too young, and she told him. This kingly bird was her lover—was king of the gods in disguise, Father Zeus himself, and the actual father of Aecus.

The next time the eagle swooped down for his mother, the young man confronted him.

"Are you Zeus?"

"If I am, young man, I could be very angry for the insolent way you address me."

"Anyone can claim he's Zeus. His transformations are well-known. So any bull or swan or stallion or eagle can go around saying, 'I'm Zeus, I'm Zeus. Be careful or I'll get angry.'"

The eagle laughed.

"You have a point there, I suppose. How can I prove to you I am what I say?"

"I'm lonely. I want some companions."

There was a roll of thunder and a flash of lightning. The

young man saw lightning shafts strike all about him; then
all was still. The eagle had disappeared; Aegina was gone.
Aecus lay on the grass trying to collect his wits. His eye was
caught by a column of ants marching across the sand dragging a dead beetle. In the distance an eagle screamed.

Before the boy's eyes those brown ants changed to youths
in brown armor, and a voice spoke like thunder from the blue
sky, "Here are your men, Aecus, comrades and soldiers, if
you make them so."

Now the Greek word for "ant" is *myrmekes,* and the men
of Aecus were called *myrmidons.* Under his leadership they
became the best troops of all the lands of the Inner Sea.
Aecus was the father of Peleus, grandfather to Achilles. Peleus had inherited the legions of Myrmidons and had passed
them on to Achilles. They still retained some antlike char-
acteristics—dressed always in brown armor; were enormously
disciplined, stubborn, tireless; some loved sweet food and
some loved fat, but they could live on very little when ra-
tions were low.

Now they followed Patroclus at a dead run. No matter
how fast the chariot was drawn by those stallions sired by
the West Wind, the Myrmidons would always catch up and
engage the Trojans at the point where Patroclus had broken
their lines.

Hector stood on a low hill under the west wall of Troy
watching his men flee. It was here that he meant to rally
them to try to prevent the Greeks from storming the wall.
But he was full of foreboding. He did not see how he could
put any heart into his terror-stricken men. Then he smelled
a sunny fragrance and heard a voice full of angry music. He
dropped to his knees to listen to the words of Apollo.

"I am disappointed in you, Hector. You were my chosen
hero, the man of men who was to combat Achilles. Through-
out this war you have plumed yourself on being the only

Trojan who would dare to close with the son of Peleus. Now what do I see? You flee his shadow."

Tears streamed down Hector's face. He felt himself burning with shame. He could not answer.

"Yes, his *shadow*," said Apollo. "I mean it not as a figure of speech, but literally. That glittering armor clothes not Achilles, but Patroclus who has borrowed his mighty friend's appearance, knowing that it alone could be enough to frighten the Trojans into fits. Well, for almost ten years now I have been trying to warm you with my own flame. I see it is hopeless. No one can help cowards! They defeat themselves. I am going to stop defying my father, Zeus, and keep aloof from this war."

"No, bright Phoebus, no," pleaded Hector. "Do not withdraw your hand from us. Lord of the moving sun, I pray you—lord of the harp, of the golden bow, heed my plea. I will prove to you I'm no coward. I faltered for a moment, it's true, but if you abide with me, I will reclaim my manhood, and straightway engage Patroclus. When I do, he is a dead man. I further swear that when Achilles comes to avenge the dead Patroclus, as come he must, I will not fear to meet him either, but will challenge him to mortal combat."

Then the sun-god appeared in all his radiance before Hector, and said, "Rise, Hector. Rise, and reclaim your manhood."

Apollo took off his golden helmet whose crest was a plume of red and blue flame.

"Dip your spear point into this plume of flame," he said, "and go, hot-handed, to meet your false foe."

Hector arose and held his spearhead in the plume of flame that sprouted from Apollo's helmet. The god became invisible again, leaving only his fragrance behind—of oranges and roses and those fruits and flowers that love the sun. This fragrance enwrapt Hector filling him with a wild exultance.

Yelling his war-cry, he rushed toward Patroclus, shouting, "Actor, Mountebank! Fraud! Descend from that borrowed chariot and fight in your own name."

Patroclus heard this bright cry and wheeled his chariot about. He remembered Achilles' warning that on no account was he to seek out Hector in single combat. But by now the mask had grown into the face. By now, aping Achilles, triumphing like Achilles, he had become Achilles—or so he thought. Ofttimes in days past had he and Achilles felt close enough to have been joined by a membrane, like a pair of unnatural twins, one bloodstream coursing through both bodies. Now he leaped from his chariot and rushed toward Hector, shouting, "Well met, son of Priam! Whether I be Achilles or Patroclus, you will never know the difference because the same blade will find your heart."

He ran so fast that he outraced the Myrmidons. Hector raced to meet him. They met with a crash of weapons like two stags breaking their antlers against each other. Brave he was, Patroclus. Fair he was. Nobly he wore Achilles' armor and handled Achilles' weapons. But he was no Achilles. And Hector at that moment, burning with Apollo's flame, was more than Hector.

Patroclus never had a chance. Swiftly, delicately, Hector handled his spear. The white-hot spearhead sheared through Patroclus's armor like a welding torch—for Hector wished not only to vanquish Patroclus, but to ease the pain of his own shame by shaming his foe.

Now, Greeks and Trojans watching this duel saw a sight never seen before. Hector's white-hot spear cut through Achilles' armor; corselet, breastplate, and greaves dropped off Patroclus, leaving him naked except for his helmet. He hurled his spear. Hector laughed as it rebounded from his shield, and leisurely advanced on his naked foe.

"You look like a plucked chick, little Patroclus," he jeered.

"If I were cruel as a Greek, I would stand here, using my sword like a butcher's knife, and joint you like a chicken. But such is not my purpose. I have bared you this way so that all men may see that it takes more than armor to make a man. Now, actor, it is time for your death scene."

With an upward stroke he speared Patroclus through the belly. It was a bad death. Patroclus fell, screaming horribly, clutching at his entrails.

ARMOR for achilles

The body of Patroclus was immediately stripped of Achilles' armor. Hector lifted his voice above the battle din.

"Take the body, men! Bear it to Troy! I shall set his head on a pike on the city wall so that Achilles may meet his friend again, face to face, if he seeks to storm the wall. As for the body, we shall throw it to the dogs!"

But before the Trojans could seize the body, Menelaus rushed up and straddled it, growling like a mastiff, fighting off everyone who approached. Other Trojans pressed forward; other Greeks pressed in to aid Menelaus. A bloody battle raged over the corpse.

What happened to the dead, in those days, was very important to the living. Bodies were not buried; they were cremated. The flames were made sacred by sacrifice to the gods, by libation, and by prayer. In the case of a great warrior or a king or any person who had earned unusual respect during his lifetime, the death ceremonies would include funeral games—chariot races, wrestling, boxing, spear throwing and archery, reflecting in play form the mourned one's aptitudes in manly pursuits. By such ceremonies and celebrations, it was felt, the dead person could depart in all honor. This sense of honor would ease his journey to the Land of the Dead and give him status in Hades' kingdom. If sufficiently honored at his funeral, he would be singled out from among death's hordes by Charon, the grim boatman, whose job it was to ferry them across the Styx. The honored one would not have to linger in a mob, sorrowfully, on this side of the Styx, but would be ferried quickly over by the status-conscious Charon to his reward in the Land of the Dead.

On the other hand, if, for some reason, a corpse went unclaimed by friend or relative—or was kept by the enemy and not given a proper send-off—then, dreadful things would happen to the survivors. The dishonored dead could not cross the Styx and enter Hades' kingdom. His spirit would cling to the site of his unregarded death. Wearing stinking rags of flesh, he would appear before family and friends, usually at night, howling, weeping, begging. Or, worst of all, simply be found standing in any sudden corner, staring at you out of empty eye sockets. If you were unfortunate enough to have dealings with a ghost, you would set out his favorite food—black beans in little pots and shallow dishes of blood. He might be appeased for a while by such delicacies, but not for long. Soon he would reappear howling, begging, or silently staring.

In the case of the Greeks, demoralized as they were at this point of the battle, they still fought savagely for Patroclus's body because they knew that Achilles would go quite berserk when he learned of his friend's death—but if he also learned that the body of his beloved companion had been taken by the Trojans, beheaded, and thrown to the dogs, then, they knew he would be capable of doing anything to friend as well as foe. In fact, it was clear, he would visit his first vengeance upon the Greeks.

Thus, despite being outnumbered by the Trojans, they formed a hedge of spears around the body and would not let the Trojans pass.

But Hector sent in more men, and the weight of their numbers must finally have broken the Greek resistance had it not been for Achilles' horses—those magically bred stallions, tall as stags, fierce as harpies, swift as the West Wind. They charged toward the knot of fighting men and burst into their midst, hurling people in all directions. Reared on their haunches, struck with their front hooves, kicked and bit until they had cleared the Trojans away from the corpse, allowing Menelaus to lift it from the dust and put it in the chariot. Then the horses galloped back toward Achilles' tent bearing their dead charioteer.

Patroclus had come very close to the Trojan wall before being killed. The fighting had been quite beyond Achilles' sight although he had been watching from the rampart, trying to follow the course of battle. All he could hear was far-off shouting; all he could see was a cloud of dust.

"Under their walls," he said to himself. "I told him not to advance so far. Still, perhaps it means that he has broken their lines and has put them to flight."

Then he saw a bright speck detach itself from the dust and fly toward him. He watched until it took shape. A chariot! Coming with such speed it could be drawn only by Xanthus and Balius, his own stallions! His heart leaped with joy.

"It's Patroclus!" he cried. "It must be he! They will obey only his hand beside mine!" He's safe! Safe! Coming to report a great victory!"

With incredible speed the West-Wind stallions galloped to the rampart, rearing and neighing when they saw Achilles there. He looked at them in amazement. Great tears were welling from their golden eyes. No one had ever seen horses cry before, and it was a terrible sight. He tried not to believe what those tears meant and stood staring at his beautiful stallions. Then they broke the long primordial silence.

"Forgive us, dear master," said Xanthus. "We bring back to you Patroclus."

"Dead," said Balius. "We bring him dead."

Achilles did not weep. His face was like a rock. Very gently he lifted the battered body from the chariot and bore it into his tent. He bound the latchets so that no one could enter. The stallions stood before the tent like watch dogs and let no one approach. Achilles remained alone with his grief through the long twilight and the hours of night and the next morning.

No one dared approach his tent and intrude upon his grief. The Greeks were afraid he might have fallen on his own sword, choosing to lie in death beside his comrade, but they did not dare approach.

"He will not kill himself," said Ulysses. "He has work to do first; he must avenge himself upon Hector. After that, perhaps, but not yet."

In the darkest hour of night his mother Thetis arose from the sea and walked through the walls of his tent. He had not wept, but mothers can hear silent grief. She had heard his even in the depths of the sea, and had come to him. All night long he crouched in her embrace, not weeping, but making low hoarse whimpering sounds. She held his head to her naked breasts as if he were a babe again, and stroked his face, and kissed him. Even in his terrible grief he was comforted by her sea-magic touch.

He spoke only at dawn, just before she left him. "Will you do something for me, mother?"

"Anything, son."

"Patroclus went to battle clad in my armor. The Trojans stripped him of it. It is worn by Hector now, that armor made by Hephaestus and given to my father as a wedding present. I mean to seek Hector out and combat him today, but I wish to appear in armor no less fine than that I lost, and to bear weapons no less fine than those taken from Patroclus when he fell. These can issue only from the smithy of the gods. Can you persuade Hephaestus to labor this morning and forge me new gear?"

"I have some influence over the lame god," said Thetis. "I was the one who nurtured him, you know, after Zeus had flung him from Olympus, and he had fallen into the sea with shattered legs, helpless as a tadpole. I took him to my cave and mended his wounds and raised him as my own child, giving him pebbles and sea shells to make jewelry so that he grew clever in that craft. He will drop what he is doing and labor this morning. Weapons and armor more beautiful than those you lost will issue from his forge. By the time you are ready to combat Hector you will find what you need here in your tent. Now farewell, dear son."

On certain evenings the sun diving through clouds forges out the shape of armed men, who burn in the western sky taller than mountains, as if guarding the horizon. Their flaming delicate armor is what Hephaestus took as his model when he yielded to Thetis's plea and worked the morning through casting new weapons for Achilles. Like the red-hot sun disk itself, written over with a tracery of cloud, was his shield. His spear was a polished volt-bright shaft that Zeus himself might have used as a lightning bolt. A corselet was woven light as cloud fleece but made of three thicknesses of pressed copper. Hephaestus dug into holy relics and pulled out the very ingot from which he had forged Hermes' sword, later given to Perseus and used by him to slay Medusa. He

THE TROJAN WAR

laid the lump of pure copper on his red-hot anvil and beat it out into a sword for Achilles that matched Perseus's weapon. Ares, some days before, had ordered a helmet of Hephaestus, who had been working in the hardest brass for the war-god. Now he took this half-made helmet, and with a few skillful hammer strokes shaped it into a helm for Achilles' head. As a crest he sheared off a plume of cloud fleece and dipped it into the colors of the sunset.

When he gave Thetis this gorgeous gear, the tall nereid scooped up the little lame god, held him in her superb white arms as if he were a child, and kissed him on the lips.

"Thank you, dear Hephaestus," she said. "Thank you for your kindness, for your quickness, and for your masterful craftsmanship. You are a great god now, artificer-in-chief for the whole flat world; your smithy is a volcano where you wreak implements for the high use of Father Zeus and the Pantheon. God though you be, you shall always remain my own dear little tadpole, my sweet maimed foster child, and from me you shall always have a mother's tenderness although I am cast in eternal flowing nymphhood and you in eternal middle age."

She kissed his seamed charcoal-grimed face again, set him down, and flew off bearing the glittering new armor made for Achilles.

THE SCROLL OF THE FATES

Every so often the gods were entitled to read in the great book of the Fates wherein was written all that had been and all that was to be. We use the word "book" but there were no books then, as we know them. This tome of the Fates was a huge scroll hung from a place in the heavens beyond man's sight and written over with starry characters. Night-blue was this scroll, made from the dark-blue hide of a heavenly beast, unknown to man, hunted by the gods once every thousand years in a great chase across the inlaid floors of heaven.

Night-blue was the scroll, and those winged crones who were the Fates, those twisted sisters whom even the gods fear, would dip their claws into starlight and scrawl their irrevocable decrees upon these dark pages. Once every several years the gods were summoned to read what was written on the scroll and to consider what they had read, then return to Olympus to conduct the affairs of men accordingly.

Usually the gods chose to keep man in ignorance of what was fated for him. Occasionally, though, when it amused them, or when they wished to seduce a mortal by special knowledge or when coaxed by artful oracles, the gods would let slip some information in riddling form. And it was this matter that the oracles uttered as prophecy. Soothsayers had different ways of trying to learn the gods' secrets. Some claimed that the future was written in the entrails of certain birds and beasts, and these creatures were slaughtered and gutted and their entrails studied. Such oracles were called *haruspex*. Other soothsayers claimed that the vault of heaven was the brow of Zeus, and the flights of birds were his thoughts drifting across the sky of his mind—and, studying the flight of birds, they would try to predict what was to come.

These oracles tended to cluster in groups called "colleges," each of them dedicated to a special god. Apollo's priestesses at Delphi were especially well known. They dwelt in a huge cave dug into a mountain at a place called Delphi. It was volcano country. Through a fissure in the rock an aromatic steam arose from the very entrails of the earth. The priestesses set their stone tripods across this fissure and squatted above it, breathing these fumes which gave them visions. These visions, they claimed, were of the future. They also chewed laurel—which we know as bay leaf—which sharpened vision, or blurred it, or whatever it is that makes a vision most real to those who have it. Their utterances were always couched in riddles, knotty ones; no one could understand what they were saying except other priestesses, who, for a fee, would interpret these riddles.

Now, prophecy about the Trojan War had made a rich tale from the very beginning. On this subject soothsayers blabbed the secrets of the gods without restraint. We have already met certain of these prophecies: The one which said the Greeks could win the war only with the help of Achilles; and the second part of it which said Achilles must die before Troy, but if he stayed at home and did not go to war, he could live a long peaceful life. We already know the choice he made, with the help of Ulysses. And Ulysses himself was the subject of a prophecy which said that if he went to Troy he could not return to Ithaca until twenty years had passed, and would return alone, beggared, unrecognized.

Now, on this day following the death of Patroclus, the gods were summoned again to the far reaches of heaven to read the great scroll. It was the first time since the war had begun that they had been so summoned, and there was much new matter to read in the flaming scrawl of the Fates. They returned to Olympus abrim with news, some chattering with each other, others sunk in meditation, all of them trying to think how they could best use this knowledge of the future to tease man into providing some special entertainment in the years that lay ahead.

They had three principle spokesmen to work through. Calchas and Chryses were professional oracles. Chryses, the Trojan, was a priest of Apollo. He was also father to Cressida. Calchas was the most influential among the Greek soothsayers. Sometimes he posed as a priest of Hera; at other times he claimed the special confidence of Athena. Actually he free-lanced—picking up clues from any god he could, and making pronouncements about what the Greeks should or should not do. When things were going well, he was listened to with half an ear; when disaster struck, his counsel was more valued. So, professionally, he was not quite averse to catastrophe.

But the one with the real heavy fatal burning talent for the future was Cassandra. Bestowed upon her by Apollo was that most terrible of gifts, a *memory* of the future. And she kept her pronouncements rare because she knew how awful they were. However, she did not disturb the Trojan peace of mind at all. It will be remembered that Apollo punished her for refusing his amorous advances by capping his gift with a curse. His sentence was that although she would be able to prophesy with the utmost accuracy and know that she was doing so, she would always be disbelieved by her own people.

Apollo came to her that night, sliding down one of the

shafts of his sister's moonlight. He entered her chamber where she lay asleep. But she had trained herself never to sleep more than a few minutes at a time because her dreams were so terrible. She awoke now and gazed upon him where he stood igniting the shadows and closed her eyes again, saying, "You are so unwelcome a sight; you must be a dream. It doesn't really matter. You have always ignored my need for privacy and walked through the walls of sleep as though they were open doors. Speak, my lord. Why do you honor me with this visit?"

"Well, basically to rape you—since you refuse any gentler overtures. However, all will not be loss. For in the bed-talk that will follow, I shall impart to you certain matters that I have read in the stary scroll of the Fates. There is much, much about Troy."

He smiled a scorching smile and stepped toward the bed. She screamed. But no one could hear. Her screams were always voiceless in the presence of Apollo.

Later, he told her what he had read in the scroll. He told her many things. The last thing he told her excited her unbearably. She knelt before him and clasped his knees.

"Oh, great Phoebus—please, please, in this let me be believed. If he believes me, perchance he will take the opportunity to save his life, brave though he be. Please let him believe what I tell him. If you do so then I will put aside the loathing I have for you, I swear I will. Somehow, I don't know how, I will school myself to respond to your lovemaking. But you must do this thing for me."

"Your idea of diplomacy, my child, will never cease to astound me. But make no rash vows. In the first place, you will be unable to keep them lest they go against your inmost nature. Secondly, even if you could, I cannot break my vow once given. This is a disability we gods suffer from. That is why we so seldom make promises. Farewell, I shall visit you again. Try to restrain your impatience until that golden hour."

Chryses found his daughter, Cressida, cutting flowers in the garden. He bustled up to her.

"A very important day, my dear," he cried. "Much business brews."

"How is that, Father?"

She was picking roses. Her slender fingers plucked and snipped, moving like white moths among the petals. Her face was flushed, making the roses look pale. Their fragrance was all about her.

"I consulted the entrails of a pigeon this morning," he said. "A very informative set of guts. They told me that the high gods had been summoned by the Fates to read the great scroll, but there was no hint, no hint at all, of what they learned."

"Perhaps another pigeon is on the way with this information."

"No, no, the matter has not been published yet. That much I know. They're being very close-mouthed, the gods. I resorted to other devices—cast dice, juggled numbers, even tried a few eastern tricks with the conjunction of the stars— but no luck at all. The gods are silent, and I don't know what to think."

"Well, keep eavesdropping. Perhaps you'll hear something." Girls in those days were very courteous to their fathers even while being bored.

"It's absolutely essential that I learn something," he said. "The war has come to a most important pass. Prince Achilles will undoubtedly rejoin the fray. He will seek out Hector, and upon the Dardanian plain beneath our walls the two greatest heroes on all the flat world will fight until one of them is killed. Now it is upon such days that oracles grow rich. If I could pick up even the tiniest scrap of information,

I would be able to prophesy to Prince Hector concerning the duel, and he would give me splendid gifts. Yes, so noble-hearted is he, this eldest and strongest son of Priam, that he would reward even a gloomy prognostication and if, by chance, the forecast should be happy, who knows what treasures he might heap upon me?"

Just then Cressida saw him look past her shoulder and pin a greasy fawning smile to his face. He made a deep bow. Cressida turned. She saw Princess Cassandra, who had entered the garden so silently it was as if she had been made to appear by magic.

Cassandra saw the priest's daughter coming toward her with an armful of roses. They seemed to be little red flames. The girl was carrying a bouquet of fire. And Cassandra saw her in the midst of smoke and shrieks and falling timber, offering a lover her corsage of flame. She spoke icily to quench the pain of the roses.

"Greetings, Cressida," she said. "I do not wish to interrupt your gardening. I have come to speak with your father."

Cressida watched her father with distaste. The man was practically jigging with pleasure and importance as he led Cassandra toward a garden seat.

"Priest," said Cassandra, "the gods last night consulted the scroll of Fate."

"I know, I know, good Princess. So I have divined."

"Have you divined what they were told?"

"Unfortunately, no."

"Your patron, Apollo, has told you nothing?"

"Not a word, not a word. I am hopeful of persuading him by my arts. But it takes time, time. . . ."

"Well, I have been told. I know now the heavy oracles concerning Troy."

"Can you perhaps, dear Princess, find your way clear to confiding them in me?"

"No, I cannot."

"A pity."

"But I have not come to your garden empty-handed. I will give you a single piece of information. It concerns my brother, Hector. I tell you so that you may tell him. If I tell him I shall, of course, be disbelieved."

"In all modesty, he will believe me," said Chryses. "He knows that I. . . ."

"Yes, yes. Listen closely now for this is a conditional prophecy. If he fights Achilles he will be killed, but Achilles cannot outlive Hector more than three days."

"You say 'if.' Is it not ordained that they must fight?"

"Try to understand the way the gods entertain themselves, oh oracle. There is always a margin of uncertainty injected into each edict concerning the future. That is the way the gods keep themselves in suspense about these affairs they themselves concoct, and make the spectacles more dramatic. This margin of uncertainty, this divine suspense, is called man's will—those decisions he makes about his own affairs. 'If,' my friend, is a tiny word of sublime proportions. If man properly taps the explosive strength of its pent possibilities he can alter circumstances and thrust the gods themselves into entirely new situations. The word 'if' heads the prophecy. *If* Hector fights, he dies. *If* Achilles kills Hector, he too dies. Make this clear to Hector. He can avoid the fight. In all honor he can do so. No one else fights Achilles. Why should he? If he avoids this duel, he will live. Go. Tell. He will reward you. Here is a gold armlet set with rubies and sapphires to pay for the time you have given me. If Hector exercises his 'if,' and refuses to fight Achilles, then I shall add to this armlet a fat bag of gold."

Cassandra pulled the heavy gold circlet off her arm and gave it to Chryses who fell to his knees when he took it. The princess nodded to Cressida and walked out of the garden.

Cressida crouched again among the roses. She was smiling a little mischievous smile, and gave off such a musk of desire that it drowned the fragrance of the roses. Bees came to buzz amorously in the calyx of her ear and among the thickets of her hair.

It was Aphrodite now tampering with affairs. She had come back from her session with the Fates teeming with mischief. Plan after plan for confounding the Greeks danced through her head.

"In my quiet way," she said to herself, "it seems to me I have been much more influential than those brawling hags, Hera and Athena. After all it was my gift of Helen to Paris that started this war. And who was it that embroiled Agamemnon and Achilles, instilling in them a desire for the same slave-girl? Look what that has led to. Now, however, with Patroclus dead, Achilles is sure to take the field. When he does, that mighty sword will shear through the delicate web of my contrivances. What then? All is not lost. Achilles must slay Hector if they fight says the scroll of the Fates, but if he does he himself must die soon afterward. If he does not combat Hector, all is as before. If he does and they both die, then a new situation prevails. Diomedes will be the most formidable hero in the Greek camp. I have a sharp grudge against that bully, Diomedes. Did he not dare to raise his lance against me—me, the Goddess of Love and Desire—and wound me on the wrist? Wait—here's an idea! I can settle my grudge with him, and in doing so throw the Greek camp into turmoil again. All this, by heaven, without even making a new plan; I'll use the old one. As I once set Agamemnon against Achilles, now, should Achilles die, I will set that Mycenaean bull in murderous rivalry against Diomedes, and do it in the very same way—through Cressida, whom Agamemnon held as a slave and whose ways intoxicated him. Now I will infect Cressida with the sweet venon of love for

Diomedes. She is already inclined that way, having watched him fight during his day of glory, and my job will be easy. Yes, I will raise admiration to passion that will burn in her veins, melt her bones, forge her into one single arrow of desire pointing toward him. And when she returns to Agamemnon's tent, nothing will keep her there. It is Diomedes she will want, Diomedes she will find her way to, hurling those two chieftains at each other's throat, dividing the Greeks into factions again, and weakening them altogether —so that they will be incapable of an assault against my Trojans."

Thereupon she took a vial of a thick gluey red ointment that smelled of honey and baking bread, which is the odor of desire. She flew to the garden of Chryses, all invisible, and smeared the thorns of the roses that Cressida was picking with this venom of desire. The thorns pricked Cressida's hands. Suddenly she burned with an itching yen for Diomedes. And knew that before the night had passed she must find a way to his tent, or be grilled, sleepless, over this terrible rosy fire.

"But will he want me?" she thought to herself. "He is in love with battle. Killing Trojans is his one passion, and murder is an absorbing business I understand. Will it leave room for gentler occupations? Agamemnon I could twist around my finger, but for this Diomedes I feel a kind of terror. I must make myself irresistible to him. But how? By giving him what he wants the most. Yes, victory over the Trojans, that is what he wants the most. If I can bring him information that will help him, then perhaps he will love me. Do I know any secrets? I know nothing that is not generally known. Chit-chat about the court, observations about the personal habits of Priam's sons and daughters—these will not be useful to him. No, I need something big, important. If, for only an hour, I could be that sour-faced Cassandra with her talent for reading the future, then I could come to him filled with the authority of an oracle, a priestess of knowledge, and could make him love me. But that's it! Cassandra! Locked in her head is what I must know. I must unlock it. But how? She despises me. Whom does she not despise? Her brother, Troilus, that's who. She dotes on him, mothers him. Watching on the wall, she has eyes only for deeds and his safety. She would tell Troilus what I want to know. Then I must try to know Troilus a little better. It should not be difficult. He has a hot roving eye. It has rested on me occasionally. And the task would not be distasteful. He's a very pretty boy."

And so, as we shall see, goddesses can be outwitted too, or rather, can outwit themselves. For Aphrodite, attempting to confound the Greeks, had kindled a tiny flame that was to grow into a fire big enough to burn Troy even unto the last timber.

Chryses visited Hector to tell him of Cassandra's prophecy, claiming it as his own. Hector interrupted him.

"If I had any doubts about fighting Achilles," said Hector, "I am quite rid of them now. I have always expected him to vanquish me. His pedigree is much finer than mine. He is not only the son of Thetis, queen of nereids, but great-grandson to Zeus himself. We lift our weapons against him in vain. With much pain we have learned that he cannot be hurt by spear-cast or sword-thrust. No arrow can wound him, no dart pierce his magically toughened hide, while in the use of weapons he has no equal. He can split an oak tree with a blow of his sword. With one thrust of his lance, shear through a shield made of nine layers of bullhide stiffened with brass. We know this; we have seen it. And I have always known that I must challenge him one day for I am the best we have, and we must counter their best with ours. To challenge him,

to meet him, to pray for strength and skill somehow to pierce
that invulnerable hide—to do this and then to die—this I
have known to be my fate ever since Paris returned with
Helen from Sparta. To meet him, to fall, and to account
myself lucky to be spared the sight of Troy being sacked—
that has been the best I could have hoped for. Now you tell
me that my death must lead to his . . . and you call this a
gloomy prophecy? My dear man, it is the best news I have
heard in almost a decade. I just hope I can trust it. I don't
take much stock in readings of the future, you know. We
have a prophetess in the family who claims to be divinely
inspired, and she is invariably wrong. However, I shall do
my best to believe what you tell me. I shall seek out Achilles
with great joy. And joy strengthens a man's arm."

"Pray, prince Hector, consider—"

"Enough, good Chryses. You have pleased me. Don't spoil
it. Take this bag of gold and go. And be sure to watch from
the wall tomorrow; it should be an interesting afternoon."

A sparrow was perched near during this conversation.
Being a great gossip like all sparrows, he flew off and tattled
to a seagull—who, being a sea-bird, loved Thetis and held
kindly feelings toward her son. The seagull flew to the Greek
camp and told Xanthus and Balius, the stallions who drew
Achilles' chariot.

"Thank you, seagull," said Xanthus. "We speak Greek, as
it happens, and we shall inform our master of this prophecy."

"Yes," said Balius. "Perhaps we can dissuade him from
meeting Hector."

But they discussed the matter again between themselves
after the seagull had flown away. They knew their master to
be a short-tempered man.

"What do you think?" said Balius. "Do we dare tell him?
He takes advice from no one, especially from horses."

"It is our duty," said Xanthus. "He burns for revenge against Hector, but Hector's death means his own death. Too high a price."

As it happens, Ulysses was passing and heard this exchange. He hurried to Diomedes and told him what he had heard.

"Well then," said Diomedes, "it is up to us to dissuade him. It will be difficult, but perhaps we can do so."

"Why should we?" said Ulysses.

"Why? Because he is our companion, our best fighter. Because Hector's life is not worth his. That's why."

"I admire your sentiments, dear Diomedes, but allow me to say this. We are engaged in a war. It has been a long war. The object of fighting a war is to win. That is why men risk their lives every day—to win. That is why they die every day—to win. By any calculation of the odds we should have been victorious long ago, but we have not been. Achilles has sulked. There has been dissension in our ranks. The last year our men have fought with half a heart, longing for home. The Trojans, on the other hand, have been unified under the command of Hector. No one challenges his leadership. He allows no one to fail in his duty. He is the very heart and soul of the Trojan effort, exerting an influence that far outweighs his own fighting ability, great though it is."

"I know all this," said Diomedes.

"Then know this: We can win without Achilles; without Hector they must lose."

"I see," said Diomedes.

"Then you will not rush to tell him of the prophecy?"

"I will be guided by you, wise Ulysses."

tHe wRAtH of AcHilles

Achilles took the field. All aglitter he was in the new armor forged by Hephaestus. His shield burned like the sun disk at dawn; his plumed crest burned with the colors of the sunset. Between dawn-colored shield and sunset crest his face burned white-hot as noon with pent fury. He leaped into his brass chariot and shouted to his horses. But instead of charging toward the enemy lines which they always did at the first sound of his war-shout, this time Xanthus and Balius tossed their heads and turned their long faces to him, rolling their great golden eyes.

"Pray, forgive us, Master," said Xanthus, "but one word before you go into battle."

"It is this," said Balius. "Do not seek Hector in single combat. If you find him, you will kill him for no one stands before you."

"And if you kill him," said Xanthus, "you must die within three days. That is the decree of the Fates."

"I cannot believe my ears," said Achilles. "In the field, no one questions my commands from the lowliest Myrmidon to the most powerful member of the War Council. I am certainly not accustomed to consulting my chariot horses concerning tactics."

"It is for love of you we speak, dear Master," said Xanthus. "Now do as you will."

"One favor," said Bailus. "Please leave instructions that we be burned on the same pyre as you. We do not wish to be driven by another master after your death."

"Noted," said Achilles. "Now be silent and obey orders. Forward!"

As Achilles took the field, Hector was being dressed for battle—not by his squire, but by his wife, Andromache, who had begged him to let her prepare him for this day's fighting. He had hesitated. She had been present at the conversation with Chryses and knew the prediction about his death, but she had not said a word to dissuade him from meeting Achilles. She had saved it all up, he was afraid, for this last hour before battle. The one thing that could weaken him, he knew, was her weeping. But she had asked to be allowed to help with his armor, and he could not refuse. Now she was dressing him in the gorgeous metal that had been Hephaestus's present to Peleus, later Achilles' armor, then worn by Patroclus, and taken from him by Hector.

"Dear Husband," she said, "I am filled with such love and admiration that my hands tremble, and I can scarcely bind the latchets of your corselet. In this heaven-forged armor you shine like the very morning star."

He looked at her in amazement, no tears, no reproaches, no mournful face. She was alight with love, brimming with serenity. Never since the beginning of the war had she exuded such confidence. He did not question her, but accepted her mood with glad heart. He would have felt differently, perhaps, had he known how she arrived at her present mood. It was a secret he was never to learn.

The night before, Andromache had left his bed. She wrapped herself in a dark cloak and made her way through the sleeping city, mounted the inner steps to the wall, and keeping to the deepest shadows, avoided the sentry and climbed down the other side of the wall. There she crossed the Dardanian plain to a bend of the river called Scamander. She unwrapped her cloak, pulled her gown over her head and stood naked, white as a birch, in the moonlight. She stepped into the river up to her knees.

"River!" she called. "Oh, tall brown god who loved me while I was yet a maid, River-god, beloved tawny sneak who surprised me swimming, and drowned my fears, and initiated me into the high rites of love, so that having passed through your flowing hands I was fit to be wife to great Hector—River-god, strong brown lover, Axius, spirit of the Scamander, answer me now, for I have come to you once again."

The river was a blackness spangled with gold in the hot moonlight. And hot gold was the color of the god who arose before her.

"Many tender maidens bathe in my stream," he said. "Which one are you?"

"Andromache."

"Oh, yes, I think I remember. Very sweet and strong-limbed. Quick to learn. How have you been since last we met?"

"Flourishing, my lord. I am wife to Hector, son of Priam, first among the princes of Troy."

"Hector, the great warrior?"

"Yes."

"Does he make love as skillfully as he fights?"

"He slays me every night."

"High praise from a wife. How long have you been wed?"

"Seven years."

"Why have you left his bed and come to seek me now?"

"He must preserve his strength. Tomorrow he fights Achilles."

"Foolish child! Hurry home, wake him up, take him into your embrace! It is your last night together."

"No."

"No? Did you say it was Achilles he was fighting?"

"Yes."

"That's what I thought you said. But, my dear child, no one, no one at all, engages Achilles in single combat and returns to his wife. It's just not done. The man is completely fatal. Couching here on my riverbed I have watched him in action now for nine years, and, believe me, he is the complete widow-maker. Go home and love your husband, Lady; tomorrow you are a widow."

"I beg leave to differ," said Andromache. "There is something in woman that rebels against these ordinances of the Fates, these absolute iron edicts concerning the future. We do not like to foreclose on possibilities. To us the future is precisely that which is pregnant with new life, new chance, new luck. I have heard the prophecy concerning Hector, but I will not accept it. And I need an ally strong as fate. That is why I have returned to you, oh River-god."

"Strong as fate? You flatter me. More powerful gods than I bow to fate. I do well enough here, but after all I am only a small local deity. Beyond the banks of this river I have no authority whatsoever."

"Ah, but rivers rise. Rivers rage. Rivers overflow their banks and extend their authority across great fields. They sweep away walls, cities. Rivers drink floods and grow to mighty torrents rivaling the sea. You are too modest, Axius. It is a new quality. I never noticed it before."

"And you are a very clever, very persuasive lady," said Axius. "Something I did notice before, but had forgotten. Speak plainly, what is it you want me to do? But let us get more comfortable. Why don't we lie on that inviting bed of reeds on my shore? Remember how we used to hide in the reeds?"

"I remember."

"Will you lie there again?"

"One does not lightly refuse a god," said Andromache. "Wives are not supposed to do these things. But what can one do if one is overpowered by a god?"

"True," said Axius. "Very true."

He lifted her in his arms and carried her to a bed of reeds that leaned from the shore, bowing to the night wind, and singing with mournful joy as they felt the wind among them.

"Now," said Axius, "ask me what you will, and if it is in my power, I shall help you."

"Trojan meets Greek upon your bank tomorrow. Hector will meet Achilles on your shore. Go into flood, my lord. Rage over your banks. But selectively. Sweep Achilles away. Drown him in his heavy armor."

"How do you know they will fight upon my bank?"

"They shall. I promise."

"Then I promise to do what I can. Sweet Andromache, you have returned to me on a night of hot moonlight when I was feeling old and stagnant, and have restored to me the lusty tides of my youth. I will do as you ask though stronger gods oppose me."

Andromache returned to the palace smelling of the river, so cool-fleshed and fragrant that Hector awoke and embraced her against his judgment. And they lay in each other's arms until morning.

Now, later that morning, as she helped him on with his armor, she still gave off the fragrance of that river which half-girdled Troy, running from the mountains to the sea, with dragonflies blue as jewels darting at its ripples, with elm tree and willow and tamarisk dipping toward their reflections, with tall reeds swaying and singing in the wind— and yet which could change its temper with brutal suddenness, drinking rain, gulping floods from the hills, and rising, raging over its banks, devouring town and village, crunching house and barn between its foamy teeth.

And Hector, donning his shining armor, felt himself fill with the strength of that river which nurtures the Trojan plain, whose presence had been brought into this room by his river-smelling wife.

She said to him, "One request. You know I never meddle into your affairs, but do me this favor. My husband, my lord, let me advise you out of a dream that came to me in the night."

"Speak, my dear."

"Do not seek Achilles beyond the Scamander. Stay within the bend of the river, and let him come to you. If you do so, according to my dream, you shall defeat the son of Peleus, win everlasting glory, and return to me after the battle is over."

She fell to the ground and hugged his knees, pressing them to her breasts.

"Promise!" she cried. "Promise, oh husband, please promise!"

"I promise," he said.

A detachment of Trojans pretended to flee before Achilles and his Myrmidons and drew them toward the Scamander. There they turned to face the Greeks within a half-circle of marshy land formed by a bend in the river. Achilles found he could not use his chariot; its wheels sank up to their hubs in the marshy ground. He dismounted and fought on foot, followed closely by his Myrmidons. But mounted or afoot, he moved through the Trojan ranks like Death itself with its scythe. Every thrust of his spear drank blood. Charging ahead he broke the Trojan ranks, and the brown columns of his Myrmidons, festive as ants, gorged their swords on the flesh of the scattered foe.

Now Hector and his picked guard charged into the marshy arc in a flank attack on the Myrmidons. Howling with ferocious joy, Achilles sought Hector through the mob of fighting men.

"Stand, son of Priam!" he roared. "Try your stolen armor against my weapon's edge! Stand and face me or my spear will find your life between your shoulder blades, and you shall die a shameful death!"

Despite himself Hector found his courage melting at the sound of that terrible voice. He did not turn and flee but retreated slowly until his back was to the river, and he could retreat no further.

"Now! Now!" shouted Achilles. "You have a narrow choice, killer of Patroclus. Death by water or death by blade!" And he drew back to hurl his spear, but Axius arose invisibly from the depths of the river and cast a cloak of mist about Hector. Achilles, poising his mighty lance saw Hector disappear, saw mist rising from the bank of the river, hiding his foe from sight. He cast his spear into the column of mist, but saw it sail harmlessly through and land in the river. For Axius had lifted Hector in his arms and borne him safely to the other side of the river. All Achilles could see was tatters of mist drifting across the face of the water, and he knew that Hector had escaped his wrath once again.

Now in terrible fury at this loss he turned upon the other Trojans and killed and killed and killed. The wet marshland grew wetter yet with running blood. Men sank to the top of their shin-greaves. Only Achilles, riding the wings of fury, remained light-footed as a demi-god, running over the surface of the mud like marsh fire. His new-moon sword rose and fell as if he were mowing a field. Every time it fell a Trojan died.

Finally, the Trojans in panic fled into the river. But Achilles followed with his Myrmidons and slaughtered them as they tried to cross the ford. Bodies fell into the river and disappeared. The water ran red as sunset. Now Axius arose

169

again from the depths of the river, in his own form this time, and Achilles found himself confronting a figure tall as a tree with greenish-coppery skin.

"Halt, Achilles," he said in a voice that rumbled like a waterfall. "Son of Peleus, halt before I drown you beneath fathoms of my outraged stream."

"You must be the god of this river," said Achilles. "Very well, I have no quarrel with you, my lord. My business is with Trojans."

"But I have a quarrel with you, you tiger in human form. How dare you stain my waters with blood? Pollute my stream with corpses? Prince of Phthia, you have offered me deadly insult, and now you yourself must die."

Axius leaned down scooping into the river with his mighty hands and flung a wave at Achilles. The heavy water hit him full, knocking him off his feet, tumbling over him. He fought for breath. Every time he tried to rise, another wave knocked him down. The river-god stood waist-deep, flinging torrents of water over the bank. Caught like a beetle in his heavy armor, unable to rise, Achilles was rolled over and over into the river itself. He must surely have drowned had not his mother been Thetis, daughter of Nereus, Old Man of the Sea, who bequeathed to all his descendants the power to breathe under water. But the Myrmidons had no such lineage; they were capable of drowning, and those that had followed Achilles into battle were caught in the rising waters and drowned, every one.

Achilles, who had stumbled to his feet, saw his men drowning about him and could not help them. He sprang into the middle of the stream and challenged Axius.

"Fight fair, you watery demon! I have contended with you in your element, and you have not killed me. Now come up on land, and fight with me with sword and spear."

But Axius uttered a cataract laugh and, knowing now he

could not drown Achilles, tried to crush him under a weight of water. Axius curled himself into a huge crested wave that towered taller than any building in Troy and smashed this entire mass of water down on Achilles who was hurled to the bottom of the river. He felt himself being pummeled, beaten, choked—felt an unbearable pressure squeezing his ribs. His arms were crushed against his sides; he could not even raise his sword.

Seeing his enemy pinned helplessly to the riverbed, Axius now scooped up boulder after boulder and rained them down on the Greek hero like a boy pelting the ground with stones, trying to squash an ant.

But Thetis, Lady of the Living Waters, knew everything that was happening in every sea and stream and river of which the earth drank. Rising swift as thought from the depths of the sea, she appeared before Hephaestus who worked at his smoky forge inside his volcano. Clasping him in her cool arms she flew the hot little lame god to the lip of the crater, and said, "Look! See what's happening! Axius is murdering my son!"

Hephaestus, blissful as a babe always at Thetis's touch, half-dazed before the sea-magic of her beauty, dived back into the volcano and returned with an armful of fire from his forge. Now this fire is hotter than man ever sees burning in any furnace. It is the essential flame, the very core of flame burning deep in the bowels of the earth, and is the source of all flame. And the lame god cast this fire that was hotter than fire down upon the riverbank. It kindled the reeds, elm trees, willows and tamarisks, heated the mud itself to a molten mass. The river boiled.

Axius, god of the river, felt his flesh scorching. While he was a god and could not die, he could feel pain, and the pain of Hephaestus's red fire was so terrible that he cried, "Hold, Hephaestus, hold! Hold off your red fire! I will break my vow to Andromache and allow the son of Thetis to escape!"

The smith-god recalled his fire. Axius dived to the river bottom to cool off his blistered shoulders. Achilles staggered to his feet, took off his helmet, emptied it of water. Then he clapped it on his head again, forded the river, and set off in chase of Hector.

Andromache, watching from the city wall, had been seized with great joy when she saw the river rise. She was filled with a marvelous laughing happiness when she saw Axius hurl his crested wave and bury Achilles in tons of water. But when she saw the banks burst into flame, and saw the river boil, and the rivergod's hair burning, and heard the pain-laden wailing of Axius—when she saw Achilles rise from the depths of the river like the spirit of vengeance itself, when she saw the terrible tin of his greaves cleaving the water, and saw him race over the plain seeking Hector, and the light flashing from his sun-disk shield and his new-moon sword— then she knew that in him was gathered the strength of a natural force, crushing all plots and stratagems and wifely schemes—then she knew that Hector was doomed.

"I will not watch him being killed," she said to herself. "I cannot bear it. No wife should be made to watch her husband being butchered. I will go back now and get my baby, and at the very moment that Hector falls, will leap with my son in my arms, dashing out our lives on the plain below. Thus father, son, and wife, will be burned on one pyre, and cheer each other on the last journey to Erebus."

She left the wall and went to her home, entered the nursery and took her babe from the nurse's arms. But when she looked into its face, her strength deserted her and she fell into a swoon.

Now, in the shadow of the wall, watched by his father and his mother and all the people of the court, Hector turned to face Achilles, breathing one last prayer as he did so.

"I call to you, Apollo. I ask not for victory for victory cannot be given, it must be taken. All I ask is that my courage lasts, that my marrow does not freeze at his terrible war-shout, that my knees do not melt before the white-hot fury of his lipless face. That I can stand my ground before his dread charge and meet him weapon upon weapon without fleeing. My father watches on the wall. The pride of Troy rides upon my shoulders. Fair Apollo, bright Phoebus, I pray you, let me face my death like a man."

Apollo heard and sent down a shaft of sunlight that hit the back of Hector's neck, gilding his helmet and bathing him in warm light, warming his courage so that he stood full to Achilles' charge—met him sword upon sword and shield upon shield, standing firmly planted before that fearful rush that no other man had ever withstood.

But Achilles felt himself being caressed by a delicious chill. He was bathed in sweet combative airs. The clash of weapons was bright music to which he moved perfectly as in a dance. He was happy to have a partner for this deadly dance, happy that Hector did not break and run before him. But that standing here he could put out the full flower of his strength and feast himself slowly and gluttonously on the death of the Trojan who had killed Patroclus. His new-moon sword flashed. It locked with Hector's sword. Intimately the blades writhed. A great shout went up from the walls of Troy as the people there saw their champion stand so stoutly against Achilles, parrying his thrusts, blade meeting blade in equal play.

"Can it be?" thought old Priam. "Will my long years be crowned by this enormous glory? Will my son really be able to stand against this monster?"

Achilles laughed aloud as he felt the force of Hector's parry.

"Well done," Achilles said. "You're as good a man as ever

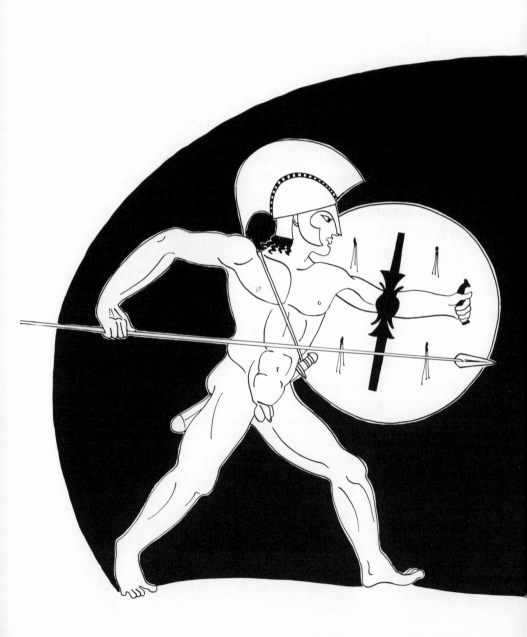

I met. Almost as good as the one you killed, but for that one you shall pay."

Hector did not answer. He saved his breath for fighting. He was putting all his strength into every parry and counter-thrust, and so far had met sword with sword and had kept the terrible new-moon blade from shearing through his armor. But every stroke now that Achilles aimed seemed to fall from a great height, seemed to fall with greater and greater weight as if it were plunging toward the center of earth. Hector felt his arms grow weary, his shoulders numb with the weight of his own muscle bunching to move his arms. Achilles' blows fell with greater and greater weight and the laughing voice grated in his ear.

"Not so soon," said Achilles. "Don't start to breathe so hard so early in the game, my fine Trojan. We have barely begun. This is only a little early swordplay; the real work is still to come."

Then, with a magnificent intricate stroke that changed direction in midair, Achilles snared Hector's blade in his own, snapped the sword from the Trojan's hand and sent it flying. A great groan went up from the watchers on the wall.

"No sword?" said Achilles. "A pity. It was my own sword too that you took from Patroclus. Never before has it been sent flying like this. But if you have lost your sword then you need no armor."

Now, coolly, relentlessly, he stepped around Hector, using his sword as delicately as though it were a small knife. And just as Hector had done to Patroclus, so did Achilles do now to Hector, shaming the Trojan hero by cutting the latchets of his armor. The breastplate fell off. The corselet fell away. The greaves were sheared away. And Hector stood naked except for his helmet.

But Hector, disencumbered of his armor, dodged away from Achilles' sword and ran for the city gate. Achilles

flashed after him. Carrying full armor he ran as lightly as
Hector did, cutting him off from the city gate and pursuing
him around the walls. Like an eagle stooping upon a lamb
was the armored Achilles striding effortlessly after the naked
Hector. Around and around three times did Achilles follow
Hector as Hecuba hid her eyes and Priam tore his beard and
all the people lamented. Striding effortlessly after his naked
prey, flashing in his armor like the evening star, Achilles pursued Hector around the city walls. And after the third circuit,
lengthened his stride and caught him.

Hector fell into the burning embrace of that bright armor
like a maiden who has run in modesty from her first suitor,
finally swooning into his arms. For Hector's wind was gone;
his marrow was frozen; the hinges of his knees were melting
with dread, and his manhood was run out. He fell into
Achilles' bright embrace. One great hand seized Hector's hair
and drew back his head, stretching the strong bronze throat
like a lamb's to the knife. The other hand raised the new-
moon sword.

And as Apollo shrieked in anger and threw a cloud across
the face of the sun so that the entire Dardanian plain darkened, Achilles with a swift merciful stroke cut Hector's
throat. Then, still immaculate, unstained, unwearied, bright
as the evening star, he bound Hector's ankles with the embroidered girdle that Ajax had given Hector after their duel.
He bound the other end of the girdle to the axle of his war-
chariot which had trundled up to him at his whistle. He
leaped into his chariot, shouted to his stallions, and they began to gallop around the walls of Troy, dragging Hector in
the dust behind them. Seven times Achilles circled the walls
of Troy dragging Hector's body behind his chariot.

Apollo threw a sleep upon Priam and Hecuba so that they
would not see the body of their son being dragged in the dust.
The sun-god also threw a magic balm upon the corpse of

THE TROJAN WAR

Hector so that the body was not broken or the flesh torn as it was dragged along the rough ground behind that terrible chariot.

With a final shout Achilles swerved his horses and headed back for the Greek camp still dragging the body of Hector.

CRESSidA

Late the next afternoon while the armies were skirmishing on the plain, Cressida crossed the lines all unseen and entered the tent of Diomedes. She found a slave-girl there heating water in a huge copper cauldron, a little pale girl whom Diomedes had captured in a raid two years before on the island of Tenos. The maidens of Tenos have squeaky voices and look like little white mice, but Diomedes had kept her as a bath-girl because her hands were so soft.

"Are you heating water for your master's bath?" asked Cressida.

"Yes, lady. He comes back all hot and grimy from the fighting. And blood-spattered—you have no idea! And he wants his bath immediately, and a cool drink, and fresh clothes."

"Heavy labor for so small a girl," said Cressida in her hoarse purring voice. "I am moved to pity. Now just disappear somewhere and I shall do your work this afternoon."

"Oh, no, lady!"

"Oh yes, little girl."

"I daren't! I daren't! He like things just so. He has to be scraped of battle-filth with this ivory stick. Then kneaded in every muscle with warm oil. Then anointed with cool scented oil; then blotted with a fleecy towel."

"These are demanding tasks requiring enthusiasm and skill," said Cressida. "Nevertheless I think I can do them passably well. Off with you!"

"No, lady, no! I cannot! I dare not! He allows no one else to bathe him. He likes the touch of my hands."

"You will be feeling the touch of my hands, little one, and you won't like the feel of them, I promise. Now get out before I lose my patience. Here are three pieces of silver for you."

"I will not take them; I will not go!"

Cressida slapped the girl across the face so hard that she knocked her off her feet. Then grasped her thin shoulders, pulled her up again, and shook her until her jaw wobbled. Seized her by the hair and dragged her from the tent. Took her to where a tree grew, and broke off a branch, then, using the slender branch as a switch, flogged the girl until she was whimpering and sobbing like a beaten child.

"Let me go!" she cried. "Don't beat me anymore! Do as you like. Take my place at the bath, but stop hitting me!"

Cressida held the little pale girl in both hands and looked down at her through the tangle of her hair. The slave-girl was like a white mouse in the clutch of a beautiful tawny cat.

"You will keep away from the tent all night," said Cressida. "Understand? If I catch a glimpse of your pasty face before morning, I'll whip you till you can't walk. Hear me, little mouse?"

"Yes, lady. Anything you say."

"Here are three pieces of silver. Go find some soldier to kiss away your tears."

When Diomedes returned to his tent after the day's skirmishing, he found Cressida there heating water in the big copper pot.

"Welcome, my lord," she said. "Did you have good sport today?"

He looked at her in amazement.

"Who are you?"

"Do you not remember me, oh Diomedes? Many a time during the past months, coming to Agamemnon's tent for a war council, you have found me there."

"Agamemnon's tent? Yes. But then you are the priest's daughter, the one that had to be returned to her father because Apollo shot arrows of plague into our camp."

"I did not ask to be returned to my father. It was his idea entirely. And now, you see, I have crossed over again. I have become attached to the Greeks, or, rather to *a* Greek. To you, my lord. I have come back to you."

He looked her up and down very carefully and said nothing.

"Let me help you off with your armor. Here is your cauldron all ready. Everything is ready, the ivory stick, the warm oil, the cool-scented oil, the fleecy towel. I have acquainted myself with your bath habits."

"Where is my bath-slave?"

"Here I am."

"I mean the little girl from Tenos."

"I sent her away."

"*You* sent her away?"

"Do not blame her. She had no choice. I bribed her; she refused the bribe. I beat her. She could not refuse the beating. You will not see her until morning."

"Do you not know that you have richly earned a beating yourself for meddling with my servants?"

"I put myself into your hands, my lord. To be touched by you, even in chastisement, would be bliss. I am parched for your touch. But why not let me take your armor off and bathe you? If you still want to beat me then I am at your disposal. But right now you must be weary."

"You are a daughter of the enemy," said Diomedes. "Your presence in our tents before brought disaster upon us, cost us hundreds of men. How do I know that you have not returned with some treachery in view?"

"Oh, I have treachery in view," she said. "You are acute, my lord. I plan a massive betrayal, but of Trojans."

As she spoke she had been undoing the latchets of his breastplate. She drew off the heavy curved piece of bronze and then began to untie the bindings of his corselet.

"After your bath, when you are rested, when you have been anointed in cool scented oils, and clothed in clean garments, when you have drunk and fed, and your mind is unclouded by fatigue—then I will tell you what you most want to know. Into the cauldron now. Let me swab the battle-grime from my lord's body. You will not flinch from my touch, I warrant. It may not be soft as a mouse's paw, but you shall find it pleasant in its own way."

Later that night when all the tents were dark, Cressida told what she had done.

"To make it brief, my lord," she began, "I come to you with those secret oracles which enwrap the fate of Troy. Certain things must happen or be made to happen before you can storm those walls and sack the city."

"How did you come by such oracles? From your father, the priest? Forgive me, but I have seen him, my girl, and I do not believe he is the kind of man the gods really entrust their secrets to."

"Not from him. But from Apollo himself through his paramour, Cassandra whom the sun-god confides in even against her will."

"And she confided in you?"

"Not at all," said Cressida. "She loathes me. With good cause. No, it was her brother, Troilus, she confided in. For I, wanting to come to you, not wishing to come empty-handed, resolved to bring you a love gift you could not refuse. So I persuaded young Troilus—who finds me quite persuasive. I asked him to go to his sister, Cassandra, and make her tell him the oracles, and bring them to me."

"Why did Cassandra, who is so clever and would know the importance of such oracles to the fate of Troy, why would she entrust them to anyone else?"

"She is clever, poor girl, but she dotes on Troilus and can refuse him nothing—even as I dote on you, dear Argive brute. Besides, the poor thing is so accustomed to her prophecies being disbelieved that she is eager to cast the future for anyone who pretends belief. And this I instructed Troilus to do."

"You are a very clever girl yourself."

"Passion has sharpened my wits. Such passion shows how stupid I am. And so cleverness can come from stupidity which gives me hope I can tease some heat even out of your icy soul, king of Argos."

"The oracles!" cried Diomedes. "Tell me the oracles. What must we do to take Troy?"

"Two conditions are necessary. One of them is couched in a riddle. It says that Troy can finally fall only through an act of 'monumental piety.' And it caps this riddle with a verse.

> *Could is should,*
> *Should is would,*
> *would is wood, of course.*
> *What began with an apple*
> *Must end with a horse.*

"Too much for me," said Diomedes. "Maybe Ulysses can figure it out. He has a head for such things. What's the other one? I hope it's a little plainer, or we'll be here for another ten years."

"The other one is quite plain, quite simple. It says Troy shall not be taken unless Troilus dies today."

"Today? Then it's too late! It is after midnight; the day has passed!"

"But before it passed, young Troilus had also passed—over the Styx into Erebus where he will join all his brothers sent before him by you and Achilles."

"You mean Troilus is dead?"

"I have had a very full day," said Cressida. "Here is a little souvenir of my day."

She handed him a dagger.

"See, my lord, it is sharp, and it has been used. It is encrusted with that which should be more precious to you than jewels, the heart-blood of Troilus."

Diomedes leaped up. He was a brave man, among the bravest who ever lived, but now he was bathed in an icy sweat of horror. "You killed him!" he cried. "He loved you, and you killed him! Why you are Hecate's own handmaid, a witch out of hell!"

"For shame," she crooned. "A warrior to be so shocked at the idea of death. How many men have you killed, my lord? How many beautiful sons have you butchered and left in the dust? Why begrudge me my one which is my love gift to you? How many times have you seen a cat who loves its master bringing him a dead bird or mouse to lay at his feet as a token of this love? So I lay Troilus at your splendid feet, my master, my king, my only love. His death is the key that unlocks the gates of Troy and brings you victory—as soon as Ulysses reads the riddle of that other oracle."

"To kill an enemy in open warfare is one thing," said Diomedes. "To slip a dagger into his back while telling him how much you love him is something else."

"Foolish man," murmured Cressida. "Your enemies die in pain and terror. Troilus died in bliss. My arms were about him, my lips burned on his. He did not even feel the blade. If so happy a death could come to all men, it would lose much of its unpopularity."

THE ENd of THE WAR

This is how the prophecy was fulfilled concerning Achilles.

Priam came to his tent to beg that Hector's body be restored to him for honorable cremation. The old king humbled himself before the mighty youth, knelt at his feet and kissed the terrible hands that had killed his son. Achilles relented and promised to return the body. This kindness was to kill him. For when he bore the body to the city gate, Paris was hiding nearby. As Achilles lifted the corpse from his chariot, Paris loosed his arrow which Apollo guided to the one vulnerable spot on Achilles, the great tendon behind the right heel. The arrow cut the tendon, killing him immediately.

Achilles had kept the promise he had made to his stallions. They were burned on the same pyre and never had to know another master's hands on their reins.

Ulysses, faced with the task of unriddling the oracle, prayed to Athena for wisdom. Whether she granted him new insight or refreshed his old cunning he never knew.

"The verse ends with these words," he said to himself. " 'What began with an apple must end with a horse.' But *what* began with an apple? This war, of course. It was started by the golden apple of discord which led to the squabble among the goddesses, to the judgment of Paris, to the abduction of Helen—which led to the thousand ships at Aulis and the siege of Troy. Then the war must end with a horse, the oracle says. What horse? What kind of horse? The verse tells, no doubt. Let's see now. . . .

> *Could is should,*
> *Should is would,*
> *Would is wood, of course.*
> *What began with an apple*
> *Must end with a horse.*

"The answer is wood! A wooden horse! This is what the oracle clearly demands, leaving everything as murky as ever. What can we accomplish with a wooden horse? What do we want to accomplish? To get inside Troy, of course. Can we ride this wooden steed, jump it over the walls of Troy? Wooden horses are not noted for their speed and agility. Looking at in another way, it's not a horse but a statue. A statue? Yes! Of course! A statue to Poseidon, father of horses! That's it! A statue so big that armed men can hide in its belly and be obligingly rolled by the pious Trojans into Troy. That is what the oracle meant by 'a monumental act of piety.' It all fits."

Thereupon Ulysses set a gigantic plan afoot, the most cunning plot he had spun in all his artful career. On a beach hidden from the sight of the walls, he ordered carpenters to build an enormous wooden horse, varnishing it to a last luster, ornamenting it with gilded mane and gilded hooves. It was set on solid wooden wheels, and a trapdoor cut into its belly which was big enough to hold twenty men.

Then Ulysses, Diomedes, Menelaus, Little Ajax, and sixteen others of the best warriors hid themselves in the belly of

185   THE TROJAN WAR

the horse. They wore no armor and carried no shields lest the clanking metal betray them; they were armed only with swords and daggers. The ships were rolled down to the water and launched. Masts were stepped, sails raised, and the fleet moved out the harbor, behind a headland, out of sight. When they were hidden from view, they moored again to wait for a signal.

When the Trojans awoke the next morning, they saw no tents on the beach, no ships, no Greeks. The camp had disappeared. Even the cattle were gone, and the fires were cold. Rejoicing with loud shouts, weeping for joy, the entire population rushed out onto the beach. No one at all was to be seen. After ten years the beach was Trojan again. The war was over! It was unbelievable, yet unbearable to believe anything else.

They marveled when they found the giant wooden horse and tried to guess its purpose.

"Read what is written!" cried Chryses.

Cut into the shoulder of the horse were these words: "An offering to Poseidon by the Greeks who after ten years of war sail for home again, and beseech fair skies and following winds."

"Clearly, an offering to Poseidon," said Chryses wisely. "If we take it into the city and set it in our temple we shall be the ones to earn the favor of the earth-shaker who has been so hostile to us."

"Brilliant," said Priam. "The very thing."

"Fatal!" shrieked Cassandra. "That horse will devour Troy!"

But no one heeded her.

Another of Priam's advisers, a man named Laocoon, had other ideas, too.

"Hear me, oh King," he said. "Beware the Greeks, even bearing gifts. I mistrust this horse. I mistrust everything an enemy does. Let us take axes and chop it to pieces."

He was a very large, impressive, deep-voiced man. His words made Priam hesitate, and he might have convinced the king but Poseidon took a hand. He sent two enormous sea-serpents gliding up onto the beach. They seized the two small sons of Laocoon and began to swallow them whole. Laocoon leaped upon the serpents, but they simply looped their coils about him and crushed him to death as they finished swallowing his sons.

"Let the impious take heed!" cried Chryses. "Those serpents were sent by Poseidon to punish the sacrilegious words of Laocoon. We must honor this wooden horse dedicated to the sea-god. Bedeck it with flowers; take it into the city; and set it in our temple."

Awestruck by the fate of Laocoon, the Trojans did what Chryses had said.

That night the Greek fleet put into shore again. Under the command of Agamemnon the men disembarked and waited on the beach while, exhausted by rejoicing, the Trojans slept in their city. In the darkest hour of night Ulysses crept out. Seeing no one he tapped on the horse's belly. Diomedes and the others slipped silently out of the trapdoor. Menelaus dashed toward the palace and Helen, followed by half the men. Ulysses led the others to the wall where they surprised and killed the drowsy sentries—then set a signal fire on the wall, summoning the army. Ulysses descended, swung open the huge gates, and the main body of troops entered Troy.

The old tales go to great lengths now giving the names of Trojans slaughtered in the sack of the city and the manner of their death. But it is sufficient to say that the men were butchered, houses looted and burned and, finally, the women and children borne off into slavery.

Andromache ended up as a slave to Neoptolemus, said to have been Achilles' son by one of the princesses of Scyros. He would have been much younger than Andromache, but it

must be remembered that his father, Achilles, had been full grown at the age of ten, and this precocity may have run in the family.

Of all the Trojan princes Aeneas was the only one to escape the massacre. Heedless of his own safety, he lifted his old father, Anchises, to his shoulders, and carried him through the burning city. And the Greeks were so struck by his courage that they let him go.

He boarded a ship and sailed away into a series of strange adventures. After years of hardship and incredible danger he came to a fair land and founded a city later to be called Rome.

Cassandra was taken back to Mycenae as Agamemnon's slave, but was murdered by his wife, Clytemnestra, on the same night she knifed her husband in his bath. Cassandra had warned Agamemnon this would happen, but he didn't believe her until it was too late.

Paris was presumed dead after the sack of Troy. But some say he fled and lived under other names in other lands, protected always by Aphrodite. He still lives, some say, still works as love's own thief and is to be found somewhere in the neighborhood whenever a beautiful woman leaves a dull husband.

Helen went back to Sparta with Menelaus and lived happily there as queen. She explained to her husband that she had been abducted by force, kept in Troy against her will, and he chose to be convinced. She kept her beauty always and was much admired by the princes of Hellas who often found occasion to visit the royal palace in Sparta, and stayed overnight.

Cressida disappears from legend after the war. It is believed that she was taken to Argos by Diomedes, but what happened to her there nobody knows.

The flames that consumed Troy burned for seven years

and were the color of blood. They burned so hotly, these blood-red flames, that the Scamander turned to steam and hissed away. And Poseidon himself retreated from their awful heat shrinking his sea. Where the beautiful waters of Troy's harbor once flowed is now a parched and empty plain.

II

THE ADVENTURES
OF ULYSSES

ships and men

After Troy was burned, Ulysses sailed for home with three ships holding fifty men each.

Three thousand years ago ships were very different; through the years they have changed much more than the men who sail them.

These beaked warships used by the pirate kingdoms of the Middle Sea were like no vessels you have ever seen. Imagine a very long narrow rowboat with twenty oars on each side. The timbers of the bow curve sharply to a prow, and this prow grows longer and sharper, becomes in fact a long polished shaft tipped by a knife-edged brass spearhead. This was called the ram, the chief weapon of ancient warships.

In battle, the opposing ships spun about each other, swooping forward, twirling on their beams, darting backward, their narrow hulls allowing them to backwater very swiftly. The object was to ram the enemy before he rammed you. And to ram first was the only defense, for the brass beak of the ramming ship sheared easily through the timbers of its victim, knocking a huge hole in the hull and sinking it before its men could jump overboard.

These warships were also equipped with sail and mast—used only for voyaging, never in battle—a square sail, and a short mast, held fast by oxhide stays. The sail was raised only for a fair wind, or could be tilted slightly for a quartering wind, but was useless against headwinds.

This meant that these ships were almost always at the mercy of the weather, and were often blown off course. Another thing that made them unfit for long voyages was the lack of cargo space. Only a few days' supply of food and water could be carried, leaving space for no other cargo. That is why these fighting ships tried to hug the coast and avoid the open sea.

Ulysses' problem was made worse by victory. When Troy was sacked, he and his men captured a huge booty—gold and jewels, silks, furs—and, after ten years of war, the men refused to leave any loot behind. This meant that each of his ships could carry food and water for a very few days.

This greed for treasure caused many of his troubles at first. But then troubles came so thick and fast that no one could tell what caused them; hardships were simply called bad luck, or the anger of the gods.

But bad luck makes good stories.

THE CICONIANS

The voyage began peacefully. A fair northeast wind blew, filling the sails of the little fleet and pushing it steadily homeward. The wind freshened at night, and the three ships scudded along joyfully under a fat moon.

On the morning of the second day Ulysses saw a blue haze of smoke and a glint of white stone. He put in toward shore and saw a beautiful little town. The men stared in amazement at this city without walls, rich with green parks and grazing cattle, its people strolling about in white tunics. Ten years of war had made Ulysses' men as savage as wolves. Everyone not a shipmate was an enemy. To meet was to fight; property belonged to the winner.

Ulysses stood in the bow, shading his eyes with his hand, gazing at the city. A tough, crafty old warrior named Eurylochus stood beside him.

"We attack, do we not?" he asked. "The city lies there defenseless. We can take it without losing a man."

"Yes, it looks tempting," said Ulysses. "But the wind blows fair, and good fortune attends us. Perhaps it will spoil our luck to stop."

"But this fat little city has been thrown into our laps by the gods, too," said Eurylochus, "and they grow angry when men refuse their gifts. It would be bad luck *not* to attack."

Ulysses heard the fierce murmur of his men behind him, and felt their greed burning in his veins. He hailed the other ships and gave orders, and the three black-hulled vessels swerved toward shore and nosed into the harbor, swooping down upon the white city like wolves upon a sheepfold.

They landed on the beach. The townsfolk fled before them into the hills. Ulysses did not allow his men to pursue them, for there was no room on the ship for slaves. From house to house the armed men went, helping themselves to whatever they wanted. Afterward they piled the booty in great heaps upon the beach.

Then Ulysses had them round up a herd of the plump, swaying, crook-horned cattle, and offer ten bulls in sacrifice to the gods. Later they built huge bonfires on the beach, roasted the cattle, and had a great feast.

But while the looting and feasting was going on the men of the city had withdrawn into the hills and called together their kinsmen of the villages, the Ciconians, and began preparing for battle. They were skillful fighters, these men of the hills. They drove brass war chariots that had long blades attached to the wheels, and these blades whirled swiftly as the wheels turned, scything down the foe.

They gathered by the thousands, an overwhelming force, and stormed down out of the hills onto the beach. Ulysses' men were full of food and wine, unready to fight, but he had posted sentries, who raised a shout when they saw the Ciconians coming down from the hills in the moonlight. Ulysses raged among his men, slapping them with the flat of his sword, driving the fumes of wine out of their heads. His great racketing battle cry roused those he could not whip with his sword.

The men closed ranks and met the Ciconians at spearpoint. The Hellenes retreated slowly, leaving their treasure where it was heaped upon the beach and, keeping their line unbroken, made for their ships.

Ulysses chose two of his strongest men and bade them lift a thick timber upon their shoulders. He sat astride this timber, high enough to shoot his arrows over the heads of his men. He was the most skillful archer since Heracles. He aimed only at the chariot horses, and aimed not to kill, but to cripple, so that the horses fell in their traces, and their furious flailing and kicking broke the enemy's advance.

Thus the Hellenes were able to reach their ships and roll them into the water, leap into the rowers' benches, and row away. But eighteen men were left dead on the beach—six from each ship—and there was scarcely a man unwounded.

Eurylochus threw himself on his knees before Ulysses and said, "I advised you badly, O Chief. We have angered the gods. Perhaps, if you kill me, they will be appeased."

"Eighteen dead are enough for one night," said Ulysses. "Our luck has changed, but what has changed can change again. Rise, and go about your duties."

The ships had been handled roughly in the swift retreat

from the Ciconian beach. Their hulls had been battered by axes and flung spears, and they had sprung small leaks. The wind had faded to a whisper, and the men were forced to row with water sloshing around their ankles. Ulysses saw that his ships were foundering, and that he would have to empty the holds. Food could not be spared, nor water; the only thing that could go was the treasure taken from Troy. The men groaned and tore at their beards as they saw the gold and jewels and bales of fur and silk being dropped overboard. But Ulysses cast over his own share of the treasure first—and his was the largest share—so the men had to bite back their rage and keep on rowing.

As the necklaces, bracelets, rings, and brooches sank slowly, winking their jewels like drowned fires, a strange thing happened. A shoal of naiads—beautiful water nymphs—were drawn by the flash of the jewels. They dived after the bright baubles and swam alongside the ships, calling to the men, singing, tweaking the oars out of their hands, for they were sleek mischievous creatures who loved jewels and strangers. Some of them came riding dolphins, and in the splashing silver veils of spray the men thought they saw beautiful girls with fishtails. This is probably how the first report of mermaids arose.

Poseidon, God of the Sea, was wakened from sleep by the sound of this laughter. When he saw what was happening, his green beard bristled with rage, and he said to himself, "Can it be? Are these the warriors whom I helped in their siege of Troy? Is this their gratitude, trying to steal my naiads from me? I'll teach them manners."

He whistled across the horizon to his son, Aeolus, keeper of the winds, who twirled his staff and sent a northeast gale skipping across the sea. It pounced upon the little fleet and scattered the ships like twigs. Ulysses clung to the helm, trying to hold the kicking tiller, trying to shout over the wind.

THE ADVENTURES OF ULYSSES

There was nothing to do but ship the mast and let the wind take them.

And the wind, in one huge gust of fury, drove them around Cythera, the southernmost of their home islands, into the open waters of the southwest quarter of the Middle Sea, toward the hump of Africa called Libya.

THE lOTUS—EATERS

Now, at this time, the shore of Libya was known as "the land where Morpheus plays."

Who was Morpheus? He was a young god, son of Hypnos, God of Sleep, and nephew of Hades. It was his task to fly around the world, from nightfall to dawn, scattering sleep. His father, Hypnos, mixed the colors of sleep for him, making them dark and thick and sad.

"For," he said, "it is a little death you lay upon man each night, my son, to prepare him for the kingdom of death."

But his aunt, Persephone, sewed him a secret pocket, full of bright things, and said: "It is not death you scatter, but repose. Hang the walls of sleep with bright pictures, so that man may not know death before he dies."

These bright pictures were called dreams. And Morpheus became fascinated by the way a little corner of man's mind remained awake in sleep, and played with the colors he had hung, mixing them, pulling them apart, making new pictures. It seemed to him that these fantastic colored shadows the sleepers painted were the most beautiful, most puzzling things he had ever seen. And he wanted to know more about how they came to be.

He went to Persephone, and said, "I need a flower that makes sleep. It must be purple and black. But there should be one petal streaked with fire-red, the petal to make dreams."

Persephone smiled and moved her long white hand in the air. Between her fingers a flower blossomed. She gave it to him.

"Here it is, Morpheus. Black and purple like sleep, with one petal of fire-red for dreams. We will call it lotus."

Morpheus took the flower and planted it in Libya, where it is always summer. The flower grew in clusters, smelling deliciously of honey. The people ate nothing else. They slept all the time, except when they were gathering flowers. Morpheus watched over them, reading their dreams.

It was toward Lotusland that Ulysses and his men were blown by the gale. The wind fell while they were still offshore. The sky cleared, the sea calmed, a hot sun beat down. To Ulysses, dizzy with fatigue, weak with hunger, the sky and the water and the air between seemed to flow together in one hot blueness.

He shook his head, trying to shake away the hot blue haze, and growled to his men to unship the oars, and row toward land. The exhausted men bent to the oars, and the ships crawled over the fire-blue water. With their last strength they pulled the ships up on the beach, past the high-tide mark, and then lay down and went to sleep.

As they slept, the Lotus-eaters came out of the forest. Their arms were heaped with flowers, which they piled about the sleeping men in great blue and purple bouquets, so that they might have flowers to eat when they awoke, for these people were very gentle and hospitable.

The men awoke and smelled the warm honey smell of the

flowers, and ate them in great handfuls—like honeycomb—
and fell asleep again. Morpheus hovered over the sleeping
men and read their dreams.

"These men have done terrible things," the god whispered
to himself. "Their dreams are full of gold and blood and fire.
Such sleep will not rest them."

And he mixed them some cool green and silver dreams of
home. The nightmares faded. Wounded Trojans stopped
screaming, Troy stopped burning; they saw their wives smile,
heard their children laugh, saw the green wheat growing in
their own fields. They dreamed of home, awoke and were
hungry, ate the honeyed lotus flowers and fell into a deeper
sleep.

Then Morpheus came to Ulysses who was stretched on the
sand, a little apart from the rest. He studied his face—the
wide grooved brow, the sunken eyes, the red hair, the jutting
chin. And he said to himself, "This man is a hero. Terrible
are his needs, sudden his deeds, and his dreams must be his
own. I cannot help him."

So Morpheus mixed no colors for Ulysses' sleep, but let
him dream his own dreams, and read them as they came. He
hovered above the sleeping king and could not leave.

"What monsters he makes," he said to himself. "Look at
that giant with the single eye in the middle of his forehead.
And that terrible spider-woman with all those legs. . . . Ah,
the things he dreams, this angry sleeper. What bloody
mouths, what masts falling, sails ripping, what rocks and
reefs, what shipwrecks . . . how many deaths?"

Ulysses awoke, choking, out of a terrible nightmare. It
seemed to him that in his sleep he had seen the whole voyage
laid out before him, had seen his ships sinking, his men
drowning. Monsters had crowded about him, clutching,
writhing. He sat up and looked about. His men lay asleep
among heaped flowers. As he watched, one opened his eyes,

raised himself on an elbow, took a handful of flowers, stuffed them into his mouth, and immediately fell asleep again.

Ulysses smelled the honey sweetness, and felt an over-powering hunger. He took some of the flowers and raised them to his mouth. As their fragrance grew stronger, he felt his eyelids drooping, and his arms grew heavy, and he thought, "It is these flowers that are making us sleep. Their scent alone brings sleep. I must not eat them."

But he could not put them down; his hand would not obey him. Exerting all the bleak force of his will, he grasped his right hand with his left—as if it belonged to someone else—and one by one forced open his fingers and let the flowers fall.

Then he dragged himself to his feet and walked slowly into the sea. He went under and arose snorting. His head had cleared. But when he went up on the beach, the sweet fragrance rose like an ether and made him dizzy again.

"I must work swiftly," he said.

One by one he carried the sleeping men to the ships, and propped them on their benches. His strength was going. The honey smell was invading him, making him droop with sleep. He took his knife and, cutting sharp splinters of wood to prop open his eyelids, staggered back among the men. He worked furiously now, lifting them on his shoulders, carrying them two at a time, throwing them into the ships.

Finally, the beach was cleared. The men lolled sleeping upon the benches. Then, all by himself, using his last strength, he pushed the ships into the water. When the ships were afloat in the shallow water, he lashed one to another with rawhide line, his own ship in front. Then he raised his sail and took the helm.

The wind was blowing from the southwest. It filled his sail. The line grew taut; the file of ships moved away from Lotusland.

The men began to awake from their dreams of home, and found themselves upon the empty sea again. But the long sleep had rested them, and they took up their tasks with new strength.

Ulysses kept the helm, grim and unsmiling. For he knew that what he had seen painted on the walls of his sleep was meant to come true, and that he was sailing straight into a nightmare.

тHE cyclops's cAVE

After he had rescued his crew from Lotusland, Ulysses found that he was running from one trouble into another. They were still at sea, and there was no food for the fleet. The men were hungry and getting dangerous. Ulysses heard them grumbling: "He should have left us there in Lotusland. At least when you're asleep you don't know you're hungry. Why did he have to come and wake us up?" He knew that unless he found food for them very soon he would be facing a mutiny.

That part of the Aegean Sea was dotted with islands. On every one of them was a different kind of enemy. The last thing Ulysses wanted to do was to go ashore, but there was no other way of getting food. He made a landfall on a small mountainous island. He was very careful; he had the ships of the fleet moor offshore and selected twelve of his bravest men as a landing party.

They beached their skiff and struck inland. It was a wild hilly place, full of boulders, with very few trees. It seemed deserted. Then Ulysses glimpsed something moving across the valley, on the slope of a hill. He was too far off to see what they were, but he thought they must be goats since the hill was so steep. And if they were goats they had to be caught. So the men headed downhill, meaning to cross the valley and climb the slope.

Ulysses had no way of knowing it, but this was the very worst island in the entire sea on which the small party could have landed. For here lived the Cyclopes, huge savage creatures, tall as trees, each with one eye in the middle of his forehead. Once, long ago, they had lived in the bowels of Olympus, forging thunderbolts for Zeus. But he had punished them for some fault, exiling them to this island where they had forgotten all their smithcraft and did nothing but fight with each other for the herds of wild goats, trying to find enough food to fill their huge bellies. Best of all, they liked storms; storms meant shipwrecks. Shipwrecks meant sailors struggling in the sea, who could be plucked out and eaten raw; and the thing they loved best in the world was human flesh. The largest and the fiercest and the hungriest of all the Cyclopes on the island was one named Polyphemus. He kept constant vigil on his mountain, fair weather or foul. If he spotted a ship, and there was no storm to help, he would dive into the sea and swim underwater, coming up underneath the ship and overturning it. Then he would swim off with his pockets full of sailors.

On this day he could not believe his luck when he saw a boat actually landing on the beach, and thirteen meaty-looking sailors disembark, and begin to march toward his cave. But here they were, climbing out of the valley now, up the slope of the hill, right toward the cave. He realized they must be hunting his goats.

THE ADVENTURES OF ULYSSES

The door of the cave was an enormous slab of stone. He shoved this aside so that the cave stood invitingly open, casting a faint glow of firelight upon the dusk. Over the fire, on a great spit, eight goats were turning and roasting. The delicious savors of the cooking drifted from the cave. Polyphemus lay down behind a huge boulder and waited.

The men were halfway up the slope of the hill when they smelled the meat roasting. They broke into a run. Ulysses tried to restrain them, but they paid no heed—they were too hungry. They raced to the mouth of the cave and dashed in. Ulysses drew his sword and hurried after them. When he saw the huge fireplace and the eight goats spitted like sparrows, his heart sank because he knew that they had come into reach of something much larger than themselves. However, the men were giving no thought to anything but food; they flung themselves on the spit, and tore into the goat meat, smearing their hands and faces with sizzling fat, too hungry to feel pain as they crammed the hot meat into their mouths.

There was a loud rumbling sound; the cave darkened. Ulysses whirled around. He saw that the door had been closed. The far end of the cavern was too dark to see anything, but then—amazed, aghast—he saw what looked like a huge red lantern far above, coming closer. Then he saw the great shadow of a nose under it, and the gleam of teeth. He realized that the lantern was a great flaming eye. Then he saw the whole giant, tall as a tree, with huge fingers reaching out of the shadows, fingers bigger than baling hooks. They closed around two sailors and hauled them screaming into the air.

As Ulysses and his horrified men watched, the great hand bore the struggling little men to the giant's mouth. He ate them, still wriggling, the way a cat eats a grasshopper; he ate them clothes and all, growling over their raw bones.

The men had fallen to their knees and were whimpering

like terrified children, but Ulysses stood there, sword in hand, his agile brain working more swiftly than it ever had before.

"Greetings," he called. "May I know to whom we are indebted for such hospitality?"

The giant belched and spat buttons. "I am Polyphemus," he growled. "This is my cave, my mountain, and everything that comes here is mine. I do hope you can all stay to dinner. There are just enough of you to make a meal. Ho, ho. . . ." And he laughed a great, choking phlegmy laugh, swiftly lunged, and caught another sailor, whom he lifted into the air and held before his face.

"Wait!" cried Ulysses.

"What for?"

"You won't enjoy him that way. He is from Attica, where the olives grow. He was raised on olives and has a very delicate oily flavor. But to appreciate it, you must taste the wine of the country."

"Wine? What is wine?"

"It is a drink. Made from pressed grapes. Have you never drunk it?"

"We drink nothing but ox blood and buttermilk here."

"Ah, you do not know what you have missed, gentle Polyphemus. Meat-eaters, in particular, love wine. Here, try it for yourself."

Ulysses unslung from his belt a full flask of unwatered wine. He gave it to the giant, who put it to his lips and gulped. He coughed violently, and stuck the sailor in a little niche high up in the cave wall, then leaned his great slab of a face toward Ulysses and said:

"What did you say this drink was?"

"Wine. A gift of the gods to man, to make women look better and food taste better. And now it is my gift to you."

"It's good, very good." He put the bottle to his lips and

swallowed again. "You are very polite. What's your name?"

"My name? Why I am—nobody."

"Nobody. . . . Well, Nobody, I like you. You're a good fellow. And do you know what I'm going to do? I'm going to save you till last. Yes, I'll eat all your friends first, and give you extra time, that's what I'm going to do."

Ulysses looked up into the great eye and saw that it was redder than ever. It was all a swimming redness. He had given the monster, who had never drunk spirits before, undiluted wine. Surely it must make him sleepy. But was a gallon enough for that great gullet? Enough to put him to sleep—or would he want to eat again first?

"Eat 'em all up, Nobody—save you till later. Sleep a little first. Shall I? Won't try to run away, will you? No—you can't, can't open the door—too heavy, ha, ha. . . . You take a nap too, Nobody. I'll wake you for breakfast. Breakfast. . . ."

The great body crashed full-length on the cave floor, making the very walls of the mountain shake. Polyphemus lay on his back, snoring like a powersaw. The sailors were still on the floor, almost dead from fear.

"Up!" cried Ulysses. "Stand up like men! Do what must be done! Or you will be devoured like chickens."

He got them to their feet and drew them about him as he explained his plan.

"Listen now, and listen well, for we have no time. I made him drunk, but we cannot tell how long it will last."

Ulysses thrust his sword into the fire; they saw it glow white-hot.

"There are ten of us," he said. "Two of us have been eaten, and one of our friends is still unconscious up there on his shelf of rock. You four get on one side of his head, and the rest on the other side. When I give the word, lay hold of the ear on your side, each of you. And hang on, no matter how he thrashes, for I am going to put out his eye. And if I am to be sure of my stroke you must hold his head still. One stroke is all I will be allowed."

Then Ulysses rolled a boulder next to the giant's head and climbed on it, so that he was looking down into the eye. It was lidless and misted with sleep—big as a furnace door and glowing softly like a banked fire. Ulysses looked at his men. They had done what he said, broken into two parties, one group at each ear. He lifted his white-hot sword.

"Now!" he cried.

Driving down with both hands, and all the strength of his back and shoulders, and all his rage and all his fear, Ulysses stabbed the glowing spike into the giant's eye.

His sword jerked out of his hand as the head flailed upward, men pelted to the ground as they lost their hold. A huge screeching curdling bellow split the air.

"This way!" shouted Ulysses.

He motioned to his men, and they crawled on their bellies toward the far end of the cave where the herd of goats were tethered. They slipped into the herd and lay among the goats as the giant stomped about the cave, slapping the walls with great blows of his hands, picking up boulders and cracking them together in agony, splitting them to flinders, clutching his eye, a scorched hole now from which the brown blood jelled. He moaned and gibbered and bellowed in frightful pain; his groping hand found the sailor in the wall, and he tore him to pieces between his fingers. Ulysses could not even hear the man scream because the giant was bellowing so.

Now Ulysses saw that the Cyclops's wild stampeding was giving place to a plan. For now he was stamping on the floor in a regular pattern, trying to find and crush them beneath his feet. He stopped moaning and listened. The sudden silence dazed the men with fear. They held their breath and

tried to muffle the sound of their beating hearts; all the giant heard was the breathing of the goats. Then Ulysses saw him go to the mouth of the cave, and swing the great slab aside, and stand there. He realized just in time that the goats would rush outside, which is what the giant wanted, for then he could search the whole cave.

Ulysses whispered, "Quickly, swing under the bellies of the rams. Hurry, hurry!"

Luckily, they were giant goats and thus able to carry the men who had swung themselves under their bellies and were clinging to the wiry wool. Ulysses himself chose the largest ram. They moved toward the mouth of the cave, and crowded through. The Cyclops's hands came down and brushed across the goats' backs feeling for the men, but the animals were huddled too closely together for him to reach between and search under their bellies. So he let them pass through.

Now, the Cyclops rushed to the corner where the goats had been tethered, and stamped, searched, and roared through the whole cave again, bellowing with fury when he did not find them. The herd grazed on the slope of the hill beneath the cave. There was a full moon; it was almost as bright as day.

"Stay where you are," Ulysses whispered.

He heard a crashing, peered out, and saw great shadowy figures converging on the cave. He knew that the other Cyclopes of the island must have heard the noise and come to see. He heard the giant bellow.

The others called to him: "Who has done it? Who has blinded you?"

"Nobody. Nobody did it. Nobody blinded me."

"Ah, you have done it yourself. What a tragic accident."

And they went back to their own caves.

"Now!" said Ulysses. "Follow me!"

He swung himself out from under the belly of the ram,

and raced down the hill. The others raced after him. They were halfway across the valley when they heard great footsteps rushing after them, and Polyphemus bellowing nearer and nearer.

"He's coming!" cried Ulysses. "Run for your lives!"

They ran as they had never run before, but the giant could cover fifty yards at a stride. It was only because he could not see and kept bumping into trees and rocks that they were able to reach the skiff and push out on the silver water before Polyphemus burst out of the grove of trees and rushed onto the beach. They bent to the oars, and the boat scudded toward the fleet.

Polyphemus heard the dip of the oars and the groaning of the oarlocks, and, aiming at the sound, hurled huge boulders after them. They fell around the ship, but did not hit. The skiff reached Ulysses' ship, and the sailors climbed aboard.

"Haul anchor, and away!" cried Ulysses. And then called to the Cyclops, "Poor fool! Poor blinded drunken gluttonous fool—if anyone else asks you, it is not Nobody, but Ulysses who has done this to you."

But he was to regret this final taunt. The gods honor courage, but punish pride.

Polyphemus, wild with rage, waded out chest-deep and hurled a last boulder, which hit mid-deck, almost sunk the ship, and killed most of the crew—among them seven of the nine men who had just escaped.

And Polyphemus prayed to Poseidon, "God of the Sea, I beg you, punish Ulysses for this. Visit him with storm and shipwreck and sorceries. Let him wander many years before he reaches home, and when he gets there let him find himself forgotten, unwanted, a stranger."

Poseidon heard this prayer, and made it all happen just that way.

keeper of the winds

Now the black ships beat their way northward from the land of the Cyclopes. And Ulysses, ignorant of the mighty curse that the blind giant had fastened upon him, was beginning to hope that they might have fair sailing the rest of the way home. So impatient was he that he took the helm himself and kept it night and day although his sailors pleaded with him to take some rest. But he was wild with eagerness to get home to his wife, Penelope, to his young son Telemachus, and to the dear land of Ithaca that he had not seen for more than ten years now.

At the end of the third night, just as the first light was staining the sky, he saw something very strange—a wall of bronze, tall and wide, floating on the sea and blocking their way. At first he thought it was a trick of the light, and he rubbed his eyes and looked again. But there it was, a towering bright wall of beaten bronze.

"Well," he thought to himself, "it cannot stretch across the sea. There must be a way to get around it."

He began to sail along the wall as though it were the shore of an island, trying to find his way around. Finally, he came to a huge gate, and even as he gazed upon it in amazement, the gate swung open and the wind changed abruptly. The shrouds snapped, the sails bulged, the masts groaned, and all three ships of the fleet were blown through the gate, which immediately clanged shut behind them. Once within the wall, the wind fell off and Ulysses found his ship drifting toward a beautiful hilly island. Suddenly there was a great howling of wind. The sun was blown out like a candle. Darkness fell upon the waters. Ulysses felt the deck leap beneath him as the ship was lifted halfway out of the water by the ferocious gust and hurled through the blackness. He tried to shout, but the breath was torn from his mouth and he lost consciousness.

Ulysses had no way of knowing this, but the mischievous Poseidon had guided his ships to the island fortress of Aeolus, Keeper of the Winds. Ages before, when the world was very new, the gods had become fearful of the terrible strength of the winds, and had decided to tame them. So Zeus and Poseidon, working together, had floated an island upon the sea, and girdled it about with a mighty bronze wall. Then they set a mountain upon the island and hollowed out that mountain until it was a huge stone dungeon. Into this hollow mountain they stuffed the struggling winds, and appointed Aeolus as their jailer. And there the winds were held captive. Whenever the gods wanted to stir up a storm and needed a particular wind, they sent a message to Aeolus, who would draw his sword and stab the side of the mountain, making a hole big enough for the wind to fly through. If the north wind were wanted, he stabbed the north side of the mountain, its east slope for the east wind, and so on. When the storm was done, he would whistle the wind home, and the huge brawling gale, broken by its imprisonment, would crawl back whimpering to its hole.

Aeolus was an enormously fat demigod with a long wind-tangled beard and a red wind-beaten face. He loved to eat and drink, and fight, play games, and hear stories. Twelve children he had, six boys and six girls. He sent them out one by one, riding the back of the wind around the world, managing the weather for each month.

And it was in the great castle of Aeolus that Ulysses and his men found themselves when they awoke from their enchanted sleep. Invisible hands held torches for them, guided them to the baths, anointed them with oil, and gave them fresh clothing. Then the floating torches led them to the dining hall, where they were greeted by Aeolus and his twelve handsome children. A mighty banquet was laid before them, and they ate like starved men.

Then Aeolus said, "Strangers, you are my guests—uninvited—but guests all the same. By the look of you, you have had adventures and should have fine stories to tell. Yes, I love a tale full of fighting and blood and tricks, and if you have such to tell, then I shall entertain you royally. But if you are such men as sit dumb, glowering, unwilling to please, using your mouths only to stuff food into—then—well, then you are apt to find things less pleasant. You, Captain!" he roared, pointing at Ulysses. "You, sir—I take you for the leader of this somewhat motley crew. Do you have a story to tell?"

"For those who know how to listen, I have a tale to tell," said Ulysses.

"Your name?"

"Ulysses—of Ithaca."

"Mmm—yes," said Aeolus. "I seem to recognize that name —believe I heard it on Olympus while my uncles and aunts up there were quarreling about some little skirmish they had interested themselves in. Near Troy I think it was. . . . Yes-s-s. . . . Were you there?"

"I was there," said Ulysses. "I was there for ten years, dear host, and indeed took part in some of that petty skirmishing that will be spoken of by men who love courage when this bronze wall and this island, and you and yours, have vanished under the sea and have been forgotten for a thousand years. I am Ulysses. My companions before Troy were Achilles,

Menelaus, Agamemnon, mighty heroes all, and, in modesty, I was not least among them."

"Yes-s-s. . . ." said Aeolus. "You are bold enough. Too bold for your own good, perhaps. But you have caught my attention, Captain. I am listening. Tell on. . . ."

Then Ulysses told of the Trojan War; of the abduction of Helen, and the chase, and the great battles; the attacks, the retreats, the separate duels. He spoke of Achilles fighting Hector, and killing him with a spear thrust, of Paris ambushing Achilles; and, finally, how he himself had made a great hollow wooden horse and had the Greek armies pretend to leave, only to sneak back and hide in the belly of the horse. He told how the Trojans had dragged the horse within their gates, and how the Greek warriors had crept out at night and taken the city and slaughtered their enemies.

Aeolus shouted with laughter. His face blazed and his belly shook. "Ah, that's a trick after my own heart!" he cried. "You're a sharp one, you are. . . . I knew you had a foxy look about you. Wooden horse—ho ho! Tell more! Tell more!"

Then Ulysses told of his wanderings after the fall of Troy, of his adventure in Lotusland, and what had happened in the Cyclops's cave. And when Aeolus heard how he had outwitted Polyphemus and blinded his single eye, he struck the table with a mighty blow of his fist, and shouted, "Marvelous! A master stroke! By the gods, you are the bravest, craftiest warrior that has ever drunk my wine." He was especially pleased because he had always hated Polyphemus. He had no way of knowing, of course, that the blinded Cyclops had prayed to his father and had laid a curse on Ulysses, and that he, Aeolus, was being made the instrument of that curse. He did not know this, for the gods move in mysterious ways. And so he roared with laughter, and shouted, "You have pleased me, Ulysses. You have told me a brave tale, a tale full of blood and tricks. . . . And now I shall grant you any favor within my power. Speak out, Ulysses. Ask what you will."

"But one thing I seek, generous Aeolus," said Ulysses, "your help. I need your help in getting home. For it has been a long weary time since we saw our homes and our families. Our hearts thirst for the sight of Ithaca."

"No one can help you better than I," said Aeolus. "You sail on ships, and I am Keeper of the Winds. Come with me."

He led Ulysses out into the night. A hot orange moon rode low in the sky, and they could see without torches. Aeolus led him to the mountain, carrying his sword in one hand and a great leather bag in the other. He stabbed the side of the mountain. There was a rushing, sobbing sound; he clapped his leather bag over the hole, and Ulysses, amazed, saw the great bag flutter and fill. Aeolus held its neck closed, strode to the east face of the mountain, and stabbed again. As the east wind rushed out, he caught it in his sack. Then he stomped to the south slope and stabbed again, and caught the south wind in the sack. Now, very carefully, he wound a silver wire about the neck of the sack. It was full now, swollen, tugging at his arm like a huge leather balloon, trying to fly away.

He said, "In this bag are the north wind, the south wind, and the east wind. You must keep them prisoner. But if you wish to change course—if a pirate should chase you, say, or a sea monster, or if an adventure beckons, then you open the bag very carefully—you and you alone, Captain—and whistle up the wind you wish, let just a breath of it out, close the bag quickly again, and tie it tight. For winds grow swiftly— that is their secret—and so they must be carefully guarded."

"I shall not change course," said Ulysses. "No matter what enemy threatens or what adventure beckons, I sail straight for Ithaca. I shall not open your bag of winds."

"Good," said Aeolus. "Then bind it to your mast, and guard it yourself, sword in hand; let none of your men approach, lest they open it unwittingly. In the meantime, I will send the gentle west wind to follow your ship and fill your sails and take you home."

"Thank you, great Aeolus, thank you, kindly keeper of the winds. I know now that the gods have answered my prayers, and I shall be able to cease this weary heartbreaking drifting over the face of the sea, having my men killed and eaten, my ships destroyed, and my hopes shattered. I will never cease thanking you, Aeolus, till the day I die."

"May that sad occasion be far off," said Aeolus politely. "Now, sir, much as I like your company, you had better gather your men and go. I shall be uneasy now until my winds return to me and I can shut them in the mountain again."

Ulysses returned to the castle and called together his men. Gladly they trooped down to the ships and went aboard. Ulysses bound the great leather sack to the mast and warned his crew that no man must touch it on pain of death. Then he himself stood with naked sword under the mast, guarding the sack.

"Up anchor!" he cried.

The west wind rolled off the mountain and filled their sails. The black ships slipped out of the harbor. Away from the island they sailed, away from the mountain and the castle, toward the wall of bronze. When they reached the wall, the great gate swung open and they sailed eastward over water oily with moonlight. Eastward they sailed for nine days and nine nights. In perfect weather they skimmed along, the west wind hovering behind them, keeping their sails full, pushing them steadily home.

And for nine nights and nine days, Ulysses did not sleep; he did not close his eyes or sheath his sword. He kept his station under the mast—food and drink were brought to him there—and never for an instant stopped guarding the sack.

Then, finally, on the morning of the ninth day, he heard the lookout cry, "Land Ho!" and strained his eyes to see. What he saw made his heart swell. Tears coursed down his face, but they were tears of joy. For he saw the dear familiar hills of home. He saw the brown fields of Ithaca, the twisted olive trees, and, as he watched, he saw them even more clearly, saw the white marble columns of his own castle on the cliff. And his men, watching, saw the smoke rising from their own chimneys.

When Ulysses saw the white columns of his palace, he knew that unless the west wind failed, they would be home in an hour, but the friendly wind blew steadily as ever. Ulysses heaved a great sigh. The terrible tension that had kept him awake for nine days and nights eased its grip. He raised his arms and yawned. Then he leaned against the mast and closed his eyes, just for a minute.

Two of the men, standing in the bow, saw him slump at the foot of the mast, fast asleep. Their eyes traveled up the mast to the great leather bag, plump as a balloon, straining against its bonds as the impatient winds wrestled inside. Then Poseidon, swimming invisibly alongside, clinked his golden armlets. The men heard the clinking, and thought it came from the bag.

One man said to the other: "Do you hear that? Those are coins, heavy golden coins, clinking against each other. There must be a fortune in that sack."

The other man said, "Yes, a fortune that should belong to all of us by rights. We shared the danger and should share the loot."

"It is true," said the first, "that he has always been generous. He shared the spoils of Troy."

"Yes, but that was then. Why does he not divide this great

sack of treasure? Aeolus gave it to him, and we know how rich he is. Aeolus gave it to him as a guest gift, and he should share it with us."

"He never will. Whatever is in that bag, he does not mean for us to see it. Did you not observe how he has been guarding it all these nights and all these days, standing there always, eating and drinking where he stands, never sheathing his sword?"

"It is in his sheath now," said the second sailor. "And his eyes are closed. Look—he sleeps like a babe. I doubt that anything would wake him."

"What are you doing? What are you going to do with that knife? Are you out of your mind?"

"Yes—out of my mind with curiosity, out of my mind with gold fever, if you must know. Ulysses lies asleep. His sword sleeps in its sheath. And I mean to see what is in that bag."

"Wait, I'll help you. But you must give me half."

"Come then. . . ."

Swiftly and silently the two barefooted sailors padded to the mast, slashed the rope that bound the bag to the spar, and bore it away.

"Hurry—open it!"

"I can't. This wire's twisted in a strange knot. Perhaps a magic knot. It won't come out."

"Then we'll do it this way!" cried the sailor with the knife, and struck at the leather bag, slashing it open. He was immediately lifted off his feet and blown like a leaf off the deck and into the sea as the winds rushed howling out of the bag and began to chase each other around the ship. The winds screamed and jeered and laughed, growing, leaping, reveling in their freedom, roaring and squabbling, screeching around and around the ship. They fell on their gentle brother, the west wind, and cuffed him mercilessly until he fled; then they chased each other around the ship again, spinning it like a cork in a whirlpool.

Then, as they heard the far summoning whistle of the Keeper of the Winds—far, far to the west on the Aeolian Island—they snarled with rage and roared boisterously homeward, snatching the ships along with them, ripping their sails to shreds, snapping their masts like twigs, and hurling the splintered hulls westward over the boiling sea.

Ulysses awoke from his sleep to find the blue sky black with clouds and his home island dropping far astern, out of sight. He saw his crew flung about the deck like dolls, and the tattered sails and the broken spars, and he did not know whether he was awake or asleep—whether this was some nightmare of loss, or whether he was awake now and had slept before, dreaming a fair dream of home. Whichever it was, he began to understand that he was being made the plaything of great powers.

With the unleased winds screaming behind him at gale force the trip back to where they had started took them only two days. And once again the black ships were hurled onto the island of the winds. Ulysses left his crew on the beach and went to the castle. He found Aeolus in his throne room, and stood before him, bruised, bloody, clothes torn, eyes like ashes.

"What happened?" cried Aeolus. "Why have you come back?"

"I was betrayed," said Ulysses. "Betrayed by sleep—the most cruel sleep of my life—and then by a wicked foolish greedy crew who released the winds from the sack and let us be snatched back from happiness even as we saw the smoke rising from our own chimneys."

"I warned you," said Aeolus, "I warned you not to let anyone touch that bag."

"And you were right, a thousand times right!" cried Ulysses. "Be generous once again. You can heal my woes, you alone. Renew your gift. Lend me the west wind to bear me home again, and I swear to you that this time I shall do everything you bid."

"I can't help you," said Aeolus. "Whom the gods detest, no one can help. And they detest you, man—they hate you. What you call bad luck is their hatred, turning gifts into punishment, fair hopes into nightmares. And bad luck is very catching. So please go. Get on your ship and sail away from this island, and never return."

"Farewell," said Ulysses, and strode away.

He gathered his weary men and made them board the ships again. The winds were pent in their mountain. The sea was sluggish. A heavy calm lay over the harbor. They had to row on their broken stumps of oars, crawling like beetles over the gray water. They rowed away from the island, through the bronze gate, and out upon the sullen sea.

And Ulysses, heartbroken, almost dead of grief, tried to hide his feelings from the men; he stood on deck, barking orders, making them mend sail, patch hull, rig new spars, and keep rowing. He took the helm himself and swung the tiller, pointing the bow eastward toward home, which once again, lay at the other end of the sea.

cannibal beach

Ulysses wished to put as much open water as possible between him and the Island of the Winds, but after six days he realized he would have to put into harbor. His ships were in very poor trim. Their hulls were gashed and splintered, the sails tattered, and the men themselves cut and bruised and half dead with fatigue. It was a terrible punishment his fleet had taken from the brawling winds.

As dusk was thickening they made a landfall. The sight of the island pleased Ulysses; it seemed perfect for his purpose. It had a natural basin of tideless water cupped by a smoothly curved outcropping of rock. And as they sailed through the narrow throat of rock into the harbor they saw a marvelous sight. The purple sky deepened to inky blue, to black, then swiftly paled. Orange bars of fire stood in the sky, then a great flooding of golden light, which purpled again, and went dark. Ulysses searched the sky; he had never seen anything like this before. For night followed day upon this island like a hound hunting a deer. The sun chased the moon across the bowl of the sky, and the beach darkened and went light again, moved from bright day to blackest night in the time that it takes to eat a meal.

"This is a wonder," said Ulysses to himself. "And truly, all my life I have sought wonders. But just now I would wish for a more ordinary course of events. All strangeness holds danger now, and we have had our bellyful of adventure for the time. What I pray for now is a space of days without surprise or wild encounter—to have a fair wind and a calm sea and a swift voyage home. Alas, I fear it is not yet to be. I fear this Island of the Racing Sun. And yet I must land here and mend my ships and rest my crew."

The Greek warriors beached their ships and dragged them onto the shore. But according to his prudent custom, Ulysses beached only two ships, keeping one moored in the harbor in the event of attack. Ulysses spoke his orders; the men broke into groups and began to work. Some built fires and began to cook food, others mended sail, some caulked hulls, and sentries kept watch.

"Climb that tall tree there," Ulysses said to one of his men. "Climb to the top and look about, then come down and tell me what you see."

"It's too dark to see," said the sailor.

"You forget where we are," said Ulysses. "Here night chases day, and day pursues night. There will be light enough by the time you reach the top."

The man went off to climb the tree. Ulysses stalked about inspecting the work being done on the ships. The sky paled; dawn bloomed. But the sailor had not returned.

"Odd," said Ulysses. "He must be asleep up there." And he dispatched another sailor to climb the tree to see what had happened to the first one.

The shadows were lengthening. The sky shed its gold; shadows yawned and swallowed the light. It was night, and the second sailor had not returned. Ulysses frowned and sent a third man to climb the tree. Then he kept guard there on the beach, in the firelight, eyes narrowed, beard bristling, like a great cat waiting.

The sun minted itself again in the sky; morning flashed. The third sailor had not returned. Ulysses decided to climb the tree himself. It was a good half-mile from where he stood, a huge solitary tree stretching up, up. When he reached it he saw that its bark was wrinkled in a most curious way; it fell in soft brown folds unlike any bark he had ever seen. And when he grasped the tree to climb it, the bark felt like a heavy cloth beneath his hands. But it made climbing easy. Up and up he went; up, up in the thickening darkness, climbing with the ease of a man of the Middle Sea who had begun to climb masts as soon as he could walk.

He climbed and climbed, rested, and climbed again. Suddenly he heard a mumbling, chuckling sound as if some beast were crouching in the branches above. He stopped climbing and peered upward. He could see no branches. Reaching up he felt a hairy foliage grazing his fingers. He clung there to the branch, right where he was, not moving, until the blackness thinned, and he began to see.

He had been climbing through darkness; now he saw against the paler sky toward what he had been climbing. The hairy foliage was a beard. A huge bushy beard, hanging some forty feet above the ground. Above that beard was a grinning of enormous teeth; above the teeth the muddy gleam of eyes as large as portholes. Ulysses' head swam with fear. Fear pried at his legs and arms, and he had to clutch the trunk with all his strength to keep from falling. But it was no trunk. He had been climbing no tree. It was a giant's leg he had been climbing, and the clothlike bark was cloth indeed, the stuff of its garment. And he realized then that the three sailors he had sent aloft had climbed to a mumbling death.

Ulysses thanked the gods then that he had begun his climb in darkness, for he understood that the giant slept standing, like a horse, and that his eyes were not yet adjusted to the new light. That is why the huge slab of hand he saw swinging there now had not trapped him like a fly. He loosened his grasp and slid down so swiftly that he tore the skin off his hands. But he was mindless of pain. He hit the ground and raised a great shout. "To the ships!" he cried. "To the ships!"

But it was too late. The sun was burning in the sky and there was too much light. A brutal bellowing yell shattered the air, and the men, paralyzed with fear, whimpering like puppies, saw a mob of giants, tall as trees, trooping toward them over the hills. And before Ulysses could rally his terrified men, the giants were upon them, trampling the ships like twigs, scooping the men up and popping them into their great mouths like children eating berries.

Ulysses did not lose his wits. Fear turned to anger in him, and anger became an icy flame that quickened him. His sword was scything the air; he hacked away at the giant hands that came at him like a flock of huge meaty gulls. He whipped his blade at their fingers, hacking them off at the knuckle joints. His sword smoked with blood.

Inspired by the sight of him fencing with the giant fingers, a small group of his men gathered around and made a hedge of steel. They hacked their way through the great grasping hands to the edge of the sea, then followed Ulysses into the water and swam to the single ship that they had left moored in the harbor. Luckily the swift night was falling again, and they were shielded by darkness. They heard the huge snuffling noise of the giants feasting upon their shipmates, but there was nothing they could do except try to save themselves. The night had brought an offshore wind. Swiftly they raised sail and darted through the throat of rock out into the open sea.

Of the three ships that had gone in, only one sailed away. Of the three crews, but one was left. The others had gone down the gullets of the giants who lived on that strange island where night hounds the golden stag of the day across the indifferent sky.

CIRCE

Now, after battling the giant cannibals on the Island of the Racing Sun, Ulysses found himself with only forty-five men left from his crew of one hundred. He was determined to bring these men home safely, or die himself.

They were sailing northward again, and on the third day came in sight of land, low lying, heavily wooded, with a good sheltering harbor. Although they had met terrible treatment everywhere they had landed since leaving Troy, they were out of food, water was running low, and once again they would have to risk the perils of the land.

Ulysses was very cautious. He moored the ship off shore, and said to the crew:

"I shall go ashore myself—alone—to see what there is to see, and make sure there are no terrible hosts, giants, man-eating ogres, or secret sorceries. If I am not back by nightfall, Eurylochus will act as captain. Then he will decide whether to seek food and water here, or sail onward. Farewell."

He lowered a small boat and rowed toward the island, all alone. He beached his skiff and struck inland. The first thing he wanted to do was find out whether he was on an island, or the spur of a mainland. He climbed a low hill, then climbed to the top of a tree that grew on the hill. He was high enough now for a clear view, and he turned slowly, marking the flash

THE ADVENTURES OF ULYSSES

of the sea on all sides. He knew that once again they had
landed on an island and that the ship was their only means
of escape if danger should strike.

Something caught his eye. He squinted thoughtfully at
what looked like a feather of smoke rising from a grove of
trees. The trees were too thick for him to see through. He
climbed down and picked his way carefully toward the
smoke, trying to make as little noise as possible. He came to
a stand of mighty trees—oak trees, thick and tall with glossy
leaves. Glimmering through the trees he saw what looked
like a small castle made of polished gray stone. He did not
dare go near, for he heard strange howling sounds, a pack of
dogs, perhaps, but different from any dogs he had ever heard.
So he left the grove and made his way back toward the beach,
thinking hard, trying to decide whether to sail away immediately or take a chance on the inhabitants being friendly. He
did not like the sound of that howling. There was something
in it that froze his marrow. He decided that he would not risk
his men on the island, but that he would return to the ship,
raise anchor, and sail away to seek food elsewhere.

Just then a tall white deer with mighty antlers stepped
across his path. The great stag had a bearing proud as a king,
and did not deign to run, but walked on haughtily as if he
knew no one would dare to attack him. Unfortunately for the
stag, however, Ulysses was too hungry to be impressed by any
animal's own opinion of himself. The warrior raised his
bronze spear and flung it with all the power of his knotted
arm. It sang through the air, pierced the stag's body, and
nailed him to a tree. The stag died standing up, still in his
pride. He was a huge animal, so large that Ulysses feared he
could not carry him back to the ship unaided. But then he
remembered how hungry his men were, and he decided to
try. He picked weeds and wove a rope which he twisted and
twisted again until it was as strong as a ship's line. Then he

bound the stag's legs together, swung the great carcass up onto his back, and staggered off using his spear as a cane.

He was at the end of his strength when he reached the beach, and let the deer slip to the sand. He signaled to his men, who left the ship moored and came ashore on five small boats. They raised a mighty shout of joy when they saw the dead stag. All hands fell to. In a twinkling the deer was skinned and cut up. Fires were lighted, and the delicious smell of roasting meat drew the gulls to the beach, screaming and dipping, begging for scraps.

The men gorged themselves, then lay on the sand to sleep. Ulysses, himself, kept guard. All that night he stood watch, leaning on his spear, looking at the moon which hung in the sky like an orange, and paled as it climbed. As he watched, he turned things over in his mind, trying to decide what to do. While he was still bothered by the eerie howling of the mysterious animals at the castle, now, with his belly full, he felt less gloomy. The more he thought about it the wiser it seemed to explore the island thoroughly and try to determine whether it was a friendly place or not. For never before had he seen a deer so large. If there was one, there must be more; and with game like that the ship could be provisioned in a few days. Also the island was full of streams from which they could fill their dry casks with pure water.

"Yes," he said to himself, "perhaps our luck has changed. Perhaps the god that was playing with us so spitefully has found other amusements. Yes, we will explore this island, and see what there is to see."

Next morning he awakened his men and divided them into two groups, one led by himself, the other by Eurylochus. He said to Eurylochus, "There is a castle on this island. We must find out who lives there. If he be friendly, or not too strong a foe, we will stay here and hunt and lay in water until the hold be full; then we will depart. Now choose, Eurylochus.

Would you rather stay here with your men and guard the ship while I visit the castle—or would you rather I keep the beach? Choose."

"O Ulysses," Eurylochus said. "I am sick of the sight of the sea. Even as my belly hungers for food, so do my eyes hunger for leaves and trees which might recall our dear Ithaca. And my foot longs to tread something more solid than a deck—a floor that does not pitch and toss and roll. Pray, gentle Ulysses, let me and my men try the castle."

"Go," said Ulysses. "May the gods go with you."

So Eurylochus and twenty-two men set out, while Ulysses guarded the ship. As the band of warriors approached the castle, they too heard a strange howling. Some of them drew their swords. Others notched arrows to their bowstrings. They pressed on, preparing to fight. They passed through the grove of oak trees, and came to where the trees thinned. Here the howling grew louder and wilder. Then, as they passed the last screen of trees and came to the courtyard of the shining gray castle, they saw an extraordinary sight—a pack of wolves and lions running together like dogs—racing about the courtyard, howling.

When they caught sight of the men, the animals turned and flung themselves upon the strangers, so swiftly that no man had time to use his weapon. The great beasts stood on their hind legs and put their forepaws on the men's shoulders, and fawned on them, and licked their faces. They voiced low muttering growling whines. Eurylochus, who stood half-embracing a huge tawny lion, said, "Men, it is most strange. For these fearsome beasts greet us as though we were lost friends. They seem to be trying to speak to us. And look— look—at their eyes! How intelligently they gleam, how sadly they gaze. Not like beasts' eyes at all."

"It is true," said one of the men. "But perhaps there is nothing to fear. Perhaps there is reason to take heart. For if wild beasts are so tame and friendly, then perhaps the master of the castle, whoever he is or whatever he is, will be friendly too, and welcome us, and give us good cheer."

"Come," said Eurylochus.

When they reached the castle gate, they stopped and listened. For they heard a woman singing in a lovely deep fullthroated voice, so that without seeing the woman they knew she was beautiful.

Eurylochus said, "Men, you go into the castle and see what is to be seen. I will stay here, and make sure you are not surprised."

"What do you mean? You come with us. Listen to that. There can be no danger where there is such song."

"Yes, everything seems peaceful," said Eurylochus. "The wild animals are friendly. Instead of the clank of weapons, we hear a woman singing. And it may be peaceful. But something says to me, be careful, take heed. Go you, then. I stay on guard. If I am attacked, and you are unharmed, come to my aid. If anything happens to you, then I shall take word back to Ulysses."

So Eurylochus stood watch at the castle gate—sword in one hand, dagger in the other, bow slung across his back— and the rest of the men entered the castle. They followed the sound of singing through the rooms and out onto a sunny terrace. There sat a woman weaving. She sat at a huge loom, larger than they had ever seen, and wove a gorgeous tapestry. As she wove, she sang. The bright flax leaped through her fingers as if it were dancing to the music in her voice. The men stood and stared. The sun seemed to be trapped in her hair, so bright it was; she wore it long, falling to her waist. Her dress was as blue as the summer sky, matching her eyes. Her long white arms were bare to the shoulders. She stood

up and greeted them. She was very tall. And the men, looking at her, and listening to her speak, began to believe that
they were in the presence of a goddess.

She seemed to read thoughts too, for she said, "No, I am
not a goddess. But I am descended from the Immortals. I
am Circe, granddaughter of Helios, a sun-god, who married
Perse, daughter of Oceanus. So what am I—wood nymph,
sea nymph, something of both? Or something more? I can
do simple magic and prophecy, weave certain homely enchantments and read dreams. But let us not speak of me, but
of you, strangers. You are adventurers, I see, men of the
sword, men of the black-prowed ships, the hawks of the sea.
And you have come through sore, sad times, and seek a haven
here on this western isle. So be it. I welcome you. For the
sweetest spell Circe weaves is one called hospitality. I will
have baths drawn for you, clean garments laid out. And
when you are refreshed, you shall come and dine. For I love
brave men and the tales they tell."

When the men had bathed and changed, Circe gave them
each a red bowl. And into each bowl she put yellow food—
a kind of porridge made of cheese, barley, honey, and wine
plus a few secret things known only to herself. The odor
that rose from the red bowls was more delicious than anything they had ever smelled before. And as each man ate, he
felt himself sinking into his hunger, *becoming* his hunger—
lapping, panting, grunting, snuffling. Circe passed among
them, smiling, filling the bowls again and again. And the
men, waiting for their bowls to be filled, looking about, seeing each other's face smeared with food, thought, "How
strange. We're eating like pigs."

Even as the thought came, it became more true. For as
Circe passed among them now she touched each one on the
shoulder with a wand, saying: "Glut and swink, eat and

drink, gobble food and guzzle wine. Too rude, I think, for humankind, quite right, I think, for *swine!*"

As she said these words in her lovely laughing voice, the men dwindled. Their noses grew wide and long, became snouts. Their hair hardened into bristles; their hands and feet became hooves, and they ran about on all fours, sobbing and snuffling, searching the floor for bones and crumbs. But all the time they cried real tears from their little red eyes, for they were pigs only in form; their minds remained unchanged, and they knew what was happening to them.

Circe kicked them away from the table. "To the sties!" she cried. She struck them with her wand, herding them out of the castle into a large sty. And there she flung them acorns and chestnuts and red berries, and watched them grubbing in the mud for the food she threw. She laughed a wild, hard, bright laugh, and went back into the castle.

While all this was happening, Eurylochus was waiting at the gate. When the men did not return he crept up to a bow slit in the castle wall and looked in. It was dark now. He saw the glimmer of torchlight, and the dim shape of a woman at a loom, weaving. He heard a voice singing, the same enchanting voice he had heard before. But of his men he saw nothing. Nor did he hear their voices. A great fear seized him. He raced off as fast as he could, hoping against hope that the beasts would not howl. The wolves and lions stood like statues, walked like shadows. Their eyes glittered with cold moonlight, but none of them uttered a sound.

He ran until the breath strangled in his throat, until his heart tried to crack out of his ribs, but he kept running, stumbling over roots, slipping on stones. He ran and ran until he reached the beach and fell swooning in Ulysses' arms. Then with his last breath he gasped out the story, told Ulysses of the lions and the wolves, of the woman singing

in the castle, and how the men had gone in and not come out. And then he slipped into blackness.

Ulysses said to his men, "You hear the story Eurylochus tells. I must go to the castle and see what has happened to your companions. But there is no need for you to risk yourselves. You stay here. And if I do not return by sunfall tomorrow, then you must board the ship and sail away, for you will know that I am dead."

The men wept and pleaded with him not to go, but he said, "I have sworn an oath that I will never leave another man behind if there is any way I can prevent it. Farewell, dear friends."

It was dawn by the time he found himself among the oak trees near the castle. He heard the first faint howling of the animals in the courtyard. And as he walked through the rose and gray light, a figure started up before him—a slender youth in golden breastplates and golden hat with wings on it, holding a golden staff. Ulysses fell to his knees.

"Why do you kneel, venerable sir?" said the youth. "You are older than I, and a mighty warrior. You should not kneel."

"Ah, pardon," cried Ulysses. "I have sharp eyes for some things. Behind your youth—so fair—I see time itself stretching to the beginning of things. Behind your slenderness I sense the power of a god. Sweet youth, beautiful lad, I know you. You are Hermes, the swift one, the messenger god. I pray you have come with good tidings for me because I fear that I have offended the gods, or one of them anyway, and he has vowed vengeance upon me."

"It is true," said Hermes. "Somebody up there doesn't like you. Can't say who, not ethical, you know. But if you *should* suspect that he may have something to do with the management of sea matters, well, you're a good guesser, that's all."

"Poseidon . . . I have offended Poseidon," muttered Ulysses, "the terrible one, the earth-shaker."

"Well," said Hermes, "what do you expect? That unpleasant Cyclops whom you first blinded, then taunted is Poseidon's son, you know. Not a son to be proud of, but blood is thicker than water, as they say, even in the god of the sea. So Polyphemus tattled to his father, and asked him to do dreadful things to you, which, I'm afraid, he's been doing. Now, this castle you're going to is Circe's and she is a very dangerous person to meet—a sorceress, a doer of magical mischief. And she is waiting for you, Ulysses. She sits at her loom, weaving, waiting. For you. She has already entertained your shipmates. Fed them. Watched them making pigs of themselves. And, finally, helped them on their way a bit. In brief, they are now in a sty, being fattened. And one day they will make a most excellent meal for someone not too fussy. Among Circe's guests are many peculiar feeders."

"Thunder and lightning!" cried Ulysses. "What can I do!"

"Listen and learn," said Hermes. "I have come to help you. Poseidon's wrath does not please all of us, you know. We gods have our moods, and they're not always kind, but somehow or other we must keep things balanced. And so I have come to help you. You must do exactly as I say, or nothing can help you. Now listen closely. First, take this."

He snapped his fingers and a flower appeared between them. It was white and heavily scented, with a black and yellow root. He gave it to Ulysses.

"It is called *moly*," he said. "It is magical. So long as you carry it, Circe's drugs will not work. You will go to the castle. She will greet you and feed you. You will eat the food which, to her amazement, will leave you unharmed. Then you will draw your sword and advance upon her as though you meant to kill her. Then she will see that you have certain powers, and will begin to plead with you. She will unveil enchantments more powerful than any she has yet used. Resist them you cannot, nor can any man, nor any god. Nor is there any counterspell that will work against such beauty. But if you wish to see your home again, if you wish to rescue your shipmates from the sty, you must resist her long enough to make her swear the great oath of the immortals—that she will not do you any harm as long as you are her guest. That is all I can do for you. From now on, it is up to you. We shall be watching you with interest. Farewell."

The golden youth disappeared just as a ray of sunlight does when a cloud crosses the face of the sun. Ulysses shook his head, wondering whether he had really seen the god, or imagined him, but then he saw that he was still holding the curious flower, and he knew that Hermes had indeed been there. So he marched on toward the castle, through the pack of lions and wolves, who leaped about him, fawning, looking at him with their great intelligent eyes, and trying to warn him in their snarling, growling voices. He stroked their heads, and passed among them, and went into the castle.

And here, he found Circe, sitting at her loom, weaving and singing. She wore a white tunic now and a flame-colored scarf, and was as beautiful as the dawn. She stood up and greeted him, saying, "Welcome, stranger. I live here alone, and seldom see anyone, and almost never have guests. So you are triply welcome, great sea-stained warrior, for I know that you have seen battle and adventure and have tales to tell."

She drew him a warm perfumed bath, and her servants bathed and anointed him, and gave him clean garments to wear. When he came to her, she gave him a red bowl full of yellow food, and said, "Eat." The food smelled delicious; its fragrance was intoxicating. Ulysses felt that he wanted to plunge his face into it and grub it up like a pig, but he held the flower tightly, kept control of himself, and ate slowly. He did not quite finish the food.

"Delicious," he said. "Your own recipe?"

"Yes," she said. "Will you not finish?"

"I am not quite so hungry as I thought."

"Then, drink. Here's wine."

She turned her back to him as she poured the wine, and he knew that she was casting a powder in it. He smiled to himself and drank off the wine, then said: "Delicious. Your own grapes?"

"You look weary, stranger," she said. "Sit and talk with me."

"Gladly," said Ulysses. "We have much to speak of, you and I. I'm something of a farmer myself. I breed cattle on my own little island of Ithaca, where I'm king—when I'm home. Won't you show me your livestock?"

"Livestock? I keep no cattle here."

"Oh, do you not? I fancied I heard pigs squealing out there. Must have been mistaken."

"Yes," said Circe. "Badly mistaken."

"But you do have interesting animals. I was much struck by the wolves and lions who course in a pack like dogs—very friendly for such savage beasts."

"I have taught them to be friendly," said Circe. "I am friendly myself, you see, and I like all the members of my household to share my goodwill."

"Their eyes," said Ulysses. "I was stuck by their eyes—so big and sad and clever. You know, as I think of it, they looked like . . . human eyes."

"Did they?" said Circe. "Well—the eyes go last."

She came to him swiftly, raised her wand, touched him on the shoulder, and said: "Change, change, change! Turn, turn, turn!"

Nothing happened. Her eyes widened when she saw him sitting there, unchanged, sniffing at the flower he had taken from his tunic. He took the wand from her gently, and snapped it in two. Then drawing his sword he seized her by her long golden hair and forced her to her knees, pulling her head until her white throat was offered the blade of the sword. Then he said, "You have not asked me my name. It is Ulysses. I am an unlucky man, but not altogether helpless. You have changed my men into pigs. Now I will change you into a corpse."

She did not flinch before the blade. Her great blue eyes looked into his. She took the sharp blade in her hand, stroked it gently, and said, "It is almost worth dying to be overcome by so mighty a warrior. But I think living might be interesting too, now that I have met you."

He felt her fingers burning the cold metal of the sword as if the blade had become part of his body. He tried to turn his head, but sank deeper into the blueness of her eyes.

"Yes, I am a sorceress," she murmured, "a wicked woman. But you are a sorcerer too, are you not? Changing me more than I have changed your men, for I changed only their bodies and you have changed my soul. It is no longer a wicked plotting soul, but soft and tender and womanly, full of love for you."

Her voice throbbed. She stroked the sword blade. He raised her to her feet, and said, "You are beautiful enough to turn any man into an animal. I will love you. But even before I am a man, I am a leader. My men are my responsibility. Before we can love each other I must ask you to swear the great oath that you will not harm me when I am defenseless, that you will not wound me and suck away my blood as witches do, but will treat me honestly. And that, first of all, you will restore my men to their own forms, and let me take them with me when I am ready to leave."

"I will try to see that you are never ready," said Circe softly.

Circe kept her promise. The next morning she took Ulysses out to the sty and called the pigs. They came trotting up, snuffling and grunting. As they streamed past her, rushing to Ulysses, she touched each one on the shoulder with her wand. As she did so, each pig stood up, his hind legs grew longer, his front hooves became hands, his eyes grew, his nose shrank, his quills softened into hair, and he was his human self once more, only grown taller and younger.

The men crowded around Ulysses, shouting and laughing. He said to them: "Welcome, my friends. You have gone a short but ugly voyage to the animal state. And while you have returned—looking very well—it is clear that we are in a place of sorceries and must conduct ourselves with great care. Our enchanting hostess, Circe, has become so fond of our company that she insists we stay awhile. This, indeed, is the price of your release from hogdom. So you will now go down to your shipmates on the beach, and tell them what has happened. Ask them to secure the ship and then return here with you to the castle. It is another delay in our journey, but it is far better than what might have been. Go, then."

The men trooped happily down to the harbor and told the others what had happened. At first, Eurylochus protested. "How do I know," he said, "that you are not still under enchantment? How do I know that this is not some new trick of the sorceress to get us all into her power, turn us all to pigs, and keep us in the sty forever?"

But the other men paid no heed to his warning. They were eager to see the castle and the beautiful witch, to taste the delicious food, and enjoy all the luxuries their friends had described. So they obeyed Ulysses' commands. They dragged the ship up on the beach, beyond reach of the tide, unstepped its mast, then marched off laughing and singing toward the castle, carrying mast and oars and folded sail. Eurylochus followed, but he was afraid.

For some time, things went well. Ulysses and Circe lived as husband and wife. The men were treated as welcome guests. They feasted for hours each night in the great dining hall. And as they ate, they were entertained by minstrels singing, by acrobats, dancing bears, and dancing girls. During the day they swam in the ocean, hunted wild boar, threw the discus, had archery and spear-throwing contests, raced, jumped, and wrestled. Then as dusk drew in they returned to the castle for their warm perfumed baths and bowls of hot wine before the feasting began again.

As for Ulysses he found himself falling deeper under Circe's spell every day. Thoughts of home were dim now. He barely remembered his wife's face. Sometimes he would think of days gone by and wonder when he could shake off this enchantment and resume his voyage. Then she would look at him. And her eyes, like blue flame, burned these pictures out of his head. Then he could not rest until he was within the scent of her hair, the touch of her hand. And he would whimper impatiently like a dog dreaming, shake his head, and go to her.

"It is most curious," she said. "But I love you more than all my other husbands."

"In the name of heaven how many have you had?" he cried.

"Ah, don't say it like that. Not so many, when you consider. I have been a frequent widow, it is true. But, please understand, I am god-descended on both sides. I am immortal and cannot die. I have lived since the beginning of things."

"Yes. How many husbands have you had?"

"Please, my dear, be fair. Gods have loved me, and satyrs and fauns and centaurs, and other creatures who do not die. But I, I have always had a taste for humankind. My favorite husbands have been men, human men. They, you see, grow old so quickly, and I am alone again. And time grows heavy, and breeds mischief."

"How many husbands have you buried, dear widow?"

"Buried? Why, none."

"I see. You cremate them."

"I do not let them die. I cannot bear dead things. Especially if they are things I have loved. Of all nature's transformations, death seems to me the most stupid. No, I do not let them die. I change them into animals, and they roam this beautiful island forevermore. And I see them every day and feed them with my own hand."

"That explains those wolves and lions in the courtyard, I suppose."

"Ah, they are only the best, the cream, the mightiest warriors of ages gone. But I have had lesser husbands. They are now rabbits, squirrels, boars, cats, spiders, frogs, and monkeys. That little fellow there. . . ." She pointed to a silvery little ape who was prancing and gibbering on top of the bedpost. ". . . he who pelts you with walnut shells every night. He was very jealous, very busy and jealous, and still is. I picked their forms, you see, to match their dispositions. Is it not thoughtful of me?"

"Tell me," said Ulysses, "when I am used up, will I be good enough to join your select band of wolves and lions, or will I be something less? A toad, perhaps, or a snail?"

"A fox, undoubtedly," she said. "With your swiftness, and your cunning ways—oh, yes, a fox. A king of foxes." She stroked his beard. "But you are the only man who ever withstood my spells," she said. "You are my conqueror, a unique hero. It is not your fate to stay with me. It is not my happy fate to arrange your last hours."

"Is it not?" said Ulysses.

"No," she said. "Unless you can wipe out of your mind all thoughts of home. Unless you can erase all dreams of battle and voyage, unless you can forget your men, and release me from my oath, and let them become animals, contented animals, then and then only, can you remain with me as husband forever. And I will give you of my immortality. Yes, that can be arranged. I know how. You will share my immortality and live days of sport and idleness and nights of love. And we will live together always, knowing no other, and we will never grow old."

"Can such a thing be?"

"Yes. But the decision is yours. I have sworn an oath, and cannot keep you against your will. If you choose, you can remain here with me, and make this island a paradise of pleasure. If not, you must resume your voyage, and encounter dangers more dreadful than any you have seen yet. You will watch friends dying before your eyes, have your own life imperiled a hundred times, be battered, bruised, torn, wave-tossed, all this, if you leave me. But it is for you to decide."

Ulysses stood up and strode to the edge of the terrace. From where he stood he could see the light dancing in a million hot little needles on the blue water. In the courtyard he saw the wolves and the lions. Beyond the courtyard, at the edge of the wood, he saw his men, happy looking, healthy, tanned; some were wrestling, some flinging spears, others drawing the bow. Circe had crossed to her loom and was weaving, weaving and singing. He remembered his wife. She also, at home in Ithaca, would sit and weave. But how different she looked. Her hair was no fleece of burning gold, but black. She was much smaller than Circe, and she did not sing.

"I have decided," he said. "I must go."

"Must you?"

"Yes."

"First let me tell you what the gods have decreed. If you sail away from this island, you cannot head for home. First you must go to the Land of the Dead."

"The Land of the Dead?" cried Ulysses. "No! No! It cannot be!"

"To the Land of the Dead. To Tartarus. This is the decree. You must go there with all your men. And there you must consult certain ghosts, of whom you will be told, and they will prophesy for you, and plan your homeward journey. And theirs is the route you must follow if you wish to see Ithaca again."

"The Land of the Dead, dark Tartarus, the realm of torment from which no mortal returns. Must I go there?"

"Unless you stay with me here, in peace, in luxury, in every pleasure but that of adventure."

"It cannot be," said Ulysses. "As you, beautiful sorceress, choose a form for your lovers that matches their natures, and which they must wear when they are no longer men, so the Fates, with their shears, have cut out my destiny. It is danger, toil, battle, uncertainty. And, though I stop and refresh myself now and again, still must I resume my voyage, for that is my nature. And to fit my nature has fate cut the pattern of my days."

"Go quickly," said Circe. "Call your men and depart. For if you stay here any longer, I shall forget all duty. I shall break my oath and keep you here by force and never let you go. Quickly then, brave one, quickly!"

Ulysses summoned his men and led them down to the beach. They stepped the mast, rigged the sails, and sailed away. They caught a northwest puff. The sails filled and the black ship ran out of the harbor. Ulysses' face was wet with Circe's last tears and his heart was very heavy. But then spray dashed into his face with the old remembered bright shock, and he laughed.

The last sound the men heard as the ship threaded through the mouth of the harbor and ran for the open sea, was the howling of the lions and wolves who had followed them down to the beach. They stood now breast-deep in the surf, gazing after the white sail, crying their loneliness.

the land of the dead

In those days men knew that the Ocean Stream was a huge river girdling the earth. Hades' kingdom, dark Tartarus, was presumed to be on the farther shore, over the edge of the visible world. But no one could be certain, for those who went there did not return.

Now it had been foretold by Circe that Ulysses would have to visit the Land of the Dead, and be advised by wise ghosts before he could resume his journey and find his way back to Ithaca. So he turned his bow westward; and a strong east wind caught his white sails and sent the ship skimming toward waters no ship had sailed before.

Night tumbled from the sky and set its blackness on the sea and would not lift. The ship sailed blindly. The men were clamped in a nameless grief. They could hardly bear the sound of their own voices, but spoke to each other in whispers. The night wore on and did not give way to dawn. There were no stars, no moon. They sailed westward and waited for dawn, but no crack of light appeared in the sky. The darkness would not lift.

Once again Ulysses lashed himself to the tiller, and stuck splinters of wood in his eye sockets to prop the weary lids. And, finally, after a week of night, a feeble light did curdle the sky—not a regular dawn, no joyous burst of sun, but a grudging milky grayness that floated down and thickened into fog. Still Ulysses did not dare to sleep, for day was no better than night; no man could see in the dense woolly folds of fog.

Still the east wind blew, pushing them westward through the curdling mist, and still Ulysses did not dare give over the helm. For he had heard that the westward rim of the world was always fog-girt, and was studded by murderously rocky islets, where dwelt the Cimmerians, who waited quietly in the fog for ships to crack upon their shores and deliver to them their natural food, shipwrecked sailors. Finally, Ulysses knew he could not keep awake any longer; yet he knew too that to give over the helm to anyone else meant almost certain death for them all. So he sent a sailor named Elpenor to climb the mast and try to see some distance ahead. No sooner had Elpenor reached the top of the mast than the ship yawed sharply. Ulysses lost his footing and stumbled against the mast.

No one saw Elpenor fall. The fog was too thick. But they heard his terrible scream turned into a choking gurgle. And they knew that he had been shaken from the mast and had fallen into the sea and been drowned. No sooner had his voice gone still than the fog thinned. They could see from one end of the ship to the other—the wet sails, the shining spar, each other's wasted faces. A white gull rose screaming and flew ahead of them.

"Follow that gull," said Ulysses. "He will lead us where we must go."

Then he stretched himself on the deck and went to sleep. Whereupon the crew began to whisper among themselves that the gull was the spirit of their shipmate, Elpenor, and that Ulysses had shaken him from the mast purposely, as you shake fruit from a tree, so that he might fall in the water and be drowned, giving them the white flight of his spirit to follow to Tartarus.

"He has murdered our shipmate," they whispered to each other, "as he will murder us all to gain his ends."

But they did not dare say it loud enough to awaken Ulysses.

All day they sailed, following the white flash of the gull, and when night came there were no stars and no moon, nothing but choking blackness. Ulysses took the helm again. But now the bow tipped forward and the stern arose, and the ship slipped through the water with a rushing rustling speed as if it were sailing downhill. The men clung to the shrouds, and wept and groaned, and pleaded with Ulysses to change course. But he answered them not at all. He planted his feet and gripped the tiller with all his strength, as the deck tilted and the ship slipped down, down. . . .

"Who has ever heard of the sea sloping?" he said to himself. "Truly this must be the waterway to the underworld, and we are the first keel to cut these fathoms. May the gods grant we cross them again going the other way."

There was a roaring of waters. The deck leveled. They sailed out of darkness as through a curtain, and found themselves in a strange place. The sea had narrowed to a river, the water was black, and the sky was black, curving downward like the inside of a bowl; the light was gray. Tall trees grew along the bank of the river—black poplars and white birches. And Ulysses knew that the black river was the Styx, and that he had sailed his ship into the Kingdom of the Dead.

There was no wind, but the sails remained strangely taut, and the ship floated easily into harbor, as if some invisible hand had taken the helm.

Ulysses bade his men disembark. He led them past a fringe of trees to a great meadow where black goats cropped black grass. He drew his sword and scraped out a shallow trench, then had his men cut the throats of two black goats and hold them over the trench until it was filled with blood. For it was ghosts he had come to counsel with, and ghosts, he knew, came only where they could find fresh blood to drink, hoping always to fill their dry veins.

The meadow was still. No birds sang. There was no shrill of insects; the goats did not bleat. The men were too frightened to breathe. Ulysses waited, leaning on his sword, gloomily watching the trench of blood. Then he heard a rustling, and saw the air thicken into spouts of steam. Steamy shapes separated, heads and shoulders of mist leaning over the trench to drink, growing more solid as they drank.

One raised its head and looked at him. He shuddered. It was his mother, Anticleia.

"Greetings, Mother. How do you fare?"

"Poorly, son. I am dead, dead, dead. I kept telling you I would die one day, but you never believed me. Now you see. But do you see? Say you see."

A thin tittering arose from the ghosts, and they spoke in steamy whispers.

"What are you doing here, man? You're still alive. Go and die properly and come back, and we will welcome you."

"Silence!" cried Ulysses. "I come for better counsel than this. I must find my way back to Ithaca past the mighty wrath of a god who reaches his strong hand and swirls the sea as a child does a mud puddle, dashing my poor twig of a ship from peril to grim peril. I need good counsel to get home. Where is the sage, Teiresias? Why is he not here to greet me?"

"Coming—coming—He is blind but he smells blood as far as any."

"Do not drink it all. Save some for him."

And Ulysses smote the ghosts with his sword, driving them back, whimpering, from the trench of blood.

But then, striding across the meadow, came certain ghosts in armor. Ulysses bowed low.

"Welcome, O Fox of War," cried the ghost of Achilles. "Tell me, do men remember me in Arcadia?"

"The gods have not allowed me to set foot upon our dear

islands," said Ulysses. "But on whatever savage shore I am thrown there are those who know the name of great Achilles. Your fame outshines all warriors who have ever handled weapons. And your son, Neoptolemus, is a hero too."

"Thank you, Ulysses," said the ghost of Achilles. "Your words are fair and courteous, as always. Now, heed this: When you leave this place, you will sail past an island where you will hear the voices of maidens singing. And the sound of their singing will be sweeter than memories of home, and when your men hear them, their wits will be scattered, and they will wish to dive overboard and swim to shore. If they do, they will perish. For these maidens are a band of witch sisters—music-mad sisters—who lure sailors to the rocks so that they may flay them, and make drums of their skin and flutes of their bones. They are the Siren sisters. When you pass their shore, steer clear, steer clear."

"Thank you, great Achilles."

Next to Achilles stood a huge ghost staring at Ulysses out of empty eye sockets. He was a giant skeleton. He wore a cloak of stiffened blood and a red plume upon his skull. His spear and sword were made of bone too. He was Ajax.

"You tricked me, Ulysses," he said. "When great Achilles here fell on the field of battle, you claimed his golden armor by craft, when I should have had it, I . . . I. . . . You took the golden armor that my heart desired and drove me mad with rage, so that I butchered cattle and captives, and then killed myself. I hate you, sly one, and have this bad news for you: If you ever do reach Ithaca, you will find your wife being courted by other men, your son a captive in your own castle, your substance devoured. This is my word to you, Ulysses. So you had simply better fall on your sword now where you stand, and save another trip to Hades."

"Thank you, great Ajax," said Ulysses. "I will remember what you have told me."

"I knew that Penelope was being wooed by other men in your absence," said Ulysses' mother. "I knew it well, but I would not speak evil of your wife, not I, not I. . . ."

"Thank you, Mother," said Ulysses.

Then came a ghost so new that his flesh had not quite turned to mist, but quivered on his bones like a pale jelly. He was Elpenor, who had fallen from the mast and had led them to Tartarus. When Ulysses saw who it was, he was taken by a great dread, and cried, "I did not push you, Elpenor. You fell. It was an accident, I swear."

"Nevertheless," said Elpenor, "my ghost will trouble you until you make my grave."

"How will I do that?"

"The first land you come to, build me a barrow and set thereon my oar. If you forget, I shall scratch at your windows and howl down your chimney and dance in your sleep."

"I will build your grave with my own hands," said Ulysses. "Have you any counsel for me?"

"Yes. Death has cleared my eyes, and I see things I would not have known. I see your ship now sailing in a narrow place between two huge rocks. Beneath the starboard rock is a cave, and in that cave squats Scylla, an unpleasant lady with twelve legs and six heads who cries with the voice of a new-born puppy. If you sail too near that rock, she will seize six sailors to feed her six mouths—"

"Then I will steer away from Scylla—toward the other rock."

"Ah, but under the other rock lurks a strange thirsty monster named Charybdis whose habit it is to drink up a whole tide of water in one gulp, and then spit it out again, making a whirlpool of such terrible sucking force that any ship within its swirl must be destroyed."

"Monster to the right and monster to the left," cried Ulysses. "What can I do then?"

"You must keep to the middle way. But if you cannot—

and indeed it will be very difficult, for you will be tacking against headwinds—then choose the right-hand rock where hungry Scylla squats. For it is better to lose six men than your ship and your entire crew."

"Thank you, courteous Elpenor," said Ulysses. "I will heed your words."

Then the air grew vaporous as the mob of ghosts shifted and swayed, making way for one who cleaved forward toward the trench of blood, and Ulysses recognized the one he was most eager to see, the blind woman-shaped ghost of Teiresias, sage of Thebes, expert at disasters, master of prophecy.

"Hail, venerable Teiresias," he cried, "all honor to you. I have journeyed far to make your acquaintance."

Teiresias came silently to the trench, knelt, and drank. He drank until the trench was empty and the misty bladder of his body was faintly pink.

"You honor me by your visit, Ulysses," he said. "Many men sought my counsel when I was alive, but you are the first client to make his way down here. You have heard these others tell you of certain petty dangers which you will do well to avoid, but I have a mighty thing to tell."

"Tell."

"Your next landfall will be a large island which men shall one day call Sicily. Here the Sun Titan, Hyperion, pastures his herds of golden cattle. Your stores will have been eaten when you reach this place, and your men will be savage with hunger. But no matter how desperate for food they are, you must prevent them from stealing even one beef. If they do, they shall never see home again."

"I myself will guard the herds of the Sun Titan," said Ulysses, "and not one beef shall be taken. Thank you, wise Teiresias."

"Go now. Take your men aboard the ship, and go. Sail up the black river toward the upper air."

"But now that I am here and have come such a long and

weary way to get here, may I not see some of the famous sights. May I not see Orion hunting, Minos judging? May I not dance with the heroes in the Fields of Asphodel? May I not see Tantalus thirsting, or my own grandfather, Sisyphus, rolling his eternal stone up the hill?"

"No," said Teiresias. "It is better that you go. You have been here too long already, I fear; too long exposed to these bone-bleaching airs. You may already be tainted with death, you and your men, making your fates too heavy for any ship to hold. Embark then. Sail up the black river. Do not look back. Remember our advice and forget our reproaches, and do not return until you are properly dead."

Ulysses ordered his men aboard. He put down the helm. There was still no wind. But the sails stretched taut, and the ship pushed upriver. Heeding the last words of the old sage, he did not look back, but he heard the voice of his mother calling, "Good-bye . . . good-bye . . ." until it grew faint as his own breath.

THE WANDERING ROCKS

They sailed out of darkness into light, and their hearts danced with joy to see blue water and blue sky again. A fair west wind plumped their sails and sped them toward home.

"If this wind keeps blowing," said Ulysses to himself, "perhaps we can skirt the dangerous islands they spoke of; sail right around these Sirens and these tide-drinking man-eating monsters, and find our way home without further mishap. True, it was foretold differently, but what of that? How reliable are such prophecies, after all? Ajax and Achilles were always better at fighting than thinking—why should they be wiser dead than alive? And Elpenor—my most inept hand? Must I take his word for what is going to happen? Why, that fall from the mast must have scattered the few wits he had. Besides, they were all ghosts down there, advising me, and ghosts are gloomy by nature, as everyone knows. They like to frighten people; it's the way they've been trained. No! By the gods, I will not accept all this evil as inevitable, but will stretch my sails to the following wind, and speed for Ithaca."

At that very moment he heard a strange sound, not a sound the wind makes, or the water, nor the voice of man or gull. He looked about, searched sky and water. He saw nothing. Then he turned over the helm to one of the sailors and climbed the mast. There he could see for miles over the dancing water. And far to the south he saw tiny black things floating, so small he could not tell whether he was imagining them or not. But they grew larger even as he watched. And as they came near, the strange moaning grinding sound grew louder and louder.

"What are they?" he said to himself. "They look like rocks, but rocks don't float. Can they be dolphins? Not whales, surely—whales spout. And all fish are voiceless. What is it then that comes and cries upon the silence of the seas? Another evil spawned by the stubborn god who pursues me? But what?"

By now the objects were close enough to see, and he saw that they were indeed rocks. A floating reef of rocks. Jagged boulders bobbing on the waves like corks. Rubbing against each other and making that moaning, grinding sound. And coming fast, driving purposefully toward the ship.

"Port the helm!" roared Ulysses.

The ship swung northward as the rocks pressed from the south.

"Floating rocks," said Ulysses. "Who has seen their like? This is a wonder unreported by any traveler. We see a new thing today, and I should like to see the last of it. Are they following us? Are they driven by some intelligence? Or are we caught in a trick of tide that moves them so? I shall soon see."

He took the helm himself then and sailed the ship in a circle to give the rocks a chance to pass by. But to his horror he saw the rocks begin to circle also, keeping always between him and the open sea to the south. They held the same distance now. He sheared off northward; they followed, keeping the same distance. But when he turned and headed south, they held their place. He saw them loom before his bow, jagged and towering, ready to crush his hull like a walnut. And he had to swing off again and dart away northward, as the crew raised a shout of terror.

So he set his course north by northwest, thinking sadly: "I see that I can avoid nothing that was foretold. I cannot bear southward around the Isle of the Sun where lurk the demons and monsters I have been warned against, but must speed toward them as swiftly as toward a rendezvous with loved ones. These rocks shepherd me; they herd this vessel as a stray sheep is herded by the shepherd's dog, driving me toward that which the vengeful gods have ordained. So be it then. If I cannot flee, then I must dare. Heroes are made, I see, when retreat is cut off. So be it."

He set his course for the Isle of the Sun Titan, which men called Thrinacia, and which we know now as Sicily.

All through the night they sailed. In the darkness they lost sight of the rocks. But they could hear them clashing and moaning, keeping pace with the ship.

THE SiRENS

In the first light of morning Ulysses awoke and called his crew about him.

"Men," he said. "Listen well, for your lives today hang upon what I am about to tell you. That large island to the west is Thrinacia, where we must make a landfall, for our provisions run low. But to get to the island we must pass through a narrow strait. And at the head of this strait is a rocky islet where dwell two sisters called Sirens, whose voices you must not hear. Now I shall guard you against their singing which would lure you to shipwreck, but first you must bind me to the mast. Tie me tightly, as though I were a dangerous captive. And no matter how I struggle, no matter what signals I make to you, *do not release me,* lest I follow their voices to destruction, taking you with me."

Thereupon Ulysses took a large lump of the beeswax which was used by the sail mender to slick his heavy thread, and kneaded it in his powerful hands until it became soft. Then he went to each man of the crew and plugged his ears with soft wax; he caulked their ears so tightly that they could hear nothing but the thin pulsing of their own blood.

Then he stood himself against the mast, and the men bound him about with rawhide, winding it tightly around his body, lashing him to the thick mast.

They had lowered the sail because ships cannot sail through a narrow strait unless there is a following wind, and now each man of the crew took his place at the great oars. The polished blades whipped the sea into a froth of white water and the ship nosed toward the strait.

Ulysses had left his own ears unplugged because he had to remain in command of the ship and had need of his hearing. Every sound means something upon the sea. But when they drew near the rocky islet and he heard the first faint strains of the Sirens' singing, then he wished he had stopped his own ears too with wax. All his strength suddenly surged toward the sound of those magical voices. The very hair of his head seemed to be tugging at his scalp, trying to fly away. His eyeballs started out of his head.

For in those voices were the sounds that men love:

Happy sounds like bird railing, sleet hailing, milk pailing. . . .

Sad sounds like rain leaking, tree creaking, wind seeking. . . .

Autumn sounds like leaf tapping, fire snapping, river lapping. . . .

Quiet sounds like snow flaking, spider waking, heart breaking. . . .

It seemed to him then that the sun was burning him to a cinder as he stood. And the voices of the Sirens purled in a cool crystal pool upon their rock past the blue-hot flatness of the sea and its lacings of white-hot spume. It seemed to him he could actually see their voices deepening into a silvery cool pool, and that he must plunge into that pool or die a flaming death.

He was filled with such a fury of desire that he swelled his mighty muscles, burst the rawhide bonds like thread, and dashed for the rail.

But he had warned two of his strongest men—Perimedes and Eurylochus—to guard him close. They seized him before he could plunge into the water. He swept them aside as if

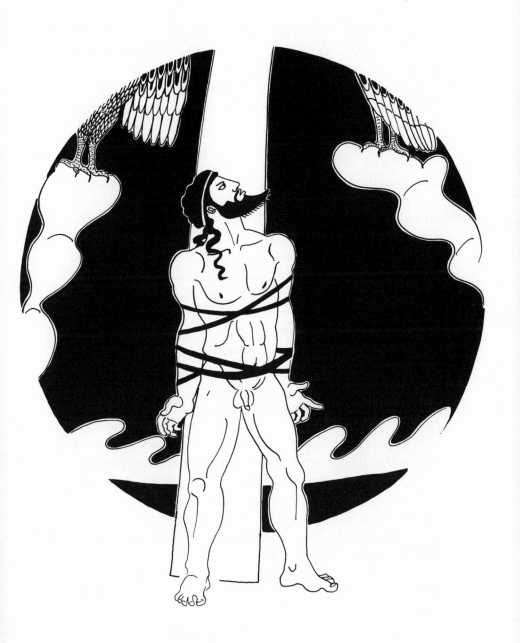

they had been children. But they had held him long enough to give the crew time to swarm about him. He was overpowered—crushed by their numbers—and dragged back to the mast. This time he was bound with the mighty hawser that held the anchor.

The men returned to their rowing seats, unable to hear the voices because of the wax corking their ears. The ship swung about and headed for the strait again.

Louder now, and clearer, the tormenting voices came to Ulysses. Again he was aflame with a fury of desire. But try as he might he could not break the thick anchor line. He strained against it until he bled, but the line held.

The men bent to their oars and rowed more swiftly, for they saw the mast bending like a tall tree in a heavy wind, and they feared that Ulysses, in his fury, might snap it off short and dive, mast and all, into the water to get at the Sirens.

Now they were passing the rock, and Ulysses could see the singers. There were two of them. They sat on a heap of white bones—the bones of shipwrecked sailors—and sang more beautifully than senses could bear. But their appearance did not match their voices, for they were shaped like birds, huge birds, larger than eagles. They had feathers instead of hair, and their hands and feet were claws. But their faces were the faces of young girls.

When Ulysses saw them he was unable to forget the sweetness of their voices because their look was so fearsome. He closed his eyes against the terrible sight of these bird-women perched on their heap of bones. But when he closed his eyes and could not see their ugliness, then their voices maddened him once again, and he felt himself straining against the bloody ropes. He forced himself to open his eyes and look upon the monsters, so that the terror of their bodies would blot the beauty of their voices.

But the men, who could only see, not hear the Sirens, were so appalled by their aspect that they swept their oars faster and faster, and the black ship scuttled past the rock. The Sirens' voices sounded fainter and fainter and finally died away.

When Perimedes and Eurylochus saw their captain's face lose its madness, they unbound him, and he signaled to the men to unstop their ears. For now he heard the whistling gurgle of a whirlpool, and he knew that they were approaching the narrowest part of the strait, and must pass between Scylla and Charybdis.

scylla and charybdis

Ulysses had been told in Tartarus of these two monsters that guard the narrow waterway leading to Thrinacia. Each of them hid beneath its own huge rock, which stood side by side and were separated only by the width of the strait at its narrowest point.

Charybdis dwelt in a cave beneath the left-hand rock. Once she had been a superbly beautiful naiad, daughter of Poseidon, and very loyal to her father in his endless feud with Zeus, Lord of Earth and Sky. She it was who rode the hungry tides after Poseidon had stirred up a storm, and led them onto the beaches, gobbling up whole villages, submerging fields, drowning forests, claiming them for the sea. She won so much land for her father's kingdom that Zeus became enraged and changed her into a monster, a huge bladder of a creature whose face was all mouth and whose arms and legs were flippers. And he penned her in the cave beneath the rock, saying, "Your hunger shall become thirst. As you once devoured land belonging to me, now you shall drink the tide thrice a day—swallow it and spit it forth again—and your name will be a curse to sailors forever."

And so it was. Thrice a day she burned with a terrible thirst, and stuck her head out of the cave and drank down the sea, shrinking the waters to a shallow stream, and then spat the water out again in a tremendous torrent, making a whirlpool near her rock in which no ship could live.

This was Charybdis. As for Scylla, who lived under the right-hand rock, she too had once been a beautiful naiad. Poseidon himself spied her swimming one day, and fell in love with her, and so provoked the jealousy of his wife, Amphitrite, that she cried, "I will make her the most hideous female that man or god ever fled from!"

Thereupon she changed Scylla into something that looked like a huge fleshy spider with twelve legs and six heads. She also implanted in her an insatiable hunger, a wild greed for human flesh. When any ship came within reach of her long tentacles, she would sweep the deck of sailors, and eat them.

Ulysses stood in the bow as the ship nosed slowly up the strait. The roaring of the waters grew louder and louder, and now he saw wild feathers of spume flying as Charybdis sucked down the tide and spat it back. He looked at the other rock. Scylla was not in sight. But he knew she was lurking underneath, ready to spring. He squinted, trying to measure distances. The only chance to come through unharmed, he saw, was to strike the middle way between the two rocks, just beyond the suction of the whirlpool, and just out of Scylla's reach. But to do this meant that the ship must not be allowed to swerve a foot from its exact course, for the middle way was no wider than the ship itself.

He took the helm, and bade his men keep a perfectly regular stroke. Then, considering further, he turned the helm over to Eurylochus, and put on his armor. Grasping sword and spear, he posted himself at the starboard rail.

"For," he said to himself, "there is no contending with the whirlpool. If we veer off our course it must be toward the other monster. I can fight any enemy I can see."

The men rowed very carefully, very skillfully. Eurylochus chanted the stroke, and the black ship cut through the waters of the strait, keeping exactly to the middle way.

They were passing between the rocks now. They watched in amazement as the water fell away to their left, showing a shuddering flash of sea bed and gasping fish, and then roared back again with such force that the water was beaten into white froth. They felt their ship tremble.

"Well done!" cried Ulysses. "A few more strokes and we are through. Keep the way—the middle way!"

But, when measuring distance, he had been unable to reckon upon one thing. The ship was being rowed, and the great sweep oars projected far beyond the width of the hull. And Scylla, lurking underwater, seized two of the oars, and dragged the ship toward her.

Dumbfounded, Ulysses saw the polished shafts of the oars which had been dipping and flashing so regularly suddenly snap like twigs, and before he knew what was happening, the deck tilted violently. He was thrown against the rail and almost fell overboard.

He lay on the deck, scrambling for his sword. He saw tentacles arching over him; they were like the arms of an octopus, but ending in enormous human hands.

He found his sword, rose to his knees, and hacked at the tentacles. Too late. The hands had grasped six sailors, snatched them screaming through the air, and into the sea.

Ulysses had no time for fear. He had to do a number of things immediately. He roared to the crew to keep the ship on course lest it be swept into the whirlpool. Then he seized an oar himself and rowed on the starboard side where the oars had been broken.

From where he sat he could see Scylla's rock, could see her squatting at the door of her cave. He saw her plainly, stuffing the men into her six bloody mouths. He heard the shrieks of his men as they felt themselves being eaten alive.

He did not have time to weep, for he had to keep his crew rowing and tell the helmsman how to steer past the whirlpool.

They passed through the strait into open water. Full ahead lay Thrinacia with its wooded hills and long white beaches, the Isle of the Sun Titan, their next landfall.

THE CATTLE OF THE SUN

Instead of landing on Thrinacia, as the crew expected, Ulysses dropped anchor and summoned his two underchiefs, Eurylochus and Perimedes, to take counsel.

He said, "You heard the warning of old Teiresias down in Tartarus. You heard him say that this island belongs to Hyperion, the Sun Titan, who uses it as a grazing land for his flocks. The warning was most dire: Whosoever of our crew harms these cattle in any way will bring swift doom upon himself, and will never see his home again."

"We all heard the warning," said Eurylochus, "and every-one will heed it."

"How can you be so sure?" said Ulysses. "If this voyage has taught you nothing else, it should have proved to you that there is nothing in the world so uncertain as man's intentions, especially his good ones. No, fair sirs, what I propose is that we change our plans about landing here and seek another island, one where death does not pasture."

"It will never do," said Eurylochus. "The men are ex-hausted. There is a south wind blowing now, which means we would have to row. We simply do not have the strength to hold the oars."

"Our stores are exhausted too," said Perimedes. "The food that Circe gave us is almost gone. The water kegs are empty. We must land here and let the men rest, and lay in fresh provisions."

"Very well," said Ulysses. "If it must be, it must be. But I am holding you two directly responsible for the safety of the sun-cattle. Post guards at night, and kill any man who goes near these fatal herds."

Thereupon the anchor was raised, and the ship put into harbor. Ulysses did not moor the ship offshore, but had the men drag it up on the beach. He sent one party out in search of game, another to fill the water kegs, and a third to chop down pine trees. From the wood was pressed a fragrant black sap, which was boiled in a big iron pot. Then he had the men tar the ship from stem to stern, caulking each crack.

The hunting party returned, downhearted. There seemed to be no game on the island, they told Ulysses, only a few wild pigs, which they had shot, but no deer, no bear, no rab-bits, no game birds. Just the pigs, and great herds of golden cattle.

The water party returned triumphantly, barrels full.

The men were so weary that Ulysses stood guard himself

that night. Wrapped in his cloak, naked sword across his knees, he sat hunched near the driftwood fire, brooding into the flames.

"I cannot let them rest here," he said to himself. "If game is so scarce, they will be tempted to take the cattle. For hungry men the only law is hunger. No, we must put out again tomorrow and try to find another island."

The next morning he routed out the men. They grumbled terribly, but did not dare to disobey. However, they were not fated to embark. A strong south wind blew up, almost gale strength, blowing directly into the harbor. There was no sailing into the teeth of it, and it was much too strong to row against.

"Very well," said Ulysses, "scour the island for game again. We must wait until the wind drops."

He had thought it must blow itself out in a day or so, but it was not to be. For thirty days and thirty nights the south wind blew, and they could not leave the island. All the wild pigs had been killed. The men were desperately hungry. Ulysses used all his cunning to find food. He had the men fish in the sea, dig the beaches for shellfish and turtle eggs, search the woods for edible roots and berries. They tore the clinging limpets off rocks and shot gulls. A huge pot was kept boiling over the driftwood fire, and in it the men threw anything remotely edible—sea polyps, sea lilies, fish heads, sand crabs—vile broth. But most days they had nothing else. And they grew hungrier and hungrier.

For thirty days the strong south wind blew, keeping them beached. Finally, one night when Ulysses was asleep, Eurylochus secretly called the men together, and said, "Death comes to men in all sorts of ways. And however it comes, it is never welcome. But the worst of all deaths is to die of starvation. And to be forced to starve among herds of fat beef is a hellish torture that the gods reserve for the greatest criminals.

So I say to you men that we must disregard the warning of that meddlesome ghost, Teiresias, and help ourselves to this cattle. We can do it now while Ulysses sleeps. And if indeed the Sun Titan is angered and seeks vengeance—well, at least we shall have had one more feast before dying."

It was agreed. They went immediately into the meadow. Now, Hyperion's cattle were the finest ever seen on earth. They were enormous, sleek, broad-backed, with crooked golden horns, and hides of beautiful dappled gold and white. And when the men came among them with their axes, they were not afraid, for no one had ever offered them any harm. They looked at the men with their great plum-colored eyes, whisked their tails, and continued grazing.

The axes rose and fell. Six fine cows were slaughtered. Because they knew they were committing an offense against the gods, the men were very careful to offer sacrifice. Upon a makeshift altar they placed the fat thighbones and burned them as offerings. They had no wine to pour upon the blazing meat as a libation, so they used water instead, chanting prayers as they watched the meat burn.

But the smell of the roasting flesh overcame their piety. They leaped upon the carcasses like wild beasts, ripped them apart with their hands, stuck the flesh on spits, and plunged them into the open fire.

Ulysses awoke from a dream of food. He sniffed the air and realized it was no dream, that the smell of roasting meat was real. He lifted his face to the sky, and said, "O mighty ones, it was unkind to let me fall into sleep. For now my men have done what they have been told they must not do."

He drew his sword and rushed off to the light of the fire.

But just then Zeus was hearing a more powerful plea. For the Sun Titan had been informed immediately by the quick spies that serve the gods, and now he was raging upon Olympus.

"O, Father Zeus," he cried, "I demand vengeance upon the comrades of Ulysses who have slaughtered my golden kine. If they are spared, I will withdraw my chariot from the sky. No longer will I warm the treacherous earth, but will go to Hades and shine among the dead."

"I hear you, cousin," said Zeus, "and promise vengeance."

Ulysses dashed among the feasting crew, ready to cut them down even as they squatted there, eating.

"Wait," cried Eurylochus. "Hold your hand. These are not the Sun God's cattle. But six stags we found on the other side of the island."

"Stags?" roared Ulysses. "What kind of monstrous lie is this? You know there are no stags on this island."

"They were there," said Eurylochus. "And now they are here. Perhaps the gods relented, and sent them as food. Come, eat, dear friend, and do not invent misdeeds where none exist."

Ulysses allowed himself to be persuaded, and sat down among the men, and began to eat with ravenous speed. But then a strange thing happened. The spitted carcasses turning over the fire began to low and moo as though they were alive, one of the flayed hides crawled over the sand to Ulysses, and he saw that it was dappled gold and white, and knew he had been tricked.

Once again he seized his sword and rushed toward Eurylochus.

"Wait!" cried Eurylochus. "Do not blame me. We have not offended the gods by our trickery. For the south wind has fallen—see? The wind blows from the north now, and we can sail away. If the gods were angry, Ulysses, would they send us a fair wind?"

"To the ship!" shouted Ulysses. "We sail immediately."

The men gathered up the meat that was left, and followed Ulysses to the beached ship. They put logs under it and rolled it down to the sea. Here they unfurled the sail, and slid out of the harbor.

Night ran out and the fires of dawn burned in the sky. The men hurried about their tasks, delighted to be well fed and sailing again, after the starving month on Thrinacia.

But then Ulysses, observing the sky, saw a strange sight. The sun seemed to be frowning. He saw that black clouds had massed in front of it. He heard a rustling noise, and looked off westward, where he saw the water ruffling darkly.

"Down sail!" he shouted. "Ship the mast!"

Too late. A wild west wind came hurtling across the water and pounced on the ship. There was no time to do anything. Both forestays snapped. The mast split and fell, laying its white sail like a shroud over the ship. A lightning bolt flared from the blue sky and struck amidship. Great billows of choking yellow smoke arose. The heat was unbearable. Ulysses saw his men diving off the deck, garments and hair ablaze and hissing like cinders when they hit the water.

He was still shouting commands, trying to chop the sail free and fighting against the gale and fire. But he was all alone. Not one man was aboard. The ship fell apart beneath him. The ribs were torn from the keel. The ship was nothing but a mass of flaming timbers, and Ulysses swam among them. He held on to the mast, which had not burned. Pushing it before him, he swam out of the blazing wreckage. He found the keel floating free. The oxhide backstay was still tied to the head of the mast; with it he lashed mast and keel together into a kind of raft.

He looked about, trying to find someone to pull aboard. There was no one. He had no way of steering the raft, but had to go where the wind blew him. And now, to his dismay, he found the wind shifting again. It blew from the south, which meant that he would be pushed back toward the terrible strait.

All day he drifted, and all night. When dawn came, it brought with it a roaring sucking sound, and he saw that he was being drawn between Scylla and Charybdis. He felt the raft being pulled toward the whirlpool. It was the very moment when Charybdis took her first drink of the day. She swallowed the tide, and held it in her great bladder of a belly. The raft spun like a leaf in the outer eddies of the huge suction, and Ulysses knew that when he reached the vortex of the whirlpool, he and the raft would be drawn to the bottom, and that he must drown.

He kept his footing on the raft until the very last moment, and just as it was pulled into the vortex, he leaped as high as he could upon the naked face of the rock, scrabbling for a handhold. He caught a clump of lichen, and clung with all his strength. He could climb no higher on the rock; it was too slippery for a foothold. All he could do was cling to the moss and pray that his strength would not give out. He was waiting for Charybdis to spit forth the tide again.

The long hours passed. His shoulders felt as though they were being torn apart by red-hot pincers. Finally he heard a great tumult of waters and saw it frothing out of the cave. The waves leaped toward his feet. And then he saw what he was waiting for—his raft came shooting up like a cork.

He dropped upon the timbers. Now he would have some hours of quiet water, he knew, before Charybdis drank again. So he kept to that side of the strait, holding as far from Scylla as he could, for he well remembered the terrible reach of her arms.

He passed safely beyond the rocks and out of the strait. For nine days he drifted under the burning sun, nine nights under the indifferent moon. With his knife he cut a long splinter from the timbers, and shaped it into a lance for spearing fish. He did not get any. Then he lay on his back, pretending to be dead, and gulls came to peck out his eyes. He caught them, and wrung their necks. He ate their flesh and drank their blood, and so stayed alive.

On the tenth day he found himself approaching another island.

He was very weak. The island grew dim as he looked at it. A black mist hid the land, which was odd because the sun was shining. Then the sky tilted, and the black mist covered him.

cAlypso

When Ulysses awoke he found himself lying on a bed of sweet-smelling grass. The sun shone hotly, but he was in a pool of delicious cool shade under a poplar tree. He was still dizzy. The trees were swaying, and bright flowers danced upon the meadow. He closed his eyes, thinking, "I am dead then. The god that hunts me took pity and shortened my hard life, and I am now in the Elysian Fields."

A voice answered, "You have not died. You are not in the Elysian Fields. You have come home."

He opened his eyes again. A woman was bending over him. She was so tall that he knew she was no mortal woman, but nymph or naiad or demigoddess. She was clad in a short tunic of yellow and purple. Her hair was yellow, and long and thick.

"You are here with me," she said. "You have come home."

"Home? Is this Ithaca? Are you Penelope?"

"This is Ogygia, and I am Calypso."

He tried to sit up. He was too weak. "But Ithaca is my home," he said. "And Penelope is my wife."

"Home is where you dwell. And wives, I am told, often change. Especially for sailors. Especially for you. And now you belong to me, because this island and everything on it is mine."

Ulysses went back to sleep. For he believed he was dreaming, and did not wish to wake up again and find himself on the raft. But when he awoke, he was still in his dream. He was strong enough now to sit up and look around. He was in a great grove hemmed by trees—alder and poplar and cypress. Across this meadow four streams ran, crossing each other, making a sound like soft laughter. The meadow was a carpet of wild flowers, violets, parsley, bluebells, daffodils, and cat-faced pansies. His bed had been made in front of a grotto, he saw. Over it a wild grapevine had been trained to fall like a curtain.

The vine curtain was pushed aside, and Calypso came out.

"You are awake," she cried, "and just in time for your wedding feast. The stag is roasted. The wine has been poured. No, don't move. You're still too weak. Let me help you, little husband."

She stooped and lifted him in her great white arms and carried him easily as though he were a child into the grotto, and set him before the hearth. A whole stag was spitted over the flame. The cave was carpeted with the skins of leopard and wolf and bear.

"Lovely and gracious goddess," said Ulysses, "tell me, please, how I came here. The last I remember I was on my raft, and then a blackness fell."

"I was watching for you," said Calypso. "I knew you would come, and I was waiting. Then your raft floated into sight. I saw you slump over and roll off the raft. And I changed you into a fish, for sharks live in this water and they are always hungry. As soon as I turned you into a fish, a gull stooped—and he would have had you—but I shot him with my arrow. Then I took my net and fished you out, restored you to your proper shape, fed you a broth of herbs, and let you sleep. That was your arrival, O man I have drawn from the sea. As for your departure, that will never be. Now eat your meat and drink your wine, for I like my husbands well fed."

Ulysses ate and drank, and felt his strength return.

"After all," he thought, "things could be worse. In fact they have been much worse. This may turn out to be quite a pleasant interlude. She is certainly beautiful, this Calypso. Rather large for my taste, and inclined to be bossy, I'm afraid. But who's perfect?"

He turned to her, smiling, and said, "You say you were waiting for me, watching for my raft. How did you know I would be coming?"

"I am one of the Titan brood," said Calypso. "Daughter of mighty Atlas, who stands upon the westward rim of the world bearing the sky upon his shoulders. We are the elder branch of the gods, we Titans. For us there is no before or after, only now, wherein all things are and always were and always will be. Time, you see, is a little arrangement man has made for himself to try to measure the immeasurable mystery of life. It does not really exist. So when we want to know anything that has happened in what you call 'before,' or what will happen in what you call 'after,' we simply shuffle the pictures and look at them."

"I don't think I understand."

"I have watched your whole voyage, Ulysses. All I have to do is poke the log in a certain way, and pictures form in the heart of the fire and burn there until I poke the log again. What would you like to see?"

"My wife, Penelope."

Calypso reached her long arm and poked the log. And in the heart of the flame Ulysses saw a woman, weaving.

"She looks older," he said.

"You have been away a long time. Only the immortals do not age. I was 2,300 years old yesterday. Look at me. Do you see any wrinkles?"

"Poor Penelope," said Ulysses.

"Don't pity her too much. She has plenty of company. She is presumed to be a widow, you know."

"Has she married again?"

"I weary of this picture. Would you like to see another?"

"My son, Telemachus."

She poked the fire again, and Ulysses saw the flickering image of a tall young man with red-gold hair. He held a spear in his hand and looked angry.

"How he has grown," murmured Ulysses. "He was a baby when I left. He is a young man now, and a fine one, is he not?"

"Looks like his father," said Calypso.

"He seems to be defying some enemy," said Ulysses. "What is happening?"

"He is trying to drive away his mother's suitors, who live in your castle now. She is quite popular—for an older woman. But then, of course, she has land and goods. A rich widow. You left her well provided, O sailor. She has many suitors, and cannot decide among them. Or perhaps she enjoys their courtship too much to decide. But your son is very proud of his father, whom he does not remember, and seeks to drive the suitors from your castle."

"I had better go home and help him," said Ulysses.

"Put that out of your mind. It simply will not happen. Forget Ithaca, Ulysses. You are a hero, a mighty hero, and heroes have many homes, and the last is always the best. Look at this. See some of your exploits. Like many warriors, you were too busy fighting to know what really happened."

She poked the log again and again, and a stream of pictures flowed through the fire. Ulysses saw himself standing on a rock in the Cyclops's cave, holding the white-hot sword above the great sleeping eye, preparing to stab it in. He saw himself wrestling with the leather bag of winds that Aeolus had given him; saw himself running with the wolves and lions who had been Circe's lovers in the dark courtyard of her castle. Then, sword in hand, he saw himself hacking at Scyllas's tentacles as she reached across the tilting deck for his men. Going back he saw himself before his homeward voyage crouched in the black belly of the wooden horse he had made. Next, climbing out of that horse after it had been dragged into the city and racing with lifted sword to slaughter the sleeping Trojan warriors. And, as he watched and saw the old battles refought, the men who had been his friends, and the monstrous enemies he had overcome, his heart sang with pride, and a drunken warmth stronger than the fumes of wine rose to his head, drowning out all the pictures of home.

He stood up, and said, "Thank you for showing me myself, Calypso. I do seem to be a hero, don't I? And worthy to love a daughter of the Titans."

"Yes," said Calypso.

Now Calypso had amused herself with shipwrecked sailors before. But she was hard to please, and none of them had lasted very long. When she was tired of someone she would throw him back into the sea. If she were feeling goodnatured she would change him to gull or fish first. Indeed, the trees of the grove were filled with nesting sea birds—gull and heron and osprey and sand owls—who called to her at night, reproaching her.

"What is that clamor of birds?" said Ulysses.

"Just birds."

"Why do they shriek so?"

"They are angry at me for loving you. They were men once, like yourself."

"How did they get to be birds?"

"Oh, well, it's no very difficult transformation, when you know how. I thought they would be happier so."

"They don't sound very happy."

"They have jealous natures."

"You are not unlike Circe in some ways," said Ulysses. "You island goddesses are apt to be abrupt with your former friends. I've noticed this."

"It's a depressing topic, dear. Let's talk about me. Do you find me beautiful today?"

"More beautiful than yesterday, if that is possible. And no doubt will find you even lovelier tomorrow, since you have shown me the penalty of any inattention."

"Do not fear," said Calypso. "You are not like the others. You are bolder and have more imagination. You are a hero."

"Perhaps you could persuade your feathered friends to nest elsewhere? They make me nervous."

"Nothing easier. I shall simply tell them to depart. If they do not, I shall change them all to grasshoppers, all save one, who will eat the rest, and then die of overeating."

"Truly, you are wise and powerful, and fair beyond all women, mortal or immortal."

She smiled. "You have such an apt way of putting things," she said.

So Ulysses made himself at home on the island, and passed the time hunting game, and fishing the sea, and reveling with the beautiful Calypso. He was happy. Thoughts of home grew dim. The nymph taught him how to poke the magic log upon her hearth so that it would cast up fire pictures. And he sat by the hour on the great hearth, reading the flickering tapestry of days gone by and days to come. But she had instructed the log never to show him scenes of Ithaca, for she wished him not to be reminded of his home in any way, lest he be tempted to depart. But Ulysses was as crafty as she was, and after he had poked the log many times, asking it to show him what was happening on his island, and the log had cast up pictures of other times, other places, he realized that Calypso had laid a magic veto upon scenes of home. And this, instead of making him forget, made him more eager than ever to know what was happening to Telemachus and Penelope.

One day he went into the wood, snared a sea crow, and asked, "Can you speak?"

"Yes," said the crow.

"Were you once a man?"

"Once . . . once . . . at the time of your grandfather, Sisyphus. I was a clever man, a spy. That's why Calypso changed me into a crow when she grew weary of me, for of all creatures we are the best for spying and prying and tattling."

"Then you're the bird for me," cried Ulysses. "Listen, I wish you to fly to Ithaca. Go to my castle and see what is happening. Then come back and tell me."

"Why should I? What will you give me?"

"Your life."

"My life? I already have that."

"But not for long. Because if you refuse to do as I ask, I shall wring your neck."

"Hmmm," said the crow. "There is merit in your argument. Very well. I shall be your spy. Only don't let Calypso know. She'll catch me and feed me to the cat before I can report to you. I have a notion she'd like you to forget Ithaca."

"Fly away, little bird," said Ulysses, "and do what you have to do. I'll take care of things here."

The next day, at dusk, as he was returning from the hunt, he heard the crow calling from the depth of an oak tree.

"Greetings," said Ulysses. "Have you done what I asked?"

"I have flown to Ithaca," said the crow. "A rough journey by sea, but not really so far as the crow flies. I flew to your castle, and perched in an embrasure, and watched and watched. Briefly, your son is grieving, your wife is weaving, and your guests are *not* leaving."

"What does my wife weave?"

"Your shroud."

"Has she decided so soon that I am dead? I have been gone scarcely twenty years."

"She is faithful. But the suitors, who are brawling, ill-mannered young men, are pressing her to choose one of them for a husband. However, she refuses to choose until she finishes the shroud. And it has been three years aweaving, for each night she rips up the work she has done by day, so the shroud is never finished. But the suitors grow impatient. They are demanding that she finish her weaving and choose a groom. Your son opposes them. And they threaten to kill him unless he steps aside."

"Thank you, crow," said Ulysses.

"What will you do now—try to escape?"

"Escape? I do not consider myself a captive, good bird. I shall simply inform Calypso that I intend to leave, and ask her to furnish transportation."

"You make it sound easy," said the crow. "Good luck."

And he flew away.

Ulysses went to Calypso in her grotto, and fell on his knees before her, and said, "Fair and gracious friend, you have made me happier than any man has a right to be, especially an unlucky one. But now I must ask you one last great favor."

Calypso frowned. "I don't like the sound of that," she said. "What do you mean 'last'? Why should I not go on doing you favors?"

"I must go home."

"This is your home."

"No. My home is Ithaca. Penelope is my wife. Telemachus is my son. I have enemies. They live in my castle and steal my goods. They wish to kill my son and take my wife. I am a king. I cannot tolerate insults. I must go home."

"Suppose you do go home, what then?"

"I will contend with my enemies. I will kill them or they will kill me."

"You kill them, say—then what?"

"Then I live, I rule. I don't know. I cannot read the future."

"I can. Look."

She poked the magic log. Fire pictures flared. Ulysses saw himself sitting on his throne. He was an old man. Penelope was there. She was an old woman.

"You will grow old . . . old. . . ." Calypso's voice murmured in his ear, unraveling in its rough purring way like raw silk. "Old . . . old. . . . You will live on memories. You will eat your heart out recalling old glories, old battles, old loves. Look . . . look into the fire."

"Is that me?"

"That's you, humping along in your old age among your hills, grown dry and cruel."

"What is that on my shoulder?"

"An oar."

"Why do I carry an oar where there is no sea?"

"If you go back to Ithaca, you will meet great trouble. You will be driven from your throne and be forced to carry an oar on your shoulder until you come to a place where no man salts his meat, and where they think the oar is a winnowing-fan. Then, if you abase yourself to Poseidon, he may forget his hatred for a while, and grant you a few more years."

"Is that me standing at the shore?"

"That is you."

"Who is that young man?"

"Your son."

"Not Telemachus?"

"Another son. A fiercer one."

"Why does his spear look so strange?"

"It is tipped with the beak of a stingray."

"Why does he raise it against me?"

"To kill you, of course. And so death will come to you from the sea at the hands of your own son. For you angered the god of the sea by wounding his son, and he does not forgive."

She tapped the log and the fire died.

"Do you still want to go back to Ithaca?" she said.

"Will my future be different if I stay here?"

"Certainly. If you stay with me, it will be entirely different. You will no longer be a mortal man. I will make you my eternal consort, make you immortal. You will not die or grow old. This will be your home, not only this island, but wherever the Titans rule."

"Never die, never grow old. It seems impossible."

"You are a man to whom impossible things happen," said Calypso. "Haven't you learned that by now?"

" 'Never'. . . ," said Ulysses. " 'Always'. . . . These are words I find hard to accept."

"Do not think you will be bored. I am expert at variety. I deal in transformations, you know. I can change our forms at will. We can love each other as lion and lioness, fox and vixen. Touch high as eagles, twine as serpents, be stallion and mare. We can fly and prowl and swim. You can be a whale once and seek me deeply, or a tomcat, perhaps, weird voice burning the night, crying murder and amour. And then . . . then . . . we can return to this bowered island as Calypso and Ulysses, goddess and hero."

"You are eloquent," said Ulysses. "And you need no eloquence, for your beauty speaks more than any words. Still, I cannot be immortal, never to die, never to grow old. What use is courage then?"

Calypso smiled at him. "Enough discussion for one night. You have time to decide. Take five or ten years. We are in no hurry, you and I."

"Five or ten years may seem little to an immortal," said Ulysses. "But I am still a man. It is a long time for me."

"That's just what I said," said Calypso. "It is better to be immortal. But, think it over."

The next morning, instead of hunting, Ulysses went to the other side of the island and built an altar of rocks and sacrificed to the gods. He poured a libation of unwatered wine, and raised his voice:

"O, great gods upon Olympus—thunder-wielding Zeus and wise Athene, earthshaking Poseidon, whom I have offended, golden Apollo—hear my prayer. For ten years I fought in Troy, and for ten more years have wandered the sea, been hounded from island to island, battered by storms, swallowed by tides. My ships have been wrecked, my men killed. But you have granted me life. Now, I pray you, take back the gift. Let me join my men in Tartarus. For if I cannot return home, if I have to be kept here as a prisoner of Calypso while my kingdom is looted, my son slain, and my wife stolen, then I do not wish to live. Allow me to go home, or strike me dead on the spot."

His prayer was carried to Olympus. Athene heard it. She went to Zeus, and asked him to call the gods into council. They met in the huge throne-room. As it happened, Poseidon was absent. He had ridden a tidal wave into Africa, where he had never been, and was visiting the Ethiopians.

Athene said, "O father Zeus, O brother gods, I wish to speak on behalf of Ulysses, who of all the mighty warriors we sent to Troy shows the most respect for our power, and the most belief in our justice. Ten years after leaving the bloody beaches of Troy he has still not reached home. He is penned now on an island by Calypso, daughter of Atlas, who uses all her Titanic enticements to keep him prisoner. This man's plight challenges our Justice. Let us help him now."

Zeus said, "I do not care to be called unjust. I am forgetful sometimes, perhaps, but then I have much to think of, many affairs to manage. And remember, please, my daughter, that this man has been traveling the sea, which belongs to my brother Poseidon, whom he has offended. Poseidon holds a heavy grudge, as you know; he does not forgive injuries. Ulysses would have been home years ago if he had not chosen to blind Polyphemus, who happens to be Poseidon's son."

"He has paid for that eye over and over again," cried Athene. "Many times its worth, I vow. And the earth-shaker is not here, as it happens. He is off shaking the earth of Africa, which has been too dry and peaceable for his tastes. Let us take advantage of his absence, and allow Ulysses to resume his voyage."

"Very well," said Zeus. "It shall be as you advise."

Thereupon he dispatched Hermes, the messenger god, to Ogygia. Hermes found Calypso on the beach singing a wild sea song, imitating now the voice of the wind, now the lisping scraping sound of waves on a shallow shore, weaving in the cry of heron and gull and osprey, tide suck and drowned moons. Now Hermes had invented pipe and lyre, and loved music. When he heard Calypso singing her wild sea song, he stood upon the bright air, ankle wings whirring, entranced. He hovered there, listening to her sing. Dolphins were drawn by her voice. They stood in the surf and danced on their tails.

She finished her song. Hermes landed lightly beside her.

"A beautiful song," he said.

"A sad song."

"All beautiful songs are sad."

"Yes. . . ."

"Why is that?"

"They are love songs. Women love men, and they go away. This is very sad."

"You know why I have come then?"

"Of course. What else would bring you here? The Olympians have looked down and seen me happy for a little while, and they have decreed that this must not be. They have sent you to take my love away."

"I am sorry, cousin. But it is fated that he find his way home."

"Fate . . . destiny . . . what are they but fancy words for the brutal decrees of Zeus. He cannot abide that goddesses should mate with mortal men. He is jealous, and that is the whole truth of it. He wants us all for himself. Don't deny it. When Eos, Goddess of Dawn, chose Orion for her lover, Zeus had his daughter, Artemis, slay him with her arrows. When Demeter, harvest wife, met Jasion in the ploughed fields, Zeus himself flung his bolt crippling him. It is always the same. He allowed Ulysses to be shipwrecked time and again. When I found him he was riding the timbers of his lost ship and was about to drown. So I took him here with me, and cherished him, and offered to make him immortal. And now Zeus suddenly remembers, after twenty years, that he must go home immediately, because it is ordained."

"You can't fight Zeus," said Hermes gently. "Why try?"

"What do you want me to do?"

"Permit Ulysses to make himself a raft. See that he has provisions. Then let him depart."

"So be it."

"Do not despair, sweet cousin. You are too beautiful for sorrow. There will be other storms, other shipwrecks, other sailors."

"Never another like him."

"Who knows?"

He kissed her on the cheek, and flew away.

iNO'S VEiL

In her generous way, Calypso went beyond what the gods had ordered, and provided Ulysses not with a raft, but with a beautiful tight little vessel, sturdy enough for a long voyage, and small enough for one man to sail.

But he would have done just as well with a raft, for his bad luck held. He was seventeen days out of Ogygia, scudding along happily, when Poseidon, on his way back from Africa, happened to notice the little ship.

The sea god scowled, and said, "Can that be Ulysses? I thought I had drowned him long ago. One of my meddlesome relatives up there must be shielding him, and I have a good notion who. Well, I'll give my owlish niece a little work to do."

His scowl deepened, darkening the sun. He shook a storm

out of his beard. The winds leaped, the water boiled. Ulysses felt the tiller being torn out of his hand. The boat spun like a chip. The sail ripped, the mast cracked, and Ulysses realized that his old enemy had found him again.

He clung to the splintered mast. Great waves broke over his head, and he swallowed the bitter water. He came up, gasping. The deck broke beneath him.

"Why am I fighting?" he thought. "Why don't I let myself drown?"

But he kept fighting by instinct. He pulled himself up onto a broken plank and clung there. Each boiling whitecap crested over him, and he was breathing more water than air. His arms grew too weak to hold the plank, and he knew that the next wave must surely take him under.

However, there was a nereid near, named Ino, who hated Poseidon for an injury he had done her long before, and now she resolved to balk his vengeance. She swam to Ulysses' timber, and climbed on.

He was snorting and gasping and coughing. Then he saw that he was sharing his plank with a green-haired woman wearing a green veil.

"Welcome, beautiful Nereid," he said. "Are you she who serves Poseidon, ushering drowned men to those caverns beneath the sea where the white bones roll?"

"No, unhappy man," she said. "I am Ino . . . and I am no servant of the windy widowmaker. I would like to do him an injury by helping you. Take this veil. It cannot sink even in the stormiest sea. Strip off your garments, wrap yourself in the veil, and swim toward those mountains. If you are bold, and understand that you cannot drown, then you will be able to swim to the coast where you will be safe. After you land, fling the veil back into the sea, and it will find its way to me."

She unwound the green veil from her body, and gave it to him. Then she dived into the sea.

"Can I believe her?" thought Ulysses. "Perhaps it's just a trick to make me leave the pitiful safety of this timber. Oh, well, if I must drown, let me do it boldly."

He pulled off his wet clothes and wrapped himself in the green veil and plunged into the sea.

It was very strange. When he had been on the raft, the water had seemed death-cold, heavy as iron, but now it seemed warm as a bath, and marvelously buoyant. He had been unable to knot the veil, but it clung closely to his body. When he began to swim he found himself slipping through the water like a fish.

"Forgive my suspicions, fair Ino," he cried. "Thank you . . . thank you. . . ."

For two days he swam, protected by Ino's veil, and on the morning of the third day he reached the coast of Phaeacia. But he could not find a place to come ashore, for it was a rocky coast, and the water swirled savagely among jagged boulders. So he was in great trouble again. While the veil could keep him from drowning, it could not prevent him from being broken against the rocks.

The current caught him and swept him in. With a mighty effort he grasped the first rock with both hands and clung there, groaning, as the rushing water tried to sweep him on. But he clung to the rock like a sea polyp, and the wave passed. Then the powerful back-tow caught him and pulled him off the rock and out to sea. He had gained nothing. His arms and chest were bleeding where great patches of skin had been scraped off against the rock.

He realized that the only thing he could do was try to swim along the coast until he found an open beach. So he swam and he swam. The veil held him up, but he was dizzy from loss of blood. Nor had he eaten for two days. Finally, to his great joy, he saw a break in the reef. He swam toward it, and saw that it was the mouth of a river. Exerting his last strength, he swam into the river, struggled against the current, swimming past the shore where the river flowed among trees. Then he had no more strength. He was exhausted.

He staggered ashore, unwrapped the veil from his body, and cast it upon the river so that it would be borne back to Ino. When he tried to enter the wood, he could not take another step. He collapsed among the reeds.

NAUSICAA

In those days, girls did not find their own husbands, especially princesses. Their marriages were arranged by their parents, and it all seemed to work out as well as any other way. But Nausicaa, sixteen-year-old daughter of the King and Queen of Phaeacia, was hard to please, and had been turning down suitors for two years now. Her father, Alcinous, and her mother, Arete, were becoming impatient. There were several hot-tempered kings and princes who had made offers—for Nausicaa was very lovely—and Alcinous knew that if he kept turning them down he might find himself fighting several wars at once. He was a fine warrior, and enjoyed leading his great fleet into battle. Still, he preferred his wars one at a time.

He told the queen that Nausicaa would have to be forced to choose.

"I was very difficult to please, too," said Arete, "but I think you'll admit I married well. Perhaps she too knows in her heart that if she bides her time the gods will send a mighty man to be her husband."

The king smiled. Arete always knew the right thing to say to him. So the discussion ended for that day. Nevertheless, the queen knew that her husband was right, and that the girl would have to choose.

That night Nausicaa was visited by a dream. It seemed to her that the goddess Athene stood over her bed, tall and gray-eyed, and spoke to her, saying, "How can you have a wedding when all your clothes are dirty? Take them to the river tomorrow and wash them."

The goddess faded slowly until all that was left was the picture on her shield—a snake-haired girl. And it seemed that the snakes writhed and hissed and tried to crawl off the shield to get at the dreamer. Nausicaa awoke, moaning. But she was a brave girl, and went right back to sleep and tried to dream the same dream again, so that she could learn more about the wedding. But the goddess did not return.

The next morning she went to her mother and told her of the dream.

"I don't understand it," she said. "What wedding?"

Yours, perhaps," said Arete.

"Mine? With whom?"

"The gods speak in riddles. You know that. Especially when they visit us in dreams. So you must do the one clear thing she told you. Take your serving girls to the river, and wash your clothes. Perhaps, if you do that, the meaning will show itself."

Thereupon Nausicaa told her serving girls to gather all the laundry in the castle, and pile it in the mule cart. She also took food, a goatskin bottle of wine, and a golden flask of oil so that they could bathe in the river. Then they set off in the red cart, and the harness bells jingled as the mules trotted down the steep streets toward the river.

It was a sparkling morning. Nausicaa felt very happy as she drove the mules. They drove past the city walls, and down the hill, and along a road that ran through a wood until they came to the river.

They dumped the clothes in the water, and stamped on them, dancing and trampling and treading them clean. Then they dragged the clothes out, and pounded them on flat stones, afterward spreading them to dry in the hot sun.

They then flung off their garments and swam in the river, scrubbing each other and anointing themselves with oil.

"Well, you look clean enough to get married," cried Nausicaa. "But it's easier to wash than to wed, isn't it, girls?"

The maidens giggled wildly, and Nausicaa shouted with laughter. She was so drunk with sun and water that she felt she could run up the mountain and dance all day and night. It was impossible to sit still. She seized a leather ball from the cart, and flung it to one of her maids, who caught it and threw it back. Then the others joined in, and the girls frisked on the riverbank, tossing the ball back and forth.

Ulysses awoke from a deep sleep. He was still dazed, and could barely remember how he had gotten among the reeds. He peered out, saw the girls playing, and then shrank back, for he did not wish to be seen as he was, naked and bruised.

But Nausicaa threw the ball so hard that it sailed over the heads of the girls and fell near the clump of reeds where Ulysses was hiding. A girl ran to pick it up, then shrank back, screaming.

"A man!" she cried. "A man—all bloody and muddy."

Ulysses reached out and plucked a spray of leaves from a fallen olive branch, and came out of the reeds.

The girls saw a naked man holding a club. His shoulders

were bleeding, his legs muddy, and his hair crusted with salt. They fled, screaming. But Nausicaa stood where she was, and waited for him.

Is this why Athene sent me here? she thought. Is this my husband, come out of the river? Is this what I am to take after all the beautiful young men I have refused? "Come back, you silly geese," she shouted to the girls. "Haven't you ever seen a man before?"

Then she turned to Ulysses, who had fallen to his knees before her.

"Speak, grimy stranger," she said, "Who are you, and what do you want?"

"Do not set your dogs upon me," said Ulysses. "I did not mean to surprise you in your glade."

"What talk is this? Are you out of your head?"

"Forgive me, but I know the fate of Actaeon, who came upon you in the wood. You turned him into a stag, and had your hounds tear him to pieces."

"Whom do you take me for?"

"Why you are Artemis, of course, Goddess of the Chase, maiden of the silver bow. I have heard poets praise your beauty, and I know you by your white arms. By your hair, and eyes, and the way you run—like light over water."

"Sorry to disappoint you, but I am not Artemis. I am Nausicaa. My father is king of this island. And I ask again—who are you?"

"An unlucky man."

"Where do you come from?"

"Strange places, princess. I am a sailor, hunted by a god who sends storms against me, wrecks my ships, kills my men. I come now from Ogygia, where I have been held captive by the Titaness, Calypso, who bound me with her spells. But as I was sailing away, a storm leaped out of the blue sky, smashing my boat. And I have been swimming in the sea for more than two days. I was dashed against the rocks of your coast, but managed to swim around it till I found this river. When I came ashore here, I had no strength to go farther, and fell where you found me."

"I suppose no one would look his best after spending two days in the sea and being beaten against rocks. You tell a good story, I'll say that for you. Why don't you bathe in the river now, and try to make yourself look human again. We can give you oil for anointing, and clean garments belonging to my brother. Then you can follow me to the castle and tell your story there."

"Thank you, sweet princess," said Ulysses.

He took the flask of oil, and went into the river and bathed and anointed himself. When he came out, he found clean garments waiting. The serving girls helped him dress, and combed out his tangled hair.

"Well," said Nausicaa, "you look much improved. I can believe you're some kind of chieftain now. Are you married?"

"Yes."

"Of course. You would have to be, at your age."

"I have not seen my wife for twenty years. She considers herself a widow."

"Has she remarried?"

"Perhaps. I do not know. Last I heard, she was being besieged by suitors."

"I am besieged by suitors too, but haven't found any I like well enough to marry."

As they spoke at the bank of the river, the serving girls had been piling the laundry into the mule cart.

"But I am thoughtless, keeping you here," said Nausicaa. "You need food and rest. You must come to the castle and finish your story there."

"The sight of your beauty is food and drink to me. And the sound of your voice makes me forget my weariness."

She laughed. "Are you courting me, stranger?"

"I am a homeless wanderer. I cannot court a princess. But I can praise her beauty."

"Come along to the castle. I want to introduce you to my father and mother. They are kind to strangers, very partial to brave men, and love to hear stories. And I want to hear more about you, too."

Now, that day, as it happened, King Alcinous had consulted an oracle, who prophesied, saying, "I see danger. I see a mountain blocking your harbor, destroying your commerce. I sense the cold wrath of the god of the sea."

"But the earth-shaker has always favored us," said the king. "He has showered blessings upon this island. Our fleets roam far, return laden. Why should he be angered now?"

"I do not know. It is not clear, it is not clear. But I say to you, O King, beware of strangers, shipwrecks, storytellers. Believe no tale, make no loan, suffer no harm."

"I don't understand."

"Neither do I. But there is no need to understand, only to obey."

The oracle departed, leaving the king very thoughtful.

Just at this time, Nausicaa was leading Ulysses into the courtyard of the castle. She bade her maids take him to the guest house.

"Wait till I send for you," she said. "Food will be brought, and wine."

She raced to her mother's chamber.

"Oh, Mother, Mother," she cried. I'm so glad I obeyed the dream and went to the river to wash our clothes. What do you think I found there? A man, hiding in the reeds, naked and wounded. I soon set him right and brought him here. Such an interesting man."

"Brought him here? Here to the castle? Paraded a naked beggar through the streets for the whole town to see? My dear child, haven't you given them enough to gossip about?"

"He's no beggar, Mother. He's a sailor or a pirate or some-thing. Such stories he tells. Listen, he landed on an island once where men eat flowers that make them fall asleep and forget who they are. So they sleep all day and pick flowers all night, and are very happy. This man's crew went ashore and ate the flowers, and forgot who they were and didn't want to go back to the ship, just sleep. But he dragged them back anyway. I'd like to try those flowers, wouldn't you?"

"Who is this man? What's his name?"

"They came to another island where the sun and moon chase each other around the sky, and day flashes on like a lamp when you pass your hand over it. But you know who lived there? Giant cannibals, tall as trees and they killed most of his men and cooked them in a big pot, and broke two of his ships—and he had only one left."

"I asked you his name."

"I don't know. He didn't tell me. It's a secret or some-thing."

"Do you believe everything he tells you?"

"Oh, yes. He's not exactly handsome, but very strong-looking, you know. Too old though, much too old. And married, of course. But I don't think he gets along with his wife. You can see he has suffered. You can see by his eyes."

"Where is he now?"

"In the guest house. Don't you think we should have a banquet for him tonight? He's a distinguished visitor, isn't he—all those things he did?"

"We don't quite know what he is, do we, dear? I think I had better meet him myself first. Your father's in a funny mood. Met with the oracle today, and something went wrong, I think."

"Yes, yes, I want you to meet him before Father does. I want to know what you think. Shall I fetch him?"

"I'll send a servant, child. You are not to see him again until I find out more about him. Do you understand?"

"Oh, yes, find out, find out! Tell me everything he says."

Queen Arete spoke with Ulysses, and then went to her husband, the king, and told him of their visitor. She was amazed to see his face grow black with rage.

"By the gods," he cried. "These are foul tidings you bring. Only today the oracle warned against strangers, shipwrecks, and storytellers. And now you tell me our daughter has picked up some nameless ruffian who combines all three—a shipwrecked stranger telling wild tales. Precisely what is needed to draw upon us the wrath of the sea god. I shall sacrifice him to Poseidon, and there will be an end to it."

"You may not do that," said Arete.

"Who says 'may not' to me? I am king."

"Exactly why you may not. Because you are king. The man comes to you as a supplicant. He is under your protection. If you harm him, you will bring down upon yourself the wrath of all gods—not just one. That is the law of hospitality."

So the king ordered a great banquet that night to honor his guest. But certain young men of the court who were skilled at reading the king's moods knew that he was displeased, and decided to advance themselves in his favor by killing the stranger, and making it seem an accident.

"We will have games in the courtyard," said Euryalus their leader. "We will hurl discus and javelin, shoot with the bow, wrestle, and challenge him to take part. And, when he does, it may be that some unlucky throw of javelin, or misshot arrow, will rid us of his company. Or, perchance, if he wrestles, he will find his neck being broken. It looks to be a thick neck, but he has been long at sea and is unused to such exercises."

So the young men began to hold their contests in the

courtyard. When Ulysses stopped to watch them, Euryalus stepped forth, and said, "There is good sport here, stranger, if you care to play."

"No, thank you," said Ulysses. "I'll just watch."

"Yes, of course," said Euryalus. "These games are somewhat dangerous. And one can see that you are a man of prudence. But then, of course, you are rather old for such sports, aren't you?"

He laughed sneeringly, picked up the heavy discus, whirled, and threw. It sailed through the air and landed with a clatter far away. All the young men laughed and cheered.

"Where I come from," said Ulysses, "such little discs are given babies to teethe on. The grown men need a bit more to test them."

He strode over to a battle chariot, and broke off one of its wheels at the axle. It was a very heavy wheel, of oak bound with brass.

He hefted it, and said, "A little light, but it will do."

For he was filled with the wild rage that make a man ten times stronger than he really is. He cradled the great wheel, whirled, and threw. It flew through the air, far past where the discus had landed, and thudded against the inner wall of the courtyard, knocking a hole in it. He turned to the others, who were paralyzed with amazement.

"Poor throw," he said. "But then, as you say, I'm rather old for such sport. However, since we are gathered here in this friendly fashion, let us play more games. If any of you would like to try me with sword or spear or dagger, or even a simple cudgel, let him step forth. Or, perchance, there is one who would prefer to wrestle?"

"That was well thrown, stranger," said Euryalus. "What is your name?"

"I do not choose to tell you my name, O athlete."

"You are not courteous."

"If you care to teach me manners, young sir, I offer again. Sword, spear, cudgel—any weapon you choose. Or no weapon at all except our hands."

"We are civilized here in Phaeacia," said Euryalus. "We do not fight with our guests. But I cannot understand why you refuse to tell us your name."

"A god hunts me. If I say my name, it may attract his notice."

The young men nodded. For this is what was believed at that time. But Euryalus ran to tell the king.

"I knew it," said Alcinous. "He carries a curse. He is the very man the oracle warned me against. I must get rid of him. But the law of hospitality forbids me to kill him under my roof. So tonight we entertain him at a banquet. But tomorrow he leaves this castle, and we shall find a way to see that he does not return."

"He is no weakling, this old sailor," said Euryalus. "He throws the discus almost as well as I."

Now, all this time, Nausicaa had been thinking about the stranger, and weaving a plan, for she was determined to find out who he was. She visited the old bard who had taught her to play the lyre, and whose task it was to sing for the guests at the royal feasts. She spoke and laughed with the old man and fed him undiluted wine until he lost his wits. Then she locked him in the stable, where he fell fast asleep on a bundle of straw, and she departed with his lyre.

At the banquet that night, when the king called for the bard to sing his tales, Nausicaa said, "The old man is ill and cannot come. However, if you permit, I shall sing for your guests."

The king frowned. But Ulysses said, "This illness is a blessing, King. I think I should rather hear your black-haired daughter sing than the best bard who ever plucked a lyre."

The king nodded. Nausicaa smiled, and began to sing.

She sang a tale of heroes. Of those who fought at Troy. She sang of fierce Achilles and mighty Ajax. Of Menelaus and his shattering war-cry. Of brave Diomedes, who fought with Ares himself when the war god came in his brazen chariot to help the Trojans.

She watched Ulysses narrowly as she sang. She saw his face soften, and his eyes grow dreamy, and she knew that he had been there, and that she was singing of his companions. But she still did not know his name.

Then she began to sing of that master of strategy, the great trickster, Ulysses. She sang of the wooden horse, and how the warriors hid inside while the Trojans debated outside, deciding what to do. Some of them wanted to chop it to pieces; others wished to take it to a cliff and push it off; still others wanted to bring it within the city as an offering to the gods—which, of course, was what Ulysses wanted them to do. She told of the men hiding in the belly of the horse, listening to their fate being debated, and of the fierce joy that flamed in their hearts when they heard the Trojans decide to drag the horse within the walls. And of how, in the blackness of the night, they came out of the horse, and how Ulysses led the charge. She sang of him fighting there by the light of the burning houses, knee-deep in blood, and how he was invincible that night and carried everything before him.

And as she sang, she kept watching the stranger's face. She saw tears steal from between his clenched eyelids and roll down his cheeks. Amazed, the banqueters saw this hard-bitten sailor put his head in his hands and sob like a child.

He raised his streaming face, and said, "Forgive me, gracious king. But the wonderful voice of your daughter has touched my heart. For you must know that I am none other than Ulysses, of whom she sings."

A great uproar broke out. The young men cheered. The

women wept. The king said, "My court is honored, Ulysses. Your deeds are known wherever men love courage. Now that I know who you are, I put all my power and goods at your disposal. Name any favor you wish, and it shall be yours."

Ulysses said, "O King, if I were the age I was twenty years ago when the ships were launched at Aulis, then the favor I would ask is your daughter's hand. For surely I have traveled the whole world over without seeing her like. I knew Helen whose beauty kindled men to that terrible war. I knew the beauties of the Trojan court whom we took captive and shared among us. And, during my wanderings I have had close acquaintance with certain enchantresses whose charms are more than human, namely Circe and Calypso. Yet never have I seen a girl so lovely, so witty, so courteous and kind as your young daughter. Alas, it cannot be. I am too old. I have a wife I must return to, and a kingdom, and there are sore trials I must undergo before I can win again what belongs to me. So all I ask of you, great king, is a ship to take me to Ithaca, where my wife waits, my enemies wait, my destiny waits."

Arete whispered to the king:

"Yes . . . yes . . . give him his ship tomorrow. I wish it could be tonight. See how your daughter looks at him; she is smitten to the heart. She is sick with love. Let him sail tomorrow. And be sure to keep watch at the wharf lest she stow away."

"It shall be as you say, mighty Ulysses," said the king. "Your ship will sail tomorrow."

So Ulysses departed the next day on a splendid ship manned by a picked crew, laden with rich goods the king had given him as hero gifts.

It is said that Athene drugged Poseidon's cup at the feast of the gods that night, so that he slept a heavy sleep and did not see that Ulysses was being borne to Ithaca. But Poseidon awoke in time to see the ship sailing back, and understood what had happened. In a rage he snatched Athene's Gorgon-head shield, the sight of which turns men to stone, and flashed it before the ship just as it was coming into port after having left Ulysses at his island. The ship and all its crew turned to stone, blocking the harbor, as the oracle had fore-told.

It is said too that Nausicaa never accepted any of the young men who came a-wooing, announcing that she was wedded to song. She became the first woman bard, and trav-eled all the courts of the world singing her song of the heroes who fought at Troy, but especially of Ulysses and of his adventures among the terrible islands of the Middle Sea.

Some say that she finally came to the court of Ithaca to sing her song, and there she stayed. Others say that she fell in with a blind poet who took all her songs and wove them into one huge tapestry of song.

But it all happened too long ago to know the truth of it.

THe RETURN

Ulysses had landed on a lonely part of the shore. His en-emies were in control of the island, and it was death to be seen. He stood on the empty beach and saw the Phaeacian ship depart. He was surrounded by wooden chests, leather bags, great bales—the treasure of gifts he had been given by Alcinous.

He looked about, at the beach and the cliff beyond, the

wooded hills, the color of the sky. He was home after twenty years, but it did not seem like home. It seemed as strange and unfriendly as any of the perilous isles he had landed on during his long wanderings. And he knew that Ithaca would not be his again until he could know it as king, until he had slain his enemies and regained his throne.

His first care was to find a cave in the cliffside, and there stow all his treasure. He moved swiftly now; he had planned his first moves on his homeward trip. It had helped him keep his thoughts away from Nausicaa. He took off his rich cloak and helmet and breastplate, and hid them in the cave he had found, then laid his sword and spear beside them. He tore his tunic so that it hung in rags. He scooped up mud and smeared his face and arms and legs. Then he huddled his shoulders together and practiced a limping walk. Finally he was satisfied, and began to hump away along the cliff road, no longer a splendid warrior, but a feeble old beggar.

He made his way to the hut of his swineherd, Eumaeus, a man his own age, who had served him all his life, and whom he trusted. Everything was the same here, he saw. The pigs were rooting in the trampled earth. There were four lanky hounds who started from their sleep and barked as he came near.

A man came out of the hut, and silenced the dogs. Ulysses felt the tears well in his eyes. It was Eumaeus, but so old, so gray.

"What do you want?" said the swineherd.

"Food, good sir. Such scraps as you throw to the hogs. I am not proud, I am hungry."

"Are you a native of these parts?" said Eumaeus.

"No. I come from Crete."

"A long way for a beggar to come."

"I was not always a begger. I was a sailor once . . . yes, and a captain of ships. I have seen better days."

"That's what all beggars say."

"Sometimes it's true. I once met a man from Ithaca, a mighty warrior, and the most generous man I have ever met. He gave me a good opinion of Ithaca. It is a place, I know, where the hungry and helpless are not spurned."

"I suppose this man you met was named Ulysses."

"Why, yes. How did you guess?"

"Because I have heard that tale so many times. Do you think you're the first beggar to come slinking around, pretending to have news of our king? Everyone knows that he vanished on his journey home from Troy. Beggars swarm all over us trying to get some supper by telling lies."

"Then you will give me no food?"

"I didn't say that. Even liars have to eat. Ulysses never turned a beggar away, and neither will I."

The swineherd fed Ulysses, and then let him rest by the fire. Ulysses pretended to sleep, but watched his host through half-closed eyes, and saw that the man was staring at him. He stretched and yawned.

"Are you sure you're a stranger to this island?" said Eumaeus. "Seems to me I've seen you before."

"No," said Ulysses. "You are mistaken. What shall I do now? Have I worn out my welcome, or may I sleep on your hearth tonight?"

"What will you do tomorrow?"

"Go to the castle and beg."

"You will not be welcome there."

"Why not? I will tell them how I met your king, and how kind he was to me. That should make them generous."

"It won't," said Eumaeus. "It will probably get you killed. Those who hold the castle now want to hear nothing about him—except the sure news of his death."

"How is that?"

"They hate him, because they do him harm. There are

more than a hundred of them—rude brawling young princes from neighboring islands and thievish young nobles of this island. They dwell in his castle as if they had taken it after a siege and seek to marry his wife, Penelope, refusing to leave until she accepts one of them. They drink his wine, devour his stores, break up the furniture for firewood, roister all night, and sleep all day. Do you know how many hogs I have to bring them? Fifty a day. That is how gluttonous they are. My herds are shrinking fast, but they say they will kill me the first day I fail to bring them fifty hogs."

"I heard he had a grown son. Why does he not defend his father's goods?"

"He's helpless. There are too many of them."

"Is he at the castle now?"

"No one knows where he is. He slipped away one night. Just as well. They were planning to kill him. The rumor is that he took ship and crew and went to seek his father. I hope he stays away. They will surely kill him if he returns."

"I go there tomorrow," said Ulysses. "It sounds like splendid begging. Such fiery young men are frequently generous, especially with other people's goods."

"You don't know them," said Eumaeus. "They are like wild beasts. But you cannot keep a fool from his folly. Go, if you must. In the meantime, sleep."

Now upon this night Telemachus was at sea, sailing toward Ithaca. He had found no news of his father and was coming home with a very heavy heart. He would have been even more distressed had he known that a party of wicked suitors were lying in wait for him aboard a swift ship full of fighting men. The ship was hidden in a cove, and the suitors meant to pounce upon him as he put into port.

But Athene saw this and made a plan. She went to Poseidon, and said, "I know you are angry with me, Uncle, for helping Ulysses. But now I wish to make it up to you. See, down there is a ship from Ithaca." She pointed to the suitors' vessel. "No doubt it holds friends of Ulysses, sailing out to meet their king. Why not do them a mischief?"

"Why not?" growled Poseidon.

And he wound a thick black mist about the suitors' ship so that it was impossible for the helmsman to see.

"Nevertheless," he said to Athene. "I still owe Ulysses himself a great mischief. I have not forgotten. In the meantime, let his friends suffer a bit."

The suitors' ship lay helpless in the mist, and Telemachus sailing past them, ignorant of danger, put into port and disembarked.

Athene then changed herself into a young swineherd, and hailed Telemachus on the beach:

"Greetings, my lord. I am sent by your servant, Eumaeus, to beg you to come to his hut before you go to the castle. He has important news to tell."

The lad set off, and Telemachus followed him toward the swineherd's hut.

Ulysses, dozing by the fire, heard a wild clamor of hounds outside, then a ringing young voice calling to them. He listened while the snarls turned to yaps of pleasure.

"It is my young master," cried Eumaeus, springing up. "Glory to the gods—he has come safely home."

Telemachus strode in. He was flushed from his walk. His face and arms were wet with the night fog, and his red-gold hair was webbed with tiny drops. To Ulysses he looked all aglitter, fledged by firelight, a golden lad. And Ulysses felt a shaft of wild joy pierce him like a spear, and for the first time he realized that he had come home.

But Telemachus was displeased to see the old beggar by the fire, for he wished to speak to Eumaeus privately to ask him how matters stood at the castle and whether it was safe for him to return.

"I do not wish to be discourteous, old man," he said, "but would you mind very much sleeping in the pig byre? You can keep quite warm there, and there are secret matters I wish to discuss."

"Be not wroth, my lord, that I have given this man hospitality," said Eumaeus. "He claims to have met your father once. A pitiful beggar's tale, no doubt, but it earned him a meal and a bed."

"Met my father? Where? When? Speak!"

But at the word "father," Ulysses could not endure it any longer. The voice of the young man saying that word destroyed all his strategies. The amazed Eumaeus saw the old beggar leap from his stool, lose his feebleness, grow wider, taller, and open his arms and draw the young man to him in a great bear hug.

"Dearest son," said the stranger, his voice broken with tears. "I am your father, Ulysses."

Telemachus thought he was being attacked, and tensed his muscles, ready to battle for his life. But when he heard these words and felt the old man's tears burning against his face, then his marrow melted, and he laid his head on his father's shoulder and wept.

Nor could the honest old swineherd say anything; his throat was choked with tears, too. Ulysses went to Eumaeus and embraced him, saying, "Faithful old friend, you have served me well. And if tomorrow brings victory, you will be well rewarded."

Then he turned to his son, and said, "The goddess herself must have led you here tonight. Now I can complete my plan. Tomorrow we strike our enemies."

"Tomorrow? Two men against a hundred? These are heavy odds, even for Ulysses."

"Not two men—four. There is Eumaeus here, who wields a good cudgel. There is the neatherd whom we can count on. And, no doubt, at the castle itself we will find a few more faithful servants. But it is not a question of numbers. We shall have surprise on our side. They think I am dead, remember, and that you are helpless. Now, this is the plan. You must go there in the morning, Telemachus, pretending great woe. Tell them you have learned on your journey that I am indeed dead, and that now you must advise your mother to take one of them in marriage. This will keep them from attacking you—for a while anyway—and will give us the time we need. I shall come at dusk, just before the feasting begins."

"What of my mother? Shall I tell her that you are alive?"

"By no means."

"It is cruel not to."

"It will prove a kindness later. Women cannot keep secrets, and we have a battle to fight. No, bid her dress in her finest garments, and anoint herself, and be as pleasant as she can to the suitors, for this will help disarm them. Understand?"

"I understand."

"Now, mark this well. You will see me being insulted, humiliated, beaten perhaps. Do not lose your temper and be drawn into a quarrel before we are ready to fight. For I must provoke the suitors to test their mettle, and see where we should strike first."

Telemachus knelt in the firelight, and said, "Sire, I shall do as you bid. I don't see how we can overcome a hundred strong men, but to die fighting at your side will be a greater glory than anything a long life can bestow. Thank you, Father, for giving me this chance to share your fortune."

"You are my true son," said Ulysses, embracing the boy tenderly. "The words you have just spoken make up for the twenty years of you I have missed."

Eumaeus banked the fire, and they all lay down to sleep.

Ulysses came to the castle at dusk the next day and followed Eumaeus into the great banquet hall which was thronged with suitors. He humped along behind the swineherd, huddling his shoulders, and limping. The first thing he saw was a dog lying near a bench. By its curious golden brown color he recognized it as his own favorite hunting hound, Argo. It was twenty-one years old, incredibly old for a dog, and it was crippled and blind and full of fleas. But Telemachus had not allowed it to be killed because it had been his father's.

As Ulysses approached, the dog's raw stump of a tail began to thump joyously upon the floor. The tattered old ears raised. The hound staggered to his feet, let out one wild bark of welcome and leaped toward the beggar. Ulysses caught him in his arms. The dog licked his face, shivered, and died. Ulysses stood there holding the dead dog.

Then Antinous, one of the most arrogant of the suitors, who fancied himself a great jokester, strode up and said, "What are you going to do with that dead dog, man, eat him? Things aren't that bad. We have a few scraps to spare, even for a scurvy old wretch like you."

Ulysses said, "Thank you, master. I am grateful for your courtesy. I come from Crete, and—"

"Shut up!" said Antinous. "Don't tell me any sad stories. Now take that thing out and bury it."

"Yes, gracious sir. And I hope I have the honor of performing a like service for you one day."

"Oho," cried Antinous. "The churl has a tongue in his head. Well, well. . . ."

He seized a footstool and smashed it over Ulysses' back. Telemachus sprang forward, blazing with anger, but Eumaeus caught his arm.

"No," he whispered. "Hold your peace."

Ulysses bowed to Antinous, and said, "Forgive me, master. I meant but a jest. I go to bury the dog."

As soon as he left the room, they forgot all about him. They were agog with excitement about the news told by Telemachus, that Ulysses' death had been confirmed, and that Penelope would now choose one of them to wed. They crowded about Telemachus, shouting questions.

He said, "Gently, friends, gently. My mother will announce her choice during the course of the night. But first she desires that you feast and make merry."

The young men raised a great shout of joy, and the feasting began. Ulysses returned and went the round of the suitors, begging scraps of food. Finally he squatted near Eurymachus, a fierce young fellow whom he recognized to be their leader. Eurymachus scowled at him, but said nothing.

Into the banquet hall strode another beggar—a giant shaggy man. He was a former smith who had decided that it was easier to beg than to work at the forge. He was well liked by the suitors because he wheedled and flattered them, and ran their errands. He swaggered over to Ulysses and grasped him by the throat.

"Get out of here, you miserable cur," he said. "Any begging around here to do, I'll do it. I, Iros."

He raised his huge meaty fist and slammed it down toward Ulysses' head. But Ulysses, without thinking, butted the man in the stomach, knocking him back against the wall.

"Look at that," cried Eurymachus. "The old souse has a head like a goat. For shame, Iros, you ought to be able to squash him with your thumb."

"Exactly what I intend to do," said Iros, advancing on Ulysses.

"A fight! A fight!" cried the suitors. "A beggar-bout. Good sport."

They crowded around the beggars, leaving just space enough for them to move.

Ulysses thought quickly. He could not risk revealing himself for what he was, yet he had to get rid of the fellow. So he shrank into his rags, as though fearful, allowing Iros to approach. Then, as the great hands were reaching for him and the suitors were cheering and jeering, he swung his right arm, trying to measure the force of the blow exactly. His fist landed on the smith's chin. The suitors heard a dry cracking sound, as when you snap a chicken bone between your fingers, and they knew that their man's jaw was broken. He fell to the floor, unconscious, blood streaming from mouth and nose. Ulysses stooped and hoisted him over his shoulder and marched out of the banquet room, saying, "I'd better let him bleed outside. It will be less unpleasant for you gentlemen."

He draped the big man over a stile, and came back.

"Well struck, old bones," said Eurymachus. "You fight well for a beggar."

"A beggar?" said Ulysses. "What is a beggar, after all? One who asks for what he has not earned, who eats others' food, uses their goods? Is this not true? If so, young sir, I think you could become a member of our guild tomorrow."

Eurymachus carefully wiped the knife which he had been using to cut his meat, and held the point to Ulysses' throat.

"Your victory over that other piece of vermin seems to have given you big ideas," he said. "Let me warn you, old fool, if you say one word more to me that I find unfitting, I will cut you up into little pieces and feed you to the dogs. Do you understand?"

"I understand, master," said Ulysses. "I meant but a jest."

"The next jest will be your last," growled Eurymachus.

Telemachus stepped between them and said, "Beggar, come with me to my mother. She has heard that you are a voyager, and would question you about the places you have seen."

"What?" cried Eurymachus. "Take this stinking bundle of rags to your mother? She will have to burn incense for hours to remove the stench."

"You forget yourself, sir," said Telemachus. "You have not yet been accepted by my mother. She is still free to choose her own company."

Eurymachus played with his knife, glaring at Telemachus. He was angry enough to kill, but he did not wish to lose his chance with Penelope by stabbing her son. So he stepped aside, and let Telemachus lead the old beggar out of the hall.

"You have done well," whispered Ulysses. "Another second and I would have been at the cur's throat, and we would have been fighting before we were ready. Besides, it is time I spoke to your mother. She enters our plans now."

When he was alone with Penelope, he sat with his face lowered. He did not wish to look at her. For her presence set up a great shuddering tenderness inside him, and he knew that he had to keep himself hard and cruel for the work that lay ahead.

"In this chamber, you are not a beggar, you are a guest," said Penelope. "So take your comfort, please. Be at ease here with me, and tell me your tidings. I understand you met my husband Ulysses once upon your voyages."

"Beautiful queen," said Ulysses. "I knew him well. Better than I have admitted. I am a Cretan. I was a soldier. When the war with Troy started I went as part of a free-booting band to sell our swords to the highest bidder. We took service with your husband, Ulysses, and I fought under his banner for many years. Now his deeds before Troy have become famous in the time that has passed since the city was destroyed. Bards sing them from court to court all over the lands of the Middle Sea. Let me tell you a little story, though, that has never been told.

"I lay with him in that famous wooden horse, you know. We crouched in the belly of the horse which was dragged into Troy and set before the altar as an offering to the gods. The Trojans were crowding around, looking at this marvelous wooden beast, wondering at it, for such a thing had never been seen. But Queen Helen knew the truth somehow and, being a mischief-loving lady always, tapped on the belly of the horse, imitating the voices of the heroes' wives. She did it so cunningly that they could have sworn they heard their own wives calling to them, and were about to leap out of the horse too soon, which would have been death.

"Now, Helen saved your voice till last. And when she imitated it, I heard Ulysses groan, felt him tremble. He alone was clever enough to know it was a trick, but your voice, even mimicked, struck him to the heart. And he had to mask his distress, and use all his force and authority to keep the others quiet. A tiny incident, madame, but it showed me how much he loved you."

Penelope said, "Truly, this is a story never told. And yet I think that of all the mighty deeds that are sung, I like this one best."

Her face was wet with tears. She took a bracelet from her wrist and threw it to him, saying, "Here is a gift. Small payment for such a tale."

"Thank you, Queen," said Ulysses. "My path crossed your husband's once again. My ship sailed past the Island of the Dawn. We had run out of water and were suffering from thirst, and there we saw a marvelous thing: A fountain of water springing out of the sea, pluming, and curling upon itself. We tasted it, and it was fresh, and we filled our water barrels. When I told about this in the next port, I learned how such a wonder had come to be. The enchantress, Circe, most beautiful of the daughters of the gods, had loved your husband and sought to keep him with her. But he told her that he must return to his wife, Penelope. After he left, she wept such tears of love as burned the salt out of the sea and turned it into a fountain of pure water."

Penelope took a necklace from her neck, and said, "I liked the first story better, but this is lovely, too."

Ulysses said, "Thank you, Queen. I have one thing more to tell. Your husband and I were talking one time around the watch fire on a night between battles, and he spoke, as soldiers speak, of home. He said that by the odds of war, he would probably leave you a widow. And, since you were beautiful, you would have many suitors, and would be hard put to decide. Then he said, 'I wish I could send her this advice: Let her take a man who can bend my bow. For that man alone will be strong enough to serve her as husband, and Ithaca as king.'"

"Did he say that—truly?"

"Truly."

"How can I ask them to try the bow? They will jeer at me. They may feel offended, and do terrible things."

"Disguise your intention. Tell them you cannot decide among such handsome charming suitors. And so you will let their own skill decide. They are to hold an archery contest, using the great bow of Ulysses, and he who shoots best to the mark will win you as wife. They cannot refuse such a challenge, their pride will not permit them to. Now, good night, lady. Thank you for your sweet company. I shall see you, perchance, when the bow is bent."

"Good night, old wanderer," said Penelope. "I shall never forget the comfort you have brought me."

As Ulysses was making his way through the dark hallway, something clutched his arm and hissed at him.

"Ulysses . . . Ulysses. . . . My master, my king . . . my baby . . . my lord. . . ."

He bent his head and saw that it was an old woman, and recognized his nurse, Eurycleia, who had known him from the day he was born, and who had tended him through his childhood.

"Dear little king," she wept. "You're back . . . you're back. I knew you would come. I told them you would."

Very gently he put his hand over her mouth, and whispered, "Silence. . . . No one must know, not even the queen. They will kill me if they find out. Silence . . . silence. . . ."

She nodded quickly, smiling with her sunken mouth, and shuffled away.

Ulysses lurked outside the banquet hall until he heard a great roar from the suitors, and knew that Penelope had come among them. He listened outside and heard her announce that she would choose the man, who, using her husband's great bow, would shoot best to the mark. He heard young men break into wild cheers. Then he hid himself as Telemachus, leading the suitors into the courtyard, began to set out torches for the shooting. Then it was that he slipped unnoticed into the castle and went to the armory where the weapons were kept. He put on a breastplate, and arranged his rags over it so that he looked as he had before. Then he went out into the courtyard.

All was ready for the contest. An avenue of torches burned, making it bright as day. In the path of light stood a row of battle-axes driven into the earth, their rings aligned. Each archer would attempt to shoot through those rings. Until now only Ulysses himself had been able to send an arrow through all twelve axe-rings.

Now, Penelope, followed by her servants, came down the stone steps carrying the great bow. She handed it to Telemachus, saying, "You son, will see that the rules are observed." Then, standing tall and beautiful in the torchlight, she said, "I have given my word to choose as husband him who best shoots to the mark, using this bow. I shall retire to my chamber now, as is fitting, and my son will bring me the name of my next husband. Now, may the gods reward you according to your deserts."

She turned and went back into the castle. The noise fell. The young men grew very serious as they examined the great bow. It was larger than any they had ever seen, made of dark polished wood, stiffened by rhinoceros horn, and bound at the tips by golden wire. Its arrows were held in a bull-hide quiver; their shafts were of polished ash, their heads of copper, and they were tailed with hawk feathers.

Ulysses squatted in the shadows and watched the suitors as they crowded around Telemachus, who was speaking.

"Who goes first? Will you try, sir?"

Telemachus handed the bow to a prince of Samos, a tall brawny man, and a skilled archer. He grasped the bow in his left hand and the dangling cord in his right, and tugged at the cord in the swift sure movement that is used to string a bow. But it did not bend. He could not make the cord reach from one end to the other. He put one end of the bow on the ground and grasped the other end and put forth all his strength. His back muscles glistened like oil in the torchlight. The bow bent a bit under the enormous pressure, and a low sighing sound came from the crowd, but when he tugged on the cord, the bow twisted in his hand as if it were a serpent, and leaped free. He staggered, and almost fell. An uneasy laugh arose. He looked wildly about, then stomped away, weeping with rage.

Telemachus picked up the bow, and said, "Next."

One by one they came; one by one they fell back. Not one of them could bend the bow. Finally, all had tried but Antinous and Eurymachus. Now Antinous was holding the bow.

He shook his head, and said, "It is too stiff; it cannot be bent. It has not been used for twenty years. It must be rubbed with tallow, and set by the fire to soften."

"Very well," said Telemachus.

He bade a servant rub the bow with tallow and set it near the fire. Ulysses kept out of sight. As they were waiting, Telemachus had a serving girl pass out horns of wine to the suitors. The men drank thirstily, but there was no laughter.

They were sullen. Their hearts were ashen with hatred; they did not believe the bow could be softened. And Ulysses heard them muttering to each other that the whole thing was a trick.

Finally, Antinous called for the bow. He tried to string it. He could not.

"It cannot be done," he cried.

"No," said Eurymachus. "It cannot be done. I will not even try. This is a trick, another miserable deceitful trick. Shroud that is never woven, bow that cannot be bent, there is no end to this widow's cunning. I tell you she is making fools of us. She will not be taken unless she be taken by force."

A great shouting and clamor arose. The suitors pressed close about Telemachus, hemming him in so tightly he could not draw his sword.

"Stop!" shouted Ulysses.

He cried it with all his force, in the great bellowing clanging battle voice that had rung over spear shock and clash of sword to reach the ears of his men on so many fields before Troy. His great shout quelled the clamor. The amazed suitors turned to see the old beggar stride out of the shadows into the torchlight. He came among them, and grasped the bow, and said, "I pray you, sirs, let me try."

Antinous howled like a wolf and sprang toward Ulysses with drawn sword. But Telemachus stepped between them, and shoved Antinous back.

"My mother watches from her chamber window," he said. "Shall she see you as cowards, afraid to let an old beggar try what you cannot do? Do you think she would take any of you then?"

"Yes, let him try," said Eurymachus. "Let the cur have one last moment in which he pretends to be a man. And when he fails, as fail he must, then we'll chop his arms off at the shoulders so that he will never again be tempted to draw bow with his betters."

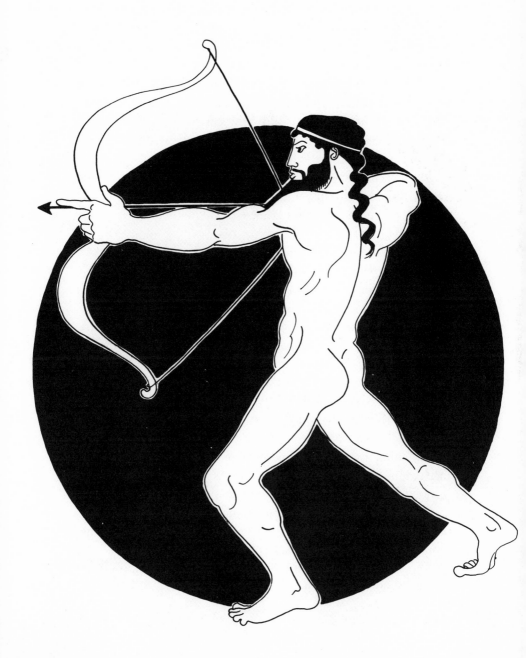

"Stand back," cried Telemachus. "Let him try."

The suitors fell back, their swords still drawn. Ulysses held the bow. He turned it lightly in his hands, delicately, tenderly, like a bard tuning his lyre. Then he took the cord and strung the bow with a quick turn of his wrist, and as the suitors watched, astounded, he held the bow from him and plucked the cord, making a deep vibrating harp note. Dumbfounded, they saw him reach into the quiver, draw forth an arrow, notch it, then bend the bow easily, powerfully, until the arrowhead rested in the circle of his fingers, just clearing the polished curve of the bow.

He stood there for a second, narrowing his eyes at the mark, then let the arrow fly. The cord twanged, the arrow sang through the air, and passed through the axe-rings, all twelve of them.

Then, paralyzed by amazement, they saw him calmly sling the quiver over his shoulder, and straighten up so that his breastplate gleamed through the rags. He stood tall and, throwing back his head, spoke to the heavens:

"So the dread ordeal ends, and I come to claim my own. Apollo, dear lord of the silver bow, archer-god, help me now to hit a mark no man has hit before."

"It is he!" cried Antinous. "Ulysses!"

He died, shouting. For Ulysses had notched another arrow, and this one caught Antinous full in the throat. He fell, spouting blood.

No suitor moved. They looked at the twitching body that had been Antinous, and felt a heavy sick fear, as if Apollo himself had come to loose his silver shaft among them.

Eurymachus found his tongue, and cried, "Pardon us, great Ulysses. We could not know you had returned. If we have done you evil, we will repay you, but hold your hand."

"Too late," said Ulysses. "Your evil can be repaid only by death. Now fight, or flee."

Then Eurymachus raised his sword and called to the suitors, "Up, men! Rouse yourselves, or he will kill us all as we stand here. Let us kill him first."

And he rushed toward Ulysses, and fell immediately with an arrow through his chest. But he had roused them out of their torpor. They knew now that they must fight for their lives, and they charged across the yard toward Ulysses in a great half-circle.

Ulysses retreated slowly, filling the air with arrows, dropping a suitor with each shaft. But still they kept coming through the heaped dead. Now he darted backward suddenly, followed by Telemachus and Eumaeus, the swineherd, who had been protecting him with their shields. They ran into the dining hall and slammed the great portal, which immediately began to shake under the axe blows of the suitors.

"Overturn the benches," cried Ulysses. "Make a barricade."

The neatherd had joined them. And now Telemachus and the two men overturned the heavy wooden benches, making a barricade. They stood behind the wall of benches and watched the huge door splintering.

It fell. The suitors poured through. Now Ulysses shot the rest of his arrows so quickly that the dead bodies piled up in the doorway making a wall of flesh through which the suitors had to push their way.

His quiver was empty. Ulysses cast the bow aside, and took two javelins. But he did not throw. For the suitors were still too far away, and he had to be sure of killing each time he threw.

A suitor named Agelaus had taken charge now, and he motioned to his men, "Let fly your spears—first you, then you, then the rest. And after each cast of spears let us move closer to the benches."

The long spears hurtled past the rampart. One grazed Telemachus's shoulder, drawing blood. And Ulysses, seeing the blood of his son, lost the battle-coldness for which he was famous among warriors. For the first time he felt the wild hot curdling rage rising in him like wine, casting a mist of blood before his eyes. Without making a decision to move, he felt his legs carrying him toward the great hearth. There he knelt, and grasped the ring of the firestone—a huge slab of rock, large enough for a roasting ox. The suitors, charging toward the wall of benches, saw him rise like a vision of the past, like some Titan in the War of the Gods holding an enormous slab of rock over his head.

They saw their danger and tried to draw back, tried to scatter. But Ulysses had hurled the slab. It fell among the suitors and crushed them like beetles in their frail armor.

Only four of the suitors were left alive. Now Ulysses and Telemachus and the two servants were upon them—one to each and each killed his man. Then Ulysses and Telemachus raised a wild exultant yell. Dappled with blood, they turned to each other, and Ulysses embraced his son.

"Well struck," he said. Then, to Eumaeus, "Thank you, good friend. Now go tell your queen, Penelope, that the contest has been decided, and the winner claims her hand."

"Father," said Telemachus. "When I reach my full strength, shall I be able to bend the great bow?"

"Yes," said Ulysses. "I promise you. I will teach you everything you have to know. I have come home."

Penelope heard her son shouting. "Mother! Mother! It's Father! He's come home!"

Slowly she descended the great stairway and entered the throne-room. She looked at the man who had slain her suitors.

Once, long ago, this same man had come to claim her from among suitors. She had been splendidly wooed before he came. Kings and the sons of kings had come courting. Doubly a princess, daughter of the royal houses of Argos and Mycenae, she was great-granddaughter to Perseus himself, the dawn hero. Princess Penelope she had been, mistress of the moon's revels, hereditary wielder of reprisals, most beautiful, most gifted, of high caprice. And the suitors had swarmed.

Then he had come, a stranger, lord of a small isle, half herdsman, half pirate. Others who sought her were richer by far, of greater renown, more beautiful. But he had come claiming her—with red bush and tricky smile and a bagful of tales. He had come to her, this husband, this stranger, and claimed her, and she had refused. But her refusal had acted upon him uncannily, turning him from a petty chieftain into a force of nature. To resist him was like shouting against the wind or swimming against a riptide. He used her own strength against her. He read her secrets and used them. Every movement she made became a movement in the courtship dance he had begun.

He packed her aboard one of the black ships and took her to Ithaca. He put her into this castle. Before her amazed eyes he battered down a stone wall and built a bridal chamber, bent a tree into a living bed. He made a summer magic. Everything obeyed. The sea was a hot blue wink. A slow night wind moved among the trees shaking out the odors of sleep. He laid a swoon upon her. He was too powerful. But she was the sole prey of that power, and this was her pride. Being owned was of priceless value; owning her, he was possessed. She was queen. Magic things kept happening. One night on the living bed he planted a prince in her. On that bed the prince was born.

Penelope looked at the man. His garments were foul. He was filthy, exhausted. His hands and forearms were bloody— like a slave who has been butchering hogs. Was this her husband? Had he come bloody-handed out of time's slaughterhouse to claim her again?

She felt herself gagging with dismay.

He was either a stranger pretending to be Ulysses, or Ulysses himself, more utter stranger, pretending to be a husband.

For he had left her. Twenty years ago, after eighteen months of marriage, he had grown restless. A war had called. A foolish unreal war, fought for a bitch and a promise. Nothing from the outside world had touched their lives. No enemy threatened—only a hunger for fame and the puniness of a vow.

So he had sailed away with three ships, voice bugling commands, sailed away from the hand-built bridal chamber and the olivetree bed. He had sailed away leaving her alone to face the consequences of enchantment.

Alone . . . for the first time in her life. After the swoon of submission and the intimacy of possession she was alone. The weight of his vigilance had lifted, and the warm shackle of his touch. She was free as death. She kept busy by day tending her son and overseeing the affairs of her island kingdom. But she could not sleep at night, and the empty hours filled with rage. A bewildering murderous nymphic rage. She understood now the old tales of the mid-summer queen who fell upon the king and dismembered him, smearing her naked thighs with his blood, and watering the furrows with his sacred gore to summon crops. It made wonderful sense. She understood that annual madness. Why had the old custom been lost? If Ulysses had returned now she would gladly have dismembered him and nourished dry outrage with his blood.

Rage parches. She felt herself parching. She began to moult. She cast off her warm bridal skin and grew a new tough skin enameled with spite. She felt herself exuding an acid. Her breath became bitter in her own nostrils; she felt nose and chin hooking toward each other; her eyes sparkled with malice. Pride kept her beautiful; she was beautiful as a lizard with diamond eyes.

After a while the suitors began to come. Young men, younger than Ulysses, her own age. Some even younger. Beautiful young men. Arrogant, wealthy. Full of wonder that any husband would leave so desirable a wife, no matter what war beckoned.

"He didn't have to go so far to find a fight," Antinous told her. "All he had to do was put in at my island. I'd have been delighted to oblige him—then come and claim the widow, as I do now."

"I am no widow; I am a wife."

"Wives have husbands. Where is yours?"

"Fighting at Troy."

"Troy has fallen."

"And he was the author of its fall. Already the harpers sing the tale. Should I not be proud to be his wife?"

"Where is he, proud wife?"

"Coming home."

"It's a long journey, but not that long."

"However long it is, I will wait."

"Not I. I am more impatient. And so are you, fairest of queens, if you but faced the truth in yourself."

The truth in herself. . . . The truth was that of all that brawling company she liked Antinous best. He was rash, brutal, joyous. Very tall with marble shoulders and a fall of wheat-colored hair. She conversed with him often, playing the older woman, permitting herself an auntly caress or two, enjoying the way he kindled at her touch, then slowly dousing him in a cascade of cool kindly words. It was diabolical coquetry, and she knew it. And a most dangerous game. He was a natural predator, a killer. She kept arousing him, although she knew it unwise. She felt herself freshening in the thwarted fire of his wrath. Besides, he was only one among many. The very multitude of suitors made for a kind of safety. Not forever, she knew. But forever was the rusty bolt of an idea she was set to unlock. Forever had been in her marriage vows, and had become the code of her deprivation. She had promised to be faithful forever. He had promised to cherish her forever. Then he had sailed away—forever. And she was expected to wait forever. Now she was determined to hunt the memory of Ulysses out of her heart forever.

She stopped weaving. One night she simply did not unravel her work, and there was nothing to reweave. She stood her spindle in the corner and locked the altar cloth away. She said nothing to anyone. But Antinous smelled out her decision like a stallion sensing the readiness of a mare across the valley. She saw him swell with stallion pride. Without knowledge, but with certainty, he knew that his season was upon him.

She was ready. The earth was ready and the weather conspired. Summer lay upon the land. The sun grew bell-mouthed as a trumpet and made summer sound for a silken green-hot rhumba wherein the wind also danced—crazy white filly of the wind stepping around a field of stallion corn. Every field in Ithaca was full of lovers. They lay in the ploughed furrows and blessed the crops. Antinous set the full weight of his attention upon her and she freshened under it as though it were hot rain. She burst into flower.

The gods, those jokers, began to laugh. Gently at first, like the west wind. Then like sails snapping, like anchor chains. They observed the stealth of her husband among suitors, and screeched with glee. They laughed like battle-cry, like arrow flight, spear shock, shield crash. They laughed with the berserk laughter of bloodlust and battle-fury. Their laughter fell to a death rattle, and all was still.

Antinous lay dismembered on a pile of stinking corpses that had been beautiful young men, and the filthy blood-

spattered butcher sat in the throne-room chatting with Telemachus, who was calling him father. She looked at the
stranger.

He arose and said, "I greet you, Penelope. I am Ulysses,
your husband."

She did not answer.

"Do you not believe me?"

She stared at him, but said nothing.

"Ah, yes. . . . Twenty years have passed. Hard years. They
have taken their price. They have aged me beyond your rec-
ognition. But you, oh queen, are more beautiful than the girl
I courted."

She said nothing. He put a hand on her shoulder. She did
not move toward him. He saw that she was looking toward
the body of Antinous.

"He angered me most," said Ulysses. "I killed him first."

"Yes," she murmured. "He deserved to be first. . . ."

The story of Ulysses was so big and so splendid that the
harpers would not let it go, but kept adding to it, giving us
many different endings to choose from.

In one version, Penelope refused to acknowledge Ulysses.
He thought it was because she did not recognize him through
his beggar's rags and his battle-grime, and he went to bathe.
While he was bathing, Athena cast a spell upon him, strip-
ping twenty years away, making him more beautiful than he
had been in his youth. When she saw him, Penelope fell in
love with him all over again.

In the most common version, Penelope kept rejecting him
despite Athena's cosmetics—until he told her something only
he could have known: how he had twisted an old olive tree
into his bedchamber, and fashioned their bed out of the living wood. In rich detail he told her how he had inlaid it with
silver and gold and ivory, and stretched a taut sling of oxhide

upon the great frame . . . and he recalled some of the words they had said to each other that first night upon the bed. When she heard that, according to this tale, Penelope welcomed him as husband and king. That night, Athena again intervened, bribing Helios to pasture the horses of the sun so that the night might last a week, prolonging the ardors of their reunion.

But other harpers sang a different tale. One tells how Penelope never would forgive Ulysses for killing her beloved suitor, Antinous. Upon the night of his return she began weaving again—a shroud. When the shroud was finished, Calypso's prophecy came true. Ulysses was killed by a young stranger who landed on his shore bearing a spear tipped with the beak of a stingray. The stranger was Telegonus, his own son by Circe. And Penelope so rejoiced in his death that she married Telegonus and made him king of Ithaca. In another variant, this tale becomes an odd quadrangle. After his mother's remarriage, Telemachus sails away, retracing his father's route—he lands on Circe's island, and marries her.

Thus, both sons of Ulysses, brave and magical warriors though they were, moved always in the shadow of the great voyager, and could love only women he had loved.

These nuptials, incidentally, would have made Circe and Penelope each other's mother-in-law—which should have inspired the minstrels to a few more verses. If so, they have been lost.

We must doubt the shroud bit though. We are told that the ancient Greeks did not bury their dead, but burned them on funeral pyres. And those hero-flames mingle with the fires that wrapped Troy on the night of the Horse, and burn still in our dreams.

Withdrawn